Start Up Telemarketing

WILEY SERIES ON BUSINESS STRATEGY

WILLIAM A. COHEN

DIRECT MARKETING SUCCESS: WHAT WORKS AND WHY
Freeman F. Gosden, Jr.

WINNING ON THE MARKETING FRONT: A CORPORATE MANAGER'S
GAME PLAN
William A. Cohen

PUBLIC SECTOR MARKETING: A GUIDE FOR PRACTITIONERS
Larry L. Coffman

THE MARKETING PROBLEM SOLVER
J. Donald Weinrauch

START UP TELEMARKETING: HOW TO LAUNCH A PROFITABLE SALES
OPERATION
Stanley Leo Fidel

START UP TELEMARKETING
How to Launch a Profitable Sales Operation

STANLEY LEO FIDEL

Fidel Communications Company
Los Angeles, California

JOHN WILEY & SONS

New York   Chichester   Brisbane   Toronto   Singapore

Library of Congress Cataloging in Publication Data:

Fidel, Stanley Leo.
  Start up telemarketing.

  (Wiley series on business strategy)
  Bibliography, p.
  1. Telemarketing.   I. Title.   II. Series.
HF5415.1265.   1987   658.8′5   87-21610
 ISBN 0-471-01064-2 cloth
 ISBN 0-471-62945-6 paper

Printed in the United States of America

10 9 8 7 6 5 4 3

658.85
F451

This book is dedicated to the memory of my father Phillip Fidel, who loved life and learning.

SERIES PREFACE

Peter Drucker said, "The future will not just happen if one wishes hard enough. It requires decision—now. It imposes risk—now. It requires action—now. It demands allocation of resources, and above all, human resources—now." The Wiley Series on Business Strategy is published to assist managers with the task of creating the future in their organizations.

Creation of the future requires application of the art and science of strategy. Strategy comes from the Greek word *strategia*, which means generalship. It has clear military roots defining how a general deployed the available forces and resources to achieve military objectives. But business and military strategy, though similar, are not identical. Business strategy is the allocation of resources to achieve a differential advantage at the time and place of decisive importance. "Resources" may be human, they may be financial, promotional, have to do with unique knowhow or have a psychological emphasis. But to be effective, these resources must be concentrated so as to be superior where it counts. This achievement is the essence of any successful business strategy and the theme of the series.

The series will investigate strategy in all of its many facets in business including marketing, management, planning, finance, communications, promotional activities, leadership, corporate culture—to note only those topics under preparation or planned. Its aim is to equip the practicing manager with the techniques and tools he or she will need for the most competitive and exciting period in business of all time.

William A. Cohen
Series Editor

PREFACE

Whenever I am asked to speak, I usually begin with something like the following: "I have read that by the year 2000, there will be 7 million people who earn their livings in the Telemarketing industry. The bad news is . . . most of them will be calling *you!*"

I don't know how many men and women will actually be employed as telephone sales people. It is apparent though, that more and more business is taking place via the telephone every year. Telemarketing has become a multi-billion dollar industry, and its growth is accelerating.

Even many of the Fortune 500 companies and those right below are foraying into telemarketing. They have the resources to succeed by employing consultants and other professionals. But what about the small and medium-sized companies? Those that do not successfully compete will be swallowed up or pass away.

This book was written for those small and medium-sized companies, whose limited resources or geographical locations inhibit employing experts who can design, develop, and implement successful telemarketing programs.

The information is based on extensive research, as well as my own experience, where for the last 7 years, I installed over a hundred telemarketing programs in a variety of industries from Insurance to Computers. The programs were both business to business, and business to consumer. They included market research, lead qualifying and appointment setting, and sales of both products and services.

Although most of the earlier programs did not make use of the computer, almost all of the ones I develop now are computer-assisted in some manner.

Telemarketing is a viable business tool. Companies that utilize it effectively will prosper. It is my hope that this book will help you launch your own successful Telemarketing program.

Stanley Leo Fidel

Los Angeles, California
September, 1987

ACKNOWLEDGMENTS

It is impossible to show the proper gratitude to all those who have helped make this book possible. I trust that those friends and associates who do not find their names here will be forgiving. Special thanks to Steve and Tom Alper, Linda Blakeley, Doug Carr, Bill Cohen, Elaine Fidel, Larry Hatterer, Norma Helms, Richard Herzog, Frank Hirsch, Mark Josephs, Ray Jutkins, Dick LeLaurin, Jamie Markowitz, Bill MacDonald, Sara Mitchell, Peter Span, Howard Stern, George Walther, and Karl Weber.

Contents

PART THREE
BUILDING A TELEMARKETING STAFF

PART FOUR
STATE-OF-THE-ART TELEMARKETING

Start Up Telemarketing

PART ONE

UNDERSTANDING TELEMARKETING

1

The Telemarketing Revolution

What if there existed a technology for your business that could:

1. Increase sales, profits, and productivity?
2. Cut down overhead?
3. Utilize personnel more effectively?
4. Provide a better follow-up and increase profits from advertising and direct mail?
5. Provide more reorders and sales of additional goods and services?

without requiring new and expensive equipment, larger offices or more overhead—and actually fewer salespeople.

Such technology does indeed exist. It is called telemarketing and is being used *now* by industries as diverse as insurance, computers, and medical equipment.

Telemarketing requires sophisticated techniques and specialized training, but, when put into practice, is an abundant source of qualified leads, confirmed appointments for your field sales force, and increased reorders—all at minimum expense.

TELEMARKETING IS THE NEW TECHNOLOGY

Let's define marketing as *everything* that relates to selling products and services. This includes identifying the needs of the market, creating an awareness of that need, and then promoting the solution in terms of the product or service.

"Tele" is derived from the Greek term meaning "at a distance." The general definition of telemarketing can include all forms of marketing at a distance, such as direct mail and video advertising. Specifically, modern telemarketing is defined as the use of *dedicated* resources, including personnel, equipment, and environments, to make or receive telephone calls for the following purposes:

Qualify prospects

Set appointments

Sell products and services

Survey markets

Test mailing lists

Support direct mail

Collect debts

Recruit personnel

Special promotions

Sales follow-up

Customer service.

"Dedicated resources" is the critical phrase. Telemarketing works best when the people, equipment, and environment are used exclusively to meet the goals of a carefully designed telemarketing plan. If other demands are made, especially on the personnel, the program usually suffers.

HOW IT ALL BEGAN

When Alexander Graham Bell invented the telephone, he probably did not foresee it would be used to sell the whole spectrum of modern commodities, products, and services, from pork bellies to office supplies and accounting.

Perhaps that is why this amazing communication instrument has not reached its full potential as a marketing tool. After a century, we are just beginning to understand the possibilities of extending our voice and ear around the world, and even outside this world, as the film *E.T.* so aptly illustrated.

Like the gold discovered in California in 1849, which precipitated a rush of fortune-hunting prospectors, business is finally discovering the telemarketing mother lode and learning how to mine its riches. Companies now are realizing the profitable efficiencies of extending their ventures into space without actually having to transport people and equipment physically to the desired location.

Although various industries—like brokerage, newspaper, and insurance—have been using the telephone to sell for many years, telemarketing has only recently become popular as a systematic method to increase sales. There are two major sources of the development of modern telemarketing:

1. AT&T
2. Innovative entrepreneurs.

In the 1960s AT&T started promoting "Phonepower," the use of the telephone to increase sales by making advance appointments instead of knocking on doors or canvassing, and by actually using the telephone to sell. Although we can assume that AT&T was promoting the use of the telephone to increase its own sales, the idea is essentially a sound one for virtually every business.

As a result of this promotion, companies began to use the telephone more widely. Salespeople were encouraged to call for appointments instead of simply dropping by their prospects' and customers' offices. Companies began to appreciate the economy of long distance telephoning versus the mail for faster action.

At the same time, the public was encouraged to use the telephone, guided by the *Yellow Pages*, for buying goods and services. "Let your fingers do the walking" is an enduring slogan that promotes the telephone as a time- and money-saving device.

In the same era, a group of businessmen reputed to have emigrated here from Europe set up a business in the basement of a building. Since they had little money, their office was actually near the boiler. Thus, the first "boiler room" was created. This operation was noted for its use of an imaginative presentation to sell office supplies. The buyer was also given an additional incentive in the form of a "gift" to help cement the sale.

Since no outside salespeople were needed to visit the customers, commissions were lowered. In addition, these telephone salespeople could contact more buyers in one hour than most outside sales representatives could see in a whole day. The result: high volumes, high profits.

Gradually, more and more companies began selling office supplies in this manner. Unfortunately, many were short-term oriented and lacked ethics and integrity. The term *boiler-room selling* developed a negative connotation in most businesspeople's minds—profitable, but unscrupulous, too.

The energy shortages of the 1970s, and the accelerating rate of inflation contributed to the need for a more efficient way to market goods and services. The high cost of traveling to the customer's location and the realization that one-on-one selling could only reach a handful of people, at most, in one day, set the stage for a new technology.

Companies like McGraw-Hill hastened the interest in telemarketing by publishing alarming statistics on the rising costs of personal sales calls. At the time of this writing, and depending on the industry involved, the average cost of one sales call varies from just under $100 to well over $200. Consider the following:

1. Most sales require five sales calls with one prospect before a sale is closed.

2. Most salespeople sell only to one out of every five of their prospects.

Think how many expensive personal calls a salesperson must make in order to complete a sale. It's no wonder companies have sought new, more cost-effective, marketing techniques.

TELEMARKETING TODAY

Because of the need to develop more profitable marketing methods, telemarketing has developed into a multibillion dollar industry showing no signs of slowing up. Telemarketing has grown because it works, and companies that ignore it will lose market share to their competitors that employ it.

Well managed, profitable, and highly respected companies like Xerox, IBM, Pacific Mutual Life, and many others now use various forms of telemarketing to increase sales and improve customer relations. Recognized as a vital component of a company's marketing mix, the use of telemarketing grows daily. Good management, proper equipment, pleasant environments, and professional training have transformed a cottage industry into a highly efficient and productive part of American business.

Every industry has its share of abusers. Unfortunately, telemarketing is no exception. Still, the modern phone room is a long way from the old boiler room. Those who neglect to explore its application to their businesses are guilty of letting an old prejudice obscure a new opportunity.

COMPUTERS HELP

Another key ingredient in the rapid growth of telemarketing is the advent of the personal computer workstation. Modern telemarketing takes advantage of the computer as a powerful support mechanism, using available software to send preapproach letters to selected companies and individuals. Then, computer reports are distributed to the telemarketers for follow-up, or the telemarketers call from computerized terminals that dial the number automatically while simultaneously showing all relevant information on a computer screen.

After the call is completed, the telemarketer simply notes the outcome on a form or enters it into the computer directly, and the system handles the follow-up, be it an order, a letter, or a change in the status of the account.

The computer system generates reports to management of all the activity involved, including the number of calls made, their duration, and the final results. Some systems even allow inventory and accounts receivable to be updated based on the outcome of the telemarketing call.

Other programs are available that synthesize one's voice and transmit personalized messages to selected individuals. This technique has produced remarkable efficiencies: Improvements of 40 percent are not uncommon. Such technological advances eliminate a great deal of the boring and repetitive facets of telemarketing, such as dialing the phone and asking for the decision maker.

THE FUTURE

By the year 2000, it has been estimated, over 7 million people will earn their living in telemarketing. As technology improves, most people will be working fewer hours and enjoying more leisure. More people will be working at home, connected to an office electronically by phone and computer. Product information will be transmitted over telephone lines or via satellite to a computer or video screen. Except for the most sensitive or critical cases, decisions will be made without the buyer and seller ever meeting face-to-face.

Imagine this scenario: You sit at your desk and turn on your computer. A prospect's record appears on your video display. You press a button and an appropriate script appears. You press another button, and the phone number is accurately dialed. When the receptionist answers, the computer, sounding exactly like you, asks to speak to the executive you've called. Your call is routed, the secretary in the executive's office answers, and the computer repeats its request. When the secretary asks a question, you pick up the phone to answer.

When the executive picks up the line, your computer begins to introduce you, again sounding exactly like you. The executive asks a question. You pick up the phone, press a button, and read the appropriate answer from your computer screen. The executive objects to an appointment. You touch another button and an answer to this objection appears on the monitor. Again you read it and he or she accepts the appointment. You say good-bye, push a button, and an appropriate confirmation letter is printed. You press another button, and the next prospect's record appears on your video display.

Does it sound too good to be true? This "future" technology is available now, and much of it is being used today.

A business associate once told me, half-facetiously, that he expected sales would be accomplished in the not too distant future by one computer (the "salesperson") selling to another computer (the "buyer"). Presumably, the one with the best program would win.

2

Telemarketing Applications

Companies that succeed in telemarketing invariably do two things: (1) They determine specific objectives, and (2) they allocate sufficient funds to accomplish those objectives. In this chapter we'll help you do both. Although there are many potential applications of telemarketing, we'll concentrate on those most profitable. Each of these applications can be handled in two ways:

1. Outgoing telemarketing
2. Incoming telemarketing.

Outgoing telemarketing—also referred to as "outbound" telemarketing—initiates the telephone call to accomplish your objective. Incoming telemarketing—also referred to as "inbound" telemarketing—means having a staff to receive the phone call.

Incoming and ougoing telemarketing may also work together. Orders or requests for information may be taken by the incoming group and then forwarded to the outgoing group for follow-up, including up-selling (increasing the sale), and cross-selling (selling additional products).

SEVEN MAJOR TELEMARKETING APPLICATIONS

The most significant uses of telemarketing are:

1. Selling
   A. Outgoing
   B. Incoming
2. Setting qualified appointments
3. Generating leads
4. Surveying
5. Customer service
6. Public relations and advertising
7. Collections.

1. Selling

A. Outgoing Telephone Sales. Selling your product or service by telephone is the most directly profitable telemarketing application. Someone picks up the phone, dials a number, speaks to a decision maker, and closes a sale. This is certainly the most desirable use of all. You can elicit reorders from existing customers, sell additional products or services, or increase the volume of products purchased. You can resell inactive customers, or you can sell new prospects. You can sell major customers auxiliary products or services. You can handle smaller customers that are not profitable to sell in person, but can be very profitable by telephone.

A trained professional telephone salesperson will average up to 15 or more phone calls per hour. At that rate, he or she can complete six presentations in that hour and average one to two sales. Compare that with outside salespeople who barely make three presentations in a day. It is certainly true that more complex products or services may require additional calls to close the sale, in which case you may elect a telemarketing strategy that includes a combination of mailing pieces, telephone calls, and even visits by outside sales reps. Experience has shown telephone selling substantially increases sales revenue.

Following are some considerations that will affect your decision to use telemarketing to sell:

1. How well known is your company?
2. How well known is your product or service?
3. How much technical information is required?
4. What price category is your product in?

If your company is very well known in the industry, it is easier to sell by telephone because you already have credibility. If your company is not so well known, it is still possible to sell; but you may need to make certain concessions like money-back guarantees or 10- to 30-day accounts, for example.

Customer awareness of your product is a favorable indicator that telemarketing will work as a selling tool. If the buyer is already acquainted with the product's benefits, education will not be necessary. Communication by telephone is easier when the discussion is about something that both the buyer and the seller know. Fewer calls will be necessary to make the sale. Products well suited to a telemarketing strategy are office supplies, vitamins, chemicals, and so on.

If your product is not familiar to your prospective buyer, or requires very technical explanation, then you will need to send good follow-up support material like catalogues, fact sheets, or samples. Given enough time and money, you can sell anything by telephone; but it is easier if you are a well known company with a familiar product that is simple to understand.

A good rule of thumb for cost/benefit analysis in telemarketing is that each telephone sale should be a minimum of $200. However, to get your foot in the door, you can sell a sample order for $50 or less. The purpose of such a sale is to make it easy for the purchaser to buy your products from then on. Do not expect your company to profit significantly until your telemarketers sell $200 or more per sale.

Whenever possible, offer billing or credit terms as an inducement to buy. But first, assemble a list of qualified prospects with good credit ratings and sell to them with easy terms. Remember, there is widespread reluctance to buy from strangers by telephone. Anything you can do to build the buyers' confidence in you and your company, while simultaneously reducing their risk, facilitates the sale. In this vein, sell "on approval." This is particularly effective when you are introducing a new product.

B. Incoming Sales. Incoming telemarketing must of course be used in conjunction with some other method of promotion: television advertising, print media, or direct mail. At this level, telemarketing is primarily order taking—the buyer sees your offer and calls to order. Good training can lead to two major enhancements in an incoming telephone program. The first is upgrading, whereby your telemarketers can increase the initial quantity by offering price discounts or establishing a sense of urgency due to a forthcoming price increase. Or, they may sell a better quality model than is first ordered.

The second enhancement in an incoming sales program is cross-selling. After the order is taken, the telemarketer sells additional products or services that are related to the buyer's initial order. For example, a customer may call to order a computer by telephone. After the order is taken, the telephone representative may also sell a service contract, some software, or a box of diskettes.

In this application, many calls that will be received will be requests for information. Your staff must be trained to record every such caller's name and phone number so they may be called back at a later time. Good training can also help them turn a request for information into an order.

There is no limit to what can be sold using telemarketing. Companies use outbound telemarketing to sell renewals of magazines when subscriptions have expired. Direct mail companies call existing customers who have not ordered in some time. Many companies allow buyers to preview books, cassettes, and videos before purchasing.

Telemarketing is especially effective in selling to existing marginal accounts and other target groups. Some companies sell automotive aftermarket products to jobbers, who then sell these products to local service stations; another company sells entrance fees to gambling tournaments at major Las Vegas and Atlantic City hotels; a business machine company sells supplies—including typewriter ribbons and daisy wheels—by telephone.

2. Setting Qualified Appointments

An important application of telemarketing is a separate telemarketing group that calls your prospects, qualifies them, and sets appointments for salespeople.

Using telemarketers to set qualified appointments for outside salespeople is a long-overdue application of the division-of-labor principle. Someone trained in setting appointments by telephone can be more effective in getting good appointments for salespeople than many salespeople themselves, because obtaining appointments is the telemarketers' major responsibility.

Salespeople have a variety of duties they must perform as part of their jobs, including preparing and giving face-to-face presentations, writing proposals, and completing a great deal of paperwork. As a result, they may have relatively little time for prospecting. A good telemarketer who does little else besides set appointments becomes more and more proficient at this job and can often outperform salespeople. Even though salespeople may have much more knowledge about the company and product, telemarketers will compensate by making *more* calls and setting more appointments.

A secondary benefit of using telemarketing for this function is that it frees your salespeople to spend more time selling one-on-one, which in turn helps them sharpen their selling skills and improve their closing ratios.

A significant improvement in morale can be realized when the sales team has a separate telemarketing group setting its appointments. Nothing is more discouraging to salespeople than repeated "no's" when prospecting. By giving your salespeople definite appointments with prospects who are open to meet with them and review their presentations, you help your salespeople avoid debilitating stress. Such support makes the sales team feel much more professional, which can lead to increased productivity and profitability.

Prospects often say to me, "I don't think telemarketing will work in setting appointments for me. My product is much too technical. I don't think a telemarketer can communicate clearly to my prospects without knowing a great deal about what we do." This is a natural first reaction, but the truth is telemarketing is useful for setting sales appointments regardless of how complex or simple your product or service is. Remember, the only thing your telemarketer is selling is the appointment. To do that, just how much does he or she actually have to know? In fact, many salespeople make the mistake of telling too much when calling for an appointment. This can boomerang because the prospect feels informed enough to make a decision without needing the appointment. That decision is usually "No."

Lack of knowledge on the part of a telemarketer can be positive. Telemarketers should be trained to say things like, "I don't really have the answer to that question, but John Jones, our representative will give you all that information when he meets with you. Are mornings or afternoons better?" Another approach is, "Well, it's a little difficult to describe on the telephone, but we could show you very clearly what it's all about when we meet with you. What's a better day for you next week, Tuesday or Thursday?"

Appointments generated by traditional methods such as advertising, direct mail, and canvassing actually cost as much as $75 to $150 each. Telemarketing can reduce appointment costs to as little as $15 to $25 each. It is also a powerful supplement to direct mail programs, increasing the response rate while lowering the cost per appointment.

Have you ever watched your sales force making appointments with potential customers? They dial the number, are put on hold, and often are then told that the decision maker is not in, not available, or on the phone. Finally, when they do get to talk to someone who can see them, more often than not, "He's not interested." In one hour of telephoning, your salespeople only manage to make one appointment or perhaps two. What could be more wasteful of a successful salesperson's time? Is it any wonder that most people don't make enough appointments?

My clients have used telemarketing appointment programs in a variety of industries, including insurance, banking, printing, accounting, computers, business machines, automatic pool cleaners, and security systems. These programs have been oriented towards selling to businesses as well as consumers. Sometimes the products and services are complex, and sometimes they are simple. It makes little difference. The bottom line for companies that use such programs is invariably a healthier balance sheet. Lower costs and greater production combine to produce additional profit.

3. Generating Leads

Sometimes it is more convenient for salespeople to schedule their own appointments. A number of factors may be involved, such as the fluctuation of the sales reps' schedules, a desire on their part to qualify the prospect or establish rapport prior to the meeting, or a downright insistence on setting their own appointments.

When this happens, one approach is to use telemarketing to qualify leads and prepare your prospects for a call by the sales rep. A lead-generating program is the next best thing to actually setting qualified appointments for salespeople. Depending on your own specific situation, you can create a lead program where the telemarketer does everything but actually set a specific appointment with an interested prospect. In this case, a prospect is told that he or she will be contacted shortly by a sales rep who will arrange a mutually convenient appointment. At the other end of the spectrum, a lead-generating program may simply provide the name and number of a prospect who has expressed some interest in learning more about your company or product.

To give your sales representative the data needed to establish rapport and qualify and close the appointment, your telemarketers should get as much information regarding your prospects and their needs as possible. Valuable information that may be gleaned by a good telemarketer includes the name of the decisionmaker, what product or service is being used now, what they like about it, what could be improved, and how long the company has been using it.

Whenever possible, appointment setting is preferred over lead generation. Once your telemarketer has an interested prospect on the telephone, a specific appointment should be made right then and there. Having a salesperson call for an appointment at a later time will only serve to delay the sale, because the salesperson will waste time attempting to reach the prospect. When the second call is made, the prospect will be in a different mood, a different frame of mind, and the salesperson will have to sell the company and its products all over again.

In cases where the salesperson's schedule is in flux, it is still better to have your telemarketing department set a specific appointment. The salesperson can always call later and reschedule. Resetting an appointment that has already been scheduled is easier than setting an appointment from a telemarketing lead. On the other hand, lead generating can be very useful for responding to questions raised by a recent advertisement or trade show "drop-bys." Your telemarketers can certainly save a good deal of your sales staff's time simply by calling and probing for potential buyers.

To assure the success of both the appointment-setting and the lead-generating programs, a lead-tracking system whereby every salesperson must account for the results of every appointment and every lead, is a vital element. Sales representatives should fill out a contact form after the appointment or after they call to follow up on the lead they were given. We will review this in more detail in a later chapter.

4. Surveying

Telemarketing can be used effectively to gather important market data, by surveying the marketplace to identify specific needs companies have and how much they would be willing to spend to fill those needs. This can be a fertile source of research on potential market acceptance of new products.

You may also take the survey a bit further into what might be an area of overlap with lead generating: calling companies to identify potential candidates for future selling. In this case you simply identify companies whose profiles relate to your marketing plan. For example, you verify the number of employees, the amount of sales revenue, whether they already buy products or services like yours, what they like about their current suppliers, what they would like to improve, and so on. This type of call can be valuable in determining logical candidates for a later sales approach.

Although surveying can be a valuable use of telemarketing, it is important to remember that information you receive on a survey may not always be as accurate or sincere as you would like. In the 1982 movie, *Tootsie,* Dustin Hoffman plays an actor masquerading as a woman. Dustin Hoffman is in love with a soap opera star and plays the role of Dorothy in the same TV show. Dorothy gains the confidence of this female star who confides that she wishes men would be more direct. She is tired of their being roundabout and playing games. She says she wishes just once, a man would just come out and say, "I'd like to go to bed with you."

This is an example of great market information. Weeks later at a party Dustin Hoffman sees the woman he's in love with. This time he's not masquerading as Dorothy. He approaches her and uses the information he received previously. He says that he thinks she's really beautiful and he would really like to make love to her. She reacts by throwing a drink in his face and turning away. So much for the reliability of survey data!

5. Customer Service

Most companies already have an incoming telemarketing program, whether or not they recognize it as such: the customer service department. Too often, customer service is a pseudonym for the complaint department. Customers call to inquire about where their order is, to complain that they've received the wrong products, or that their shipment has been damaged. You can convert these "complaint" calls into true customer service with good use of telemarketing people. You do this by training them to handle your customer's request or solve their problem. Then they can announce a special promotion that is taking place (cross-selling) and/or notify your customer of additional quantity discounts that are available (upselling).

Your customer service people may also take this opportunity to do additional promotion for your company. They can announce new products or product modifications and upgrades, they can inform your customer of new styles that have become available, and communicate the price information.

If you are concerned about appearing too aggressive to your customers by attempting to sell them something after they've called to complain about something else, remember Zig Zigler's statement: "The best way to show a customer you're not mad at him for complaining is to sell him something else."

6. Public Relations and Advertising

Telemarketing can be equivalent to buying a newspaper ad or a radio spot, or hiring a public relations firm: Get a list of companies or individuals that could benefit from your product or service and call them. You can script this call in much the same way you would write ad copy. You communicate whatever it is you wanted to say about your new product or service or modification to an existing product or service. No sales attempt is made on this kind of call. You just inform the other party of something they should find of interest.

Direct your call to the person who makes purchasing decisions regarding your product or service. If that is not possible, speak to an assistant or secretary to that person. Follow up with a letter summarizing the information you've conveyed.

You can also use this kind of call to build traffic in a retail organization. You call consumers in your area and notify them of some new products that have recently arrived. You can also entice them to visit your store by offering them a special free gift or discount if they mention the fact that they were called by the telemarketing department.

Just as companies include coupons in direct-mail pieces or newspaper ads to attract new customers, your telemarketing advertisement can offer verbal coupons. The most vital ingredient in this type of campaign is a good list of consumers likely to be interested in your company's offering.

7. Credit Department

Although the major intent of any telemarketing program is to promote the sale of your company's products and services, an important component of any marketing program is receiving payment. If you don't get paid, you would have been better off not making the sale. Telemarketing can help you collect payments. You can check the credit of your new customers by telephone before your products are shipped or your services begin. When you take their order, you can ask your new customers for trade and banking references and then call those prior to completing the transaction. Banking references are of course more reliable than trade—almost everyone has someone who will furnish them with a good reference; banks almost always provide accurate information.

Another telemarketing application in the credit department is collections. A telephone collection call is especially useful after several written requests for payment have been ignored. Telemarketers can be trained to make collection calls that get results. The script for this program always should include the question, "When will you be sending your check, please?" Some companies even go so far as to tape the conversation, and notify the person from whom they're collecting that this part of the call is being taped. This encourages them to make a promised payment on time.

CHOOSING YOUR OWN TELEMARKETING APPLICATION

There are so many potential uses of telemarketing that you may wonder where you should begin. The most practical uses of telemarketing follow:

1. Telephone sales (outgoing)
2. Order taking (incoming)
3. Setting appointments (outgoing)
4. Generating leads (outgoing or incoming)

To help you decide which application would be best, take some time to identify your priorities and objectives. The questions in Figure 2–1 should help you crystallize your needs.

After you review your answers to the questions in Figure 2–1, you will be in a position to determine which telemarketing application to use. If your product or service is familiar to your buyers, your company is well known, and your market is widely dispersed geographically, you may certainly create a sales program.

If, on the other hand, your product or service is new, or complex, or requires physical demonstration by a sales person, you should choose an appointment-setting or lead-generating program. If you have direct control of your sales staff, an appointment-setting program is preferable. If you use outside manufacturers' representatives, lead generating is necessary, since you cannot know their individual schedules on a timely basis.

If you do not have enough data regarding your market, a surveying program may be worthwhile. After you have accumulated sufficient data, you can then implement one or more additional programs. For best results, take it one step at a time. After you have successfully installed your first application, you can consider a second, and so on. But one at a time to begin with.

PLANNING YOUR PROGRAM

A good telemarketing program, like any other good business project, needs to be planned properly, by either a member of the company or an outside specialist. Either way, there is a cost. You will pay your employee for salaried time or pay a consultant a fee. The cost should be added to your budget.

Your investment in telemarketing will include the following:

COMPANY PROFILE

1. How do you get your sales now?
2. How many salespeople do you have?
   Inside? _____   Outside? _____
3. How many customers do you have?
4. What is your market potential?
5. How well known is your company?
6. What is an average customer worth in terms of sales?
7. What is your annual sales revenue?
8. What do you like about the way your sales are going?
9. What would you like to change or improve?

PRODUCT PROFILE

10. What products/services do you sell?
11. What is your best seller?
12. What would you like to sell more of?
13. What is the major benefit of your product/service?
14. List other features and benefits that really count.
15. How does your pricing compare to your competition?
16. What is your delivery time?
17. Why should your customers buy from you?
18. What markets are you selling to currently?
    ☐ Local?   ☐ Regional?   ☐ National?
19. What markets would you like to penetrate further?
20. Can you produce a profile of your typical or good customer?
21. What qualification data would you like to have regarding your prospects?
22. What are the major needs of your prospects?
23. On what basis do they mostly make their decision?
    ☐ Price   ☐ Quality   ☐ Service   ☐ Delivery
24. What prospect lists or directories do you use?
25. Who is the initial prospect contact?
26. Who is the major decision maker?

MARKETING PROFILE

27. Do you have a marketing plan?
28. Have you ever used an outside marketing firm? If yes, what were the results of their work?
29. What marketing intelligence would be valuable to your company?
30. What other marketing do you do?
    ☐ Print Advertising   ☐ Direct Mail   ☐ Trade shows   ☐ Other
31. Could telemarketing enhance those programs?
32. What sort of literature do your prospects receive about your company?
33. What would you expect to accomplish with telemarketing?
34. What other assistance would you like?
    ☐ Sales Training   ☐ Computerization   ☐ Telephone System
35. What would you need to see, hear, and feel to know that your programs were successful?

FIGURE 2-1 Telemarketing planning questionnaire

1. Program design
   A. Identify objectives
   B. Plan resources
   C. Determine key application
   D. Decide upon manual or computer-assisted program
2. Development
   A. Entry level approach
   B. Script/presentation
   C. List acquisition
   D. Testing
   E. Tracking system
3. Implementation
   A. Hire and train personnel
      1. Manager
      2. Telemarketers
      3. Sales support
   B. Telephone equipment
   C. Telephone charges
   D. Facility
   E. Miscellaneous

This outline gives you an idea of the major components in a telemarketing operation, as well as an overview of the steps to be accomplished in developing a successful program. Let's examine them in some detail.

1. Program Design

The program design is the over all plan of how, when, and where you will use telemarketing. As noted earlier, whether you elect to develop a telemarketing program in-house or with the aid of outside specialists, there definitely will be costs involved, and they will vary.

A. Objective Objectives. Telemarketing specialists should be consulted to help you identify objectives and examine your resources to determine your key application. They can also help you make objective decisions regarding the details of your specific telemarketing program, as well as provide training for your staff later.

Consultants are available for $500 to as much as $5000 a day. Many will provide a package of services where they design, develop, and implement your telemarketing program for you. If you decide to undertake this as an in-house project, remember you are using your existing management and their salary is certainly one consideration. Another is whether their other responsibilities will suffer.

In general, you may expect that the program design phase will require anywhere from $1500 to $25,000. This of course depends on the size of your company and the scope of your objectives.

B. Resourceful Resources. What resources will be available to create your program? You must decide where you will physically locate your telemarketers, what furniture and equipment they may use, what support will be provided in terms of people, brochures, and so forth. If your company is small, or your budget is tight, I recommend using your existing phones and furniture at the outset. Once the program has made a promising start, you may upgrade your phone system and enhance your environment with new telemarketing furniture.

If you have a healthy balance sheet, it is to your advantage to make the necessary upgrades immediately.

C. Choose Your Application. Choosing the initial application is a most important decision. Your choice is directly related to your major objectives and your resources. Do you want to increase sales or costs? To achieve your goal, what telemarketing application should be used? Is it sales, surveys, or collections?

D. Manual or Computer-Assisted Program. There are now available many computer-assisted telemarketing systems that increase efficiency. They eliminate much paperwork, maximize customer contacts, and maintain easy access to information. These systems allow your people to follow up their calls with computer-generated letters that foster customer relations and enhance credibility. Such systems require an additional investment of from $5000 to $50,000.

A decision must be made to begin manually or use modern automation. Manual systems are faster to implement, require less initial investment, and are easier for most telemarketers to use without special training. Automated systems are more efficient, allow better tracking of leads and sales activity, and promote greater thoroughness in customer communication.

2. Development

Once your program has been planned, it will go through a period of evolution as you attend to the many requisite details. In this development phase you will give most of your consideration to the following:

A. Entry Level Approach. What will be your initial "door-opener" approach? For example, if your product line consists of 20 different items, which one will you sell first? If you are calling to set appointments, what products and product benefits will you mention to the prospect to elicit a commitment of time and interest?

B. The Script's the Thing. Script preparation is another vital ingredient of your program. A good telephone presentation can change a marginal program into a major success. This is another area where outside expertise is very helpful. In place of a script, some companies choose to use a telechart, key phrases organized in a logical sequence. A script is a word-for-word presentation. There are advantages and disadvantages to both.

Scripts make it very easy for telemarketers to communicate all the relevant information effectively. Actual word-for-word delivery assures that the important information will be communicated in the right sequence. However, script technique must be practiced and refined by the telemarketers to prevent a canned, monotonous delivery. While telecharts, usually do not sounding like they are being read, you must rely on the ability of the telemarketers to use good judgment in their delivery to fill in around the key phrases.

Regardless of which you use, eventually telemarketers will fashion their individual presentation in a way that adapts the initial script or telechart to their own styles. But, at the beginning of the program, a prepared presentation helps your telemarketers get off to a good start.

C. The Right List. The next step is acquiring appropriate prospect lists with telephone numbers. These vary considerably in price. They are available for $25 per 1000 names to $500 per 1000 names, depending on your source and length of use. Generally, the more expensive lists are more accurate and provide more information, such as chief executive officer's name, number of employees, SIC codes, and so on. The least expensive lists usually provide names, addresses, and telephone numbers. You must evaluate your own needs and make an appropriate decision.

If you have a small, select market, for example, and your dollar potential in an individual sale is high, the more expensive lists are a worthwhile investment. If your market is large, and you are not sure of the title of the decision maker, less expensive lists may be adequate.

D. Test It First. Once you have your script and a list, you should begin testing the program. You can test in-house or use an outside telemarketing service. Depending on whether you have selected several variables in terms of lists, scripts, and approaches, your test can be as few as 10 hours to as many as 200 hours. Completing several different tests will help you identify your best direction. Outside services charge from $35 to $75 per hour for testing. A telemarketing specialist helping you design, develop, and implement your telemarketing program may include the test as part of his fee.

E. Tracking Makes It Work. Finally, you should spend some time developing and monitoring or tracking system to enable management to determine exactly what the telemarketing program is accomplishing and at what costs.

By monitoring your program in terms of number of calls made, contacts with decision makers, presentations, and resulting sales or appointments, you learn what parts of your program need to be adjusted. If there are many contacts, but few presentations, your script needs to be enhanced. If there are many presentations, but very few sales, your offer needs to be reviewed, or your people better trained in closing the sale.

A vital part of monitoring the program is the creation of forms or computer reports that track all phone activity on a daily basis. It need not take more than several hours to produce such forms. Sample forms and reports are included in the appendix.

3. Implementation

Once you have devoted time and energy to plan and develop your program, it is time to put it into effect. If your planning and development phases have been accomplished with attention to detail, there is a high probability of realizing a successful program.

Remember, even if your program does not do all you had expected at first, you can use your tracking and monitoring system to make adjustments that will lead ultimately to success.

A. Hire and Train Well. Hiring and training personnel will be part of your daily operational costs. Your costs will vary according to whether you are selling, surveying, or setting appointments. Your initial investment for telemarketers will be $5 to $10 per hour plus bonuses. Many companies have found that paying a commission only usually fosters a boiler-room environment and hard-sell approach. I find in modern telemarketing programs, it is better to pay a salary plus commissions and bonuses. Eventually, after you have established a nucleus of effective telemarketers, you can convert them from salary to straight commission.

If your telemarketing program will exceed five telemarketers, you need a manager to oversee the operation. Managers expect to earn anywhere from $1500 a month plus an override to $5000 a month plus override. The manager's compensation depends on the particular industry and other factors such as gross sales volume and costs of sales. The greater the profit margins, the more money your telemarketers and managers will expect to earn.

B. Calling Equipment. Telephone lines and instruments will be an additional one-time cost in many applications. You want to be sure there are enough telephone sets and lines to accommodate your new program. In addition, there are installation charges for the lines and the extra telephone connections. These vary from city to city. You may want to take advantage of your telemarketing program as an opportunity to obtain a new telephone system for the entire company. Since the divestiture of AT&T, many fine phone systems are being marketed by independent vendors. These systems have advanced features and functions that save time, and they can be leased or purchased relatively inexpensively. For example, a system of six speakerphone units that handle up to six lines plus intercom may be leased for under $80 per month, or purchased for under $3000. An alternative is simply to install additional phones as part of your existing telephone system.

C. Telephone Use Charges. If you are calling long distance you may expect your monthly phone bill to be approximately $1000 to $1500 per telemarketer. Some economies are possible by using WATS lines and long distance services such as MCI, Sprint, and many others. You should expect your long distance charges to be around $12 per person per hour.

If you are making local calls only, your telephone bill will be considerably less. In a local telephone program, you could expect charges of approximately $7 per hour per person.

Surprisingly, interstate calls are usually less expensive than intrastate calls. Don't expect a statewide program to be less expensive than a national one.

D. Facility. The calling environment is another integral part of your budget. Your staff requires desks, chairs, files, and all the typical accouterments found in an office.

In response to the rapid development of the telemarketing industry, companies are manufacturing lines of furniture and dividers to optimize the phone room environment at a cost of up to $2000 per station. This cost is justified in terms of the added comfort it brings to support the telemarketer, which leads to greater efficiency.

As mentioned earlier, management may be more comfortable, however, with using the company's existing furniture, at least in the initial stages of development.

E. Miscellaneous. A thriving phone program generates a good deal of support activity. With this activity, additional costs are incurred. These include additional brochures, catalogs, data sheets, and postage. People are required to mail literature or file customer information. These functions may produce a strain on your existing staff, which can be eased by hiring additional part-time help.

THE BOTTOM LINE

While operational costs vary depending upon location and whether or not your facility is computerized, you can expect to average approximately $25 to $30 per hour per person.

If your people can sell at the rate of $200 per hour, while costs are kept at $30 per hour or less, your selling costs are 15 percent or less. This should be more than acceptable in most businesses.

As mentioned earlier, you may only be averaging $100 per hour in sales when you first begin. With training and experience your sales average will continue to climb and should in time exceed $200 per hour per person.

AUTOMATING YOUR PROGRAM

There are three major components to an automated telemarketing program:

1. *Hardware*—the computer and ancillary equipment

2. *Software*—the programs that make it work
3. *People*—the humans who tailor the system to your needs and train your staff

If you elect to use computer-assisted telemarketing, your initial investment could be from $5000 to in excess of $100,000. This great variance depends on the number of people on your telemarketing staff and whether or not you want a fully integrated computerized system or one personal computer to help control your program. Larger companies definitely should consider an investment in computerized telemarketing. The additional cost generally can be as little as 50 cents to $2 per hour per person. The corresponding increase in sales can be considerable. Some companies have seen sales increase as much as 100 percent because of timely follow-up, the ability to make more phone calls due to automation of paperwork, and increased efficiency.

The major benefit of automation is increased profitability due to increased sales and reduced costs. More information is also available to management on a timely basis. The major drawbacks are the size of the initial investment and the time spent in training people to use the system properly.

Those who are simply considering telemarketing in itself can find the prospect of automating a telemarketing program intimidating. Nevertheless, it is an excellent investment.

3

In-House Telemarketing Versus Telephone Service Bureaus

Once you have decided to institute a telemarketing program, there is one additional decision that must be made: Should you develop your telemarketing program in-house, use a telemarketing service bureau, or begin it at a service bureau and then transfer your program in-house?

Every situation is unique and requires individual attention. In this chapter, I present the relative advantages and disadvantages inherent in each case. I must warn you that my own preference, as a telemarketing consultant, is generally in favor of the in-house approach. To offset what may be my own prejudice in this instance, I have drawn heavily from information provided by Richard Herzog, vice-president of sales for Telephone Marketing Services, Incorporated. His company is a telephone service bureau that also provides in-house consulting services to companies developing their own telemarketing programs.

PRO SERVICE BUREAU

Service bureaus are fast paced, production-oriented operations. They specialize in handling a high volume of calls, whether incoming or outgoing. Because their business is based primarily on telemarketing, they tend to utilize the most advanced technology available to help make that business efficient. The better telephone service bureaus use computer systems to promote efficiency and provide appropriate environments to increase telemarketing success.

Certainly, service bureaus should be considered for special projects where large numbers of phone calls must be made in a short period of time, such as a special announcement to 20,000 customers within five days. This would be an impossible task for most companies, but could be accomplished easily by a service bureau.

Another clear-cut application for a service bureau is handling incoming telemarketing in response to a new television campaign or another similar advertising program. This is especially true if you don't have an accurate projection of the number of calls you will receive as a result of your advertising. In-house facilities may be totally inadequate in the event your advertising is more effective than you expected.

When your company is involved in many simultaneous telemarketing projects, again the advantage clearly is with an outside center. They are equipped to handle a multitude of projects in an organized matter.

Another application that lends itself to an outside service center is a secondary project that is not so vital that it must be handled internally.

In addition, some conditions may exist that make it imperative to use an outside service—lack of space to accommodate a telemarketing program, for example, or being located in an area where an appropriate labor force is unavailable. These are all easy situations in that the decision is inherent in the situation. On the other hand, let's examine some situations that clearly favor an in-house approach.

PRO IN-HOUSE

If you are selling a product or service that is extremely technical in nature and requires detailed product knowledge to answer complex questions, your decision should be in favor of an in-house telemarketing program for both incoming and outgoing telemarketing. If your product or service is highly confidential and there is proprietary information involved, you should certainly lean in favor of an in-house operation. The potential for an unwanted information leak is certainly greater in a service center.

If you are selling a high-priced product or service to a relatively small market, and the sales process demands repetitive telephone and mail contact, you would do better with an in-house program. This will allow you to build a relationship between your in-house telemarketer and your prospect.

Telemarketing service centers are more apt to have high employee turnover, making it difficult to communicate a complex product or service well. Telemarketing service bureaus generally do not pay the kind of salaries and commissions that attract the best achievers in the industry. If your product or service demands a very high level of professional communications, you will definitely want to decide in favor of an in-house program.

SERVICE BUREAU ADVANTAGES

There are several advantages to using an outside service bureau to conduct your Telemarketing program. These include:

1. Low initial investment
2. Fixed operating costs
3. Quick start
4. Time flexibility

1. Low Initial Investment. If you elect to use a service bureau, you only pay for the program on a limited basis. There is no large investment for creating an additional environment, adding telephones and lines, hiring a manager and a group of employees, and hiring a consultant. Indeed, if you're starting from scratch, the costs can be considerable. Richard Herzog has furnished relevant information in Figures 3-1 to 3-4.

2. Fixed Operating Costs. A service bureau offers a clearly defined rate schedule, allowing you to project exactly what your operations will cost. Typically there is a set-up charge of $100 to $5000. The size of this one-time fee depends on whether your program is inbound or outbound and the nature of its complexity. (See Figure 3-2.)

You may be charged on a per-call or per-hour basis. Inbound programs generally charge on a per-call basis, taking into consideration the amount of information that is required and the projected length of call. A typical inbound program may charge anywhere from $1 to $4 per call, again depending on what is required. Most inbound programs conducted by service bureaus also charge a minimum guaranteed fee.

Outbound calls may average anywhere from $2 to $9 per call. Most outbound programs are based on a set hourly charge that varies from a low of $25 to a high of $60 or more. Many service bureaus offer a test agreement. This is for a specified length of time, anywhere from 30 to 200 hours. While paying $60 per hour for a telemarketing program may seem high, there are many hidden costs in creating an in-house program. Figure 3-3 presents a comprehensive view of virtually every conceivable cost factor. In all candor, this full list would rarely apply to every in-house telemarketing program. Usually one begins by utilizing the existing resources and then gradually adding additional items. The list is intended to show the maximum costs you can expect.

In a computerized telemarketing operation with 10 telemarketers, one supervisor and one manager, Herzog has indicated that hourly operation expenses can run as high $45.37. (See Figure 3-4.) I would caution the reader that these figures are definitely high. For small and medium-size companies, you would generally not begin with both a manager and supervisor. In addition, it is likely your program would not be computer assisted initially. Still, the hourly expenses are higher than one might expect without careful analysis.

Phone	Hiring charges
Installation	Newspaper ads
Equipment	Agency fees
Monitoring facilities	Interviewing expense
Construction	*Miscellaneous*
Furniture & fixtures	Printing support material & forms
Office space	Professional services
	Training
	Computers/data processing
	Office equipment

FIGURE 3-1. Telemarketing start-up costs

SERVICE BUREAU COSTS

OUTBOUND

Set-up	$1,500 to $5,000
Day calling	$33.00 to $60.00
Evening/weekend calling	$25.00 to $35.00
Average business call	$ 5.00 to $ 9.00
Average consumer call	$ 2.00 to $ 5.00

INBOUND

Set-up	$100 to $500
Name & address	$1.00 to $1.25
Telephone number or source	$ .10 to $ .15
Credit card	$ .35 to $ .40
Catalogue orders	$1.70 to $2.50
Referral	$ .95 to $2.00
First minute	$1.20 to $1.40
Subsequent minutes	$1.10 to $1.20

Note: Per-call charges depend on complexity, length of call, and volume of calls.

FIGURE 3-2. Cost comparison of in-house program versus service bureaus

TELEMARKETERS	ACD
Salary	Auto dialers
Commission	Head sets
Incentives	*MISCELLANEOUS*
Training	Management
PHYSICAL PLANT	Supervisory
Rent	Secretarial
Utilities	Clerical
Maintenance	Data processing personnel
Alterations	Lists
Furniture	Stationery
Fixtures	Forms
Computer terminals	Supplies
Additional security	Script development
TELEPHONE COSTS	Programming of special reports
Installation	Professional fees (lawyers, consultants, etc.)
Equipment costs	Fulfillment costs
Long distance line usage	Computer costs
Local line usage	Data processing equipment
	Delivery
	Vendor supervision costs

FIGURE 3-3.   Telemarketing operating expenses

3. Quick Start. Telephone service bureaus are organized to develop and institute new programs rapidly. This means that, in general, you can implement a telemarketing program at a service bureau within one to three weeks, depending on its complexity and the service bureau's existing projects.

4. Time Flexibility. As a matter of course, service centers, especially inbound telemarketing bureaus, offer 24-hour, seven day a week service. This is certainly much more convenient for consumer-oriented programs where responses to advertising may take place at night and on weekends. It is also advantageous for business-to-business programs where calls need to be made early in the morning on the West Coast to reach the East Coast, for example. It is certainly easier to install such programs at a service bureau than possibly disrupt your own company's business hours.

DIRECT EXPENSES

Labor

Manager (1/10th)	$2.16
Supervisor (1/10th)	1.44
Telemarketer —salary	7.50
Telemarketer —incentive (40%)	3.00
Administrators (2) (1/10th)	1.30
Tax & fringe (33%)	5.13
Sub Total	20.53

Phone

Equipment & service	.28
Usage (40% connect time)	11.00
Sub Total	11.28
Computer (1/40th of $200)	5.00
Miscellaneous	1.00
Total Direct Expenses	37.81
OVERHEAD (General & Administrative 20%)	7.56
Total Expenses	45.37

BASIS FOR EXPENSE ESTIMATE

Manager	$45,000/yr or $865.38/wk or $21.63/hr
Supervisor	$30,000/yr or $576.92/wk or $14.42/hr
Telemarketer	base (40 hrs) of $300/wk or $15,600/yr
Computer	$200 per station per month

FIGURE 3-4. Hourly expense estimates outbound 9:00 A.M.–5:00 P.M.

Service Bureau Disadvantages

On the other side of the coin, disadvantages of using an outside service bureau include:

1. Lack of direct control
2. Lack of security

3. Lack of employee loyalty

4. Mass market approach

5. Caliber of personnel

1. Lack of Direct Control. When you use an outside service center, you forfeit direct control of your operation to that entity. Granted, they may be highly efficient; yet there is always a feeling of not quite knowing exactly what is happening at the other location.

2. Lack of Direct Security. Although most modern telephone service bureaus pride themselves on their modern security measures and systems, the fact that the service bureau is at an external location affords less security than if your valuable records were kept under your own lock and key. You are never really sure about what is happening to your own customer and prospect lists.

3. Lack of Employee Loyalty. The employees at a service bureau are primarily loyal to that service bureau. They are motivated and compensated by that company, not yours. In addition, they may have several telemarketing jobs they perform for several different clients of the service bureau. Yours is just another application.

4. Mass Market Approach. The attitude of a service bureau, by its very nature, is that of high volume, which is not necessarily accompanied by high quality. Service bureaus handle thousands of calls, both outgoing or incoming. These large numbers do not always bring with them the attention to detail that one might desire.

5. Caliber of Personnel. Service Bureaus that charge their clients an hourly or per-call fee are likely to keep their costs down by paying the lowest possible wages to their telemarketing staff. After all, their profits are certainly influenced by their direct labor costs. They will not always attract the most motivated people to do this kind of work.

What To Do

Each company's requirements are different and need to be reviewed individually. Service bureaus are valuable resources that may or may not be appropriate in a particular instance. As mentioned earlier, some cases are obvious, others demand more analysis.

Companies that need a custom approach and are committed to telemarketing will probably do better to create their own program and use a consultant to help assure its success.

Companies that can use a mass approach and are not certain of whether or not telemarketing will work for them should certainly try it at a telemarketing service bureau. Later, they may decide to bring their program in-house.

4

Telemarketing and Other Marketing Methods

Although telemarketing can be used successfully, independently from any other kinds of marketing, results often can be significantly enhanced when telemarketing is synchronized with your total marketing mix. The major forms of marketing are print media advertising, radio and TV advertising, and direct mail. When telemarketing is carefully planned and carried out as part of a total marketing strategy that includes media advertising, the results multiply synergistically. Each of the various media have peculiarities, strengths, and weaknesses. Let's briefly review and analyze their respective qualities.

TV ADVERTISING

Television advertising is extremely expensive in both production and presentation, requiring an investment of many thousands of dollars to produce a broadcast-quality television commercial. A one-minute spot, which takes about a day to shoot, requires producers, directors, actors, camera crew, lighting people, writers—the list goes on and on. Then considerable time and expertise are required to edit and produce the final commercial. All this for a 1-minute, or perhaps 30-second message. You can be sure this message must have tremendous impact, if it is to compete with all the other 30-second and 1-minute commercials that strive for your attention while you watch your favorite television show.

Broadcasting, like other media advertising, is not very cost-effective in terms of targeting your audience, because a large portion of the viewing audience is not a potential consumer of your product or service. This is true even if the commercial has a great deal of humor, drama, or otherwise appealing characteristics. For example, much as I enjoyed the cleverness of the Wendy's "Where's the beef?" commercial, I don't eat at fast-food restaurants. Therefore, that commercial was wasted on me. Costs may be prohibitive, since commercials must be repeated many times to gain attention from and have an impact on the viewer.

On the other hand, TV advertising develops the identity and enhances the credibility of the company and its products or services. Consumers recognize companies that use professional television advertising as already successful and therefore worthwhile, at least to some extent. When a commercial is strong enough to elicit full attention, it has tremendous power in presenting both a visual and an auditory message that is highly persuasive. It is understandable that companies spend billions of dollars on TV advertising. It does work.

So, TV ads are expensive, reach a vast audience, and through repetition can be very effective. Telemarketing can increase the results of your TV ads when used to support your media campaign and hone in on prospective customers.

Inbound Telemarketing

Use your television ad to trigger a response, by giving the viewer a telephone number, preferably a toll-free, 800 number, to call for more information: a brochure, the name and address of the nearest dealer, or more technical data regarding what your company has to offer.

The viewer can also call to order your product or service, paying by credit card or C.O.D. You recognize this method as the way some companies sell nostalgia record albums and steak knives. If your business sells consumer items priced under $100, it may be worthwhile to use television commercials in conjunction with telemarketing. Because the consumer's decision to buy is impulsive or spontaneous, a bank of phone operators must be ready to take the order. Even higher priced items, such as audio and video tapes and book programs, can be sold successfully in this way. Several companies sell such programs for over $250 using a telemarketing-supported TV campaign. With the advent of cable television and narrow casting it is possible to target your market more specifically and control your costs. People who watch cable TV, for example, are accustomed to less-than-broadcast-quality commercials and will respond positively if they are interested in what you have to offer.

Outbound Telemarketing

Your television campaign can be reinforced significantly when you develop an outbound telemarketing program to support it. This can be accomplished in two distinct ways.

1. *Pre-commercial.* Let us suppose you have an ad or program running on a local cable station. You can get a list of cable subscribers in that market, then have your telemarketers call those households, inviting them to watch your program or commercial. Doing this within two to three days of scheduled airing will increase the number of viewers and will pave the way for a positive response.

2. *Post-commercial.* After your commercial or cable program has aired, your telemarketers call cable subscribers and refer to the commercial or program. This will improve credibility and rapport, and can facilitate an increase in sales. An additional sales boost will come from having the telemarketers offer added incen-

tive, in the form of a free gift or additional discount, for orders placed with them.

RADIO ADVERTISING

Radio, as another broadcast medium, is very similar to television, with two exceptions:(1) It is much less expensive to produce and air a professional radio spot; and (2) Audience impact generally is not as great as with television. However, telemarketing can support a radio campaign much as it does television.

One major disadvantage of radio advertising is that many listeners also are driving at the same time, making it almost impossible for them to make note of a telephone number, much less make an impulsive telephone call. Unless they are truly motivated by what they hear, it is unlikely that they will remember the number and call later. Making the telephone number easy to remember and repeating it often are two ways to overcome this obstacle.

PRINT ADS

Advertising space in newspapers, journals, or magazines competes for a few seconds of the readers' attention. Consumers have less time to read, and a wider selection of reading material than ever before. People who read magazines, journals, and newspapers often skim rather than read every word on every page. Entire ads may be overlooked or never even reached. Although print ads don't cost as much as TV commercials to produce and present, like TV they don't reach your best customers specifically, except in the case of trade journals. They generally cost under 14 cents per contact, but cost per qualified response and sale is much higher. As in TV advertising, they rely on clever or dramatic copy and art which may get attention but not provoke a response.

In spite of print advertising's drawbacks, telemarketing can be used to synergize results from a print campaign. When appropriate, include a toll-free number so the reader can call for additional information. Your advertising strategy should not be oriented necessarily to the sale of a specific product or service, especially if you are dealing on a business–to–business level. Rather, your strategy should be to get the buyer to the *next step:* asking for more information. As this chapter develops, we'll review a strategy that ties print advertising in with direct mail and telemarketing. For now, let's think of your print ad as the first contact to a wide audience to ferret out a potential market in that audience. In this application, the print ad works as a sieve, filtering out all who are uninterested and allowing the interested parties to receive further information by making a telephone call, mailing a coupon, or circling a number on a reader response card. It is important to add that, like TV advertising, print advertising creates credibility and recognition for the company and its products or services. Good advertising in a recognized newspaper, journal, or magazine conveys an impression of respectability.

In magazines to a greater extent than newspapers, you have the capacity to target your advertising. In a women's magazine, for example, the advertising will of course relate to the needs and desires of women. In a business magazine, the ads will relate to the needs and desires of businesspeople, and so on. Still, print ads are wasteful in that many of the people who read them are not really potential customers.

DIRECT MAIL

Direct mail advertising is where marketing begins to be more cost effective in terms of reaching a targeted audience. Although direct mail pieces cost much more per contact—anywhere from 20 cents to $1.50—they have a higher direct response rate. Direct mail is used for selling. In most forms of direct mail, the consumer receives a personally addressed letter that has been carefully designed to attract attention and elicit a response. Every piece of a direct mail offer, from the envelope to the order card, serves a purpose in clinching the sale. Unlike a TV commercial, which is over in seconds, direct mail potentially has a shelf life. An interested customer may set a direct mail offer aside for later study and a decision.

Although it is certainly true that the volume of direct mail people now receive prevents them from reading it all, a good mail offer sent to the right list will attract attention and get results. To the extent that much direct mail is thrown away unread, it is certainly a wasteful form of communication. On the other hand, direct mail is less wasteful than TV, radio, and print ads in that it is targeted to an audience that is more likely to be a market for the products and services. For example, the company selling business machines can develop a profile of its existing customers, acquire a list of businesses that match this profile, and then mail an offer to those businesses. This is an extremely effective use of marketing dollars.

Similar to other forms of advertising, direct mail is also an excellent first contact to a wide audience. Interested parties simply return a business reply card or make a call to receive additional information—or even purchase your product or service. Telemarketing can be used both before and after a direct mail offer in the same way you would use it before and after a television campaign—to advise customers to watch their mail and to follow up once the offer has reached the customer. This will improve results.

Prior to sending your direct mail promotion, you can use telemarketing to test the lists, calling about 200 names on your mailing list. You make the same offer that appears in the direct mail piece and explain the same features and benefits of your products and/or services. The results of your telephone testing will be anywhere from 2 to 10 times as great as your direct mail program. So, if your telephone program has a success rate of 5 percent, you can expect no better than a 2.5 percent success rate from your direct mail program—perhaps as little as .5 percent. This valuable technique will enable you to determine in advance the cost effectiveness of your direct mail promotion. If the test is not promising, then find another list and repeat it. If results still elude you, it is time to reevaluate the offer.

Another use of telemarketing with direct mail, especially when your target audience is relatively small, is a preapproach phone call. You make an initial telephone contact wherein you advise that you are sending a letter and ask the person to watch for and read it. This is an excellent method for avoiding the circular file treatment for your mailing piece.

After the mailing piece has been received, you may also make a follow-up phone call to reinforce the effect of your mailing and obtain the response you want. Perhaps this has happened to you: You receive something in the mail that interests you, but you want to think about it before you decide to take advantage of the offer. You put it aside, intending to return to it at a more favorable time. Time goes on and it gradually slips from your mind, due to countless other demands and decisions that take priority. Eventually you return to the direct mail piece that once was so interesting; but now perhaps the time limit has passed, or for some other reason your initial enthusiasm has lessened—you simply crumple and throw away the offer that once beckoned you.

Imagine if you had received a phone call within a day or two of the mailing piece. Suppose the person calling gave just a bit of additional information in an enthusiastic manner and asked you to act in a specific manner—say yes to an appointment or approve a C.O.D. shipment, or a 30-day trial order, or furnish your credit card number. Might he or she have obtained your agreement? This is how telemarketing can work for you. When you follow your mailing with a planned persuasive telephone call, you can multiply your results tenfold.

TELEMARKETING

Telemarketing is the second most powerful method of marketing and the second most expensive on a per-contact basis. Its impact is possibly one-tenth that of a face-to-face sales call by an outside salesperson. Yet it costs only from $2.50 to $10.00 per call, compared with over $200.00 for every outside sales call by a company representative. Telemarketing, like outside selling, is personal and direct. Because the call is made on a one-to-one basis from a person to a person, it has much greater impact than TV or radio, a print ad or a direct mail piece. It allows for immediate dialogue. The telemarketer can ascertain the level of interest of each prospect and determine if it is worthwhile to continue the sales process or not. The telemarketer also has an opportunity to understand the needs and desires of each prospect and relate the company's product or service to those needs and desires. The telemarketer can respond instantly to each prospect's questions and objections. Thus, the telephone call is an extremely effective marketing tool. To maximize your marketing results, follow up your phone call with a letter or brochure and call again after it is received. The combination of telephone calls and mail is the most cost-effective program of all. We will later review specific combinations of telephone calls and letters in a variety of contexts

OUTSIDE SALES

The personal sales call by an outside representative is the most powerful marketing tool of all. Today's outside sales people are highly professional. They have been schooled in product knowledge and presentation technique. Their people skills have been refined to a science. They are not the hucksters of yesterday, inventing scams to boost their commissions.

Because of this, sales representatives have the ability to call upon an available storehouse of communication tools. Appearance, eye contact, a firm handshake, and body language all are used to produce rapport and develop a relationship. All these nonverbal techniques combined with the advantages of speech make the outside salesperson the most powerful agent of persuasion the company has in the marketplace, albeit the most expensive. When we consider that an outside sales call costs well over $200, most sales don't occur until after three to five calls; and further that salespeople sell no more than one out of five prospects, we begin to realize just how expensive it is to sell by using outside salespeople.

I am not suggesting that telemarketing be used to replace a professional outside sales force. On the contrary, I recommend using telemarketing to support outside salespeople, helping them become more effective and efficient. This is done in several ways. To begin with, telemarketing can be used to qualify prospects. Your telemarketers can call your target universe, seeking those customers whose profiles fit your company's target client profile. Further, your telemarketers can set appointments with qualified prospects, thus freeing a great deal of your salespeople's time. Remember, your salespeople are best at selling face-to-face.

Another important use of telemarketing in a support role is calling existing customers for reorders. This allows your salespeople more time to meet new prospects and adds to your market share. You can set up a definite cycle where your existing customers will be called on a regular basis by your inside telemarketing group, alternated with personal visits to your better customers by your outside salespeople. This development of a team consisting of an inside salesperson and an outside salesperson increases the contact you have with more of your customers, and generates more sales.

SYNERGISTIC SEQUENCING

Let's examine a strategy of using the various marketing components that are most cost effective for you. As we go through the individual steps in this process, be aware that the strategy here is that each step simply takes you to the next step in sales process. In other words, your first contact is not intended to sell your product or service. Its purpose is simply to develop enough interest so that your prospect will consider getting more information, and that way you are gradually developing a relationship with your prospects and helping them get more and more involved with your company and its product.

Many companies think they are using synergistic sales because they employ a combination of print media, direct mail, and telephone follow-up (see Figure 4-1) that begins with an ad in a newspaper or trade journal advertising their product and asking interested parties to call an 800 number for more information or fill out and return a coupon. The company receives the call or the coupon and sends out a brochure or some other information package. Then the salesperson is supposed to follow up.

Ostensibly this appears to be a valid approach, a combination

Traditional Marketing Sequence

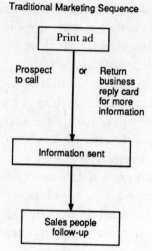

FIGURE 4-1

of the print ad to attract attention, fulfillment package to develop interest further and the call by the salesperson to follow up.

Unfortunately, this process is largely ineffective for several reasons. Many of the people who respond to the ad are either not decisionmakers or are simply gathering information for the future. Time and again, when salespeople follow up only to find the customer nowhere near the point of making a buying decision, they learn not to spend their time exploring these leads. According to media experts, 30 percent of these leads are never followed up.

Telemarketing is the missing ingredient that can turn a marginal marketing strategy into a powerfully effective one. (See Figure 4-2). As previously, your print ad generates some reader response. Either the prospect calls for additional information or returns a completed coupon. In the case of the telephone query, an incoming telemarketing representative takes the call, gets a name, address and telephone number, and then proceeds to ask questions that qualify the caller as someone simply gathering information, someone who has a moderate interest perhaps for a later time, or a real prospect genuinely interested in learning more about your product with a clear intent to act.

Those prospects disqualified as information gatherers can be

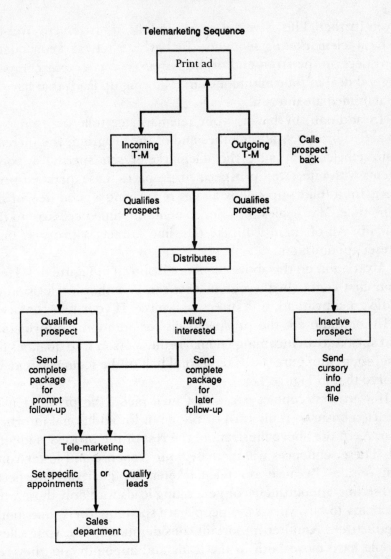

Telemarketing Sequence

FIGURE 4-2

sent a cursory information package and then be placed in an inactive file. Those identified as having moderate interest can be sent a complete package of information and their names filed for later follow-up by your sales staff. Those prospects with a more immediate need can be sent the more complete package of information and their names forwarded to your telemarketing staff to set a specific appointment for a salesperson or qualify the lead even further. This system is a tremendous improvement over the typical telemarketing sequence. By having a telemarketer qualify prospects in the front end of the system, you save your company a good deal of time and money in following up leads that have no real immediate interest.

In addition, by having your telemarketer follow up on your qualified prospects at the other end of the program, you increase your efficiency because the telemarketer sets specific appointments with interested prospects or prepares these qualified prospects for a follow-up call by a sales rep, saving a good deal of the rep's time. Many sales reps don't spend the time necessary to follow up. All of them will take the time to meet a prospect on a preset appointment.

A variation on the above sequence is shown in Figure 4-3. Here your first contact with your market can be either a television or radio ad, a print ad, or a direct mail piece. If your first contact is a TV or radio ad, the prospect calls for additional information and speaks to an incoming telemarketing person who qualifies his interest, as in Figure 4-2. The second half of the sequence is identical to that in Figure 4-2.

If your first contact is a direct mail piece, the prospect may return a business reply card or phone in for additional information. As in the above illustration, the rest of the process is identical. These sequences will increase your response and lower your costs of sales. Because your telemarketers are qualifying prospects and setting appointments or generating leads with only those who are ready to buy, your sales people are spending their time more productively. Another important consideration is that your salespeople have more faith in the leads and appointments they receive because they are the result of this qualifying process.

Another valuable byproduct of utilizing telemarketing in this process is that it lends itself to systematic tracking of results. We will discuss this in greater detail in another chapter.

TELEPHONE AND MAIL COMBINATION

One of the most powerful combinations that can be used synergistically in the marketing process is a combination of telephone

Telemarketing Sequence Variation

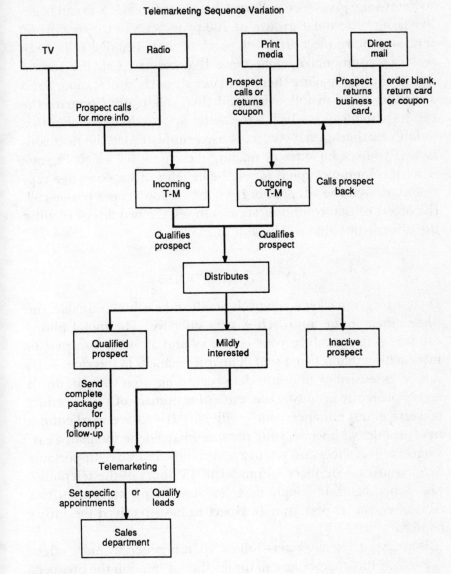

FIGURE 4-3

calling and letter writing. Ronald Mock of Scientific Marketing Inc. goes so far as to say that a combination of three letters, two telephone calls, and one sales visit is equivalent to three personal sales calls.

The question is invariably asked, which comes first: the letter or the phone call? This is many times a matter of trial and error to determine just which will work best in your case. You can begin by taking two similar groups of 200 prospects. To the first group send a mailing piece first, followed up with a phone call. Then send an additional mailing piece if necessary. Call the second group without mailing them any preapproach information. Send a mailing piece to follow-up, and then call again. Compare the results to determine which is the better approach. Remember that in both methods, each contact is used simply to sell the next contact. If you send a letter or mailing piece first, the object of your written communication is to sell the benefits of speaking to a representative on the telephone. If your first contact is a phone call, the object of that communication is to sell the benefits of reading the information that will be sent by mail.

Phone/Mail/Phone

If your target market is relatively small and easily identifiable, the phone/mail/phone approach is very effective. The initial phone call serves to introduce your company and alert the prospect to information that is being sent. The information, in this case, need not be extensive or in depth data regarding what you can do. It serves primarily to convey the sense of legitimacy of your product or service and enhance your credibility. If you are marketing a new product with which your prospect may not be familiar, a catalogue or fact sheet and photo are certainly desirable. Important: Send your mailing piece within 24 to 48 hours of the telephone call. Schedule your telephone follow-up for no more than two days after you expect your prospect to have received the information.

When your telemarketers follow up, it is generally more effective to conduct the phone call under the assumption the prospect has received the mailing piece. Do not ask if they have seen or received your material, but proceed as if they have.

The exception to this is if your sales process requires sending a sample or preview of your product. In this case, the telemarketer should determine if that was received before going any further.

Whatever the result of the follow-up phone call, it is good solid business practice to send a letter confirming whatever agreement was reached on the telephone. (We will see later how computer-assisted telemarketing can accomplish this with tremendous efficiency and cost-effectiveness).

This approach works extremely well when you are able to send samples of your products or permit people to preview them. It is also very effective if you allow a small initial order. The combination of telephone calls and letters establishes and develops a relationship between your salespeople and your customers. This relationship helps you get down to business and make the sale.

Mail/Phone/Mail

If your potential source of customers is large and you are selling a relatively expensive product or service, your sales strategy can begin with a mail piece first, which can include a business reply card and/or an 800 number. The mailing piece sells the benefit of calling to get useful information. You add to the effectiveness of your mailing piece by identifying a problem that you know is of concern of your prospect, and your understanding of the problem helps establish your credibility. Don't make the mistake, however, of giving a detailed solution to that problem. If you do that, your prospect may feel informed decision. Simply sell the benefit of finding out more about the solution you have for this problem. It's usually worthwhile to include a short "P. S." to emphasize an additional benefit, or make a special or limited offer. The P. S. is often read before the rest of the copy. Although a business reply card is enclosed, and there is a request made for your prospect to pick up the phone for further information, you should not expect a great response to your initial mailing. Today, a 2 percent return is considered excellent. One-tenth of 1 percent is more realistic. Your letter serves to establish some credibility, and when the phone call is made, you will then increase your percentage of positive responses. Using mail and telephone in combination definitely reinforce each other.

If your company receives orders by mail, you can increase orders 10 percent or more by having a telemarketing group call your customers and announce additional products that are available for sale at an excellent price. They can also increase the order by notifying your customers of discounts available for a larger order. Or you can offer prepaid freight or additional premium items if the total order reaches a specified amount. Using these techniques, it is not unusual to increase your sales by 20 percent or more.

It's worthwhile to create a new offer or promotion each month. This way, when orders come in, your telemarketing staff always has something new to promote or a special discount to encourage purchasing now. The proper procedure is first, take the order, then discuss the promotion.

Telephone and Outside Sales

The combination of telemarketing and outside sales is the most powerful of all. In this strategy, you make use of two high-impact communications methods: the telephone call and the personal visit. The key ingredient in making this approach successful is an application of the division-of-labor principle. You use telemarketers to contact each prospect and customer by phone. You use your sales force to visit them. You can develop a team approach that motivates each group to work harmoniously with the other. This approach is readily applicable to the following three applications:

1. Lead generating
2. Appointments
3. Sales

1. Lead Generating. Your telemarketers make outgoing calls to targeted prospect lists. They introduce themselves and your company. They develop rapport first and then ask several questions to determine the prospect's profile and whether or not it matches the company's target market profile. For example, when selling business machines, the telemarketers determine what kind of equipment the prospect is using now, how old it is, and when they expect to upgrade. The telemarketer identifies the decision maker and the major uses of their existing equipment. This infor-

mation is then passed on to a salesperson who will follow up in person.

This technique saves a good deal of the salesperson's time. Prospecting is one of the most time consuming and frustrating tasks a salesperson performs. While the representatives know it is necessary to contact new companies and understand their income will increase as their customer lists increase, prospecting is so undesirable a function in most salespeople's minds that they will do anything to avoid picking up the phone and talking to strangers.

On the other hand, telemarketing groups can be trained and compensated to make these time-consuming and frustrating calls. Thus, we take an undesirable function for the salesperson and make it a desirable function for the telemarketer. After all, the telemarketer is paid to make lead-generating calls, and can receive a bonus for the successful calls and possibly commission for each lead that results in a sale. We will deal with compensation later in the book.

2. Setting Appointments. Setting appointments is similar to qualifying leads with one important addition. The telemarketer, instead of referring the lead to the sales department, actually sets a specific appointment for the salesperson. Most salespeople learn to love this process.

When appointments are preset for a salesperson, the whole approach to selling improves. It gives salespeople a greater sense of professionalism. After all, they are seeing people who have indicated an interest in seeing them, rather than wasting a lot of energy and time trying to identify qualified leads. As a result, salespeople are more positive and have more energy that can be applied directly to the sale. And, there are more sales calls. They don't have to spend hours on the phone making appointments. Those hours can be spent instead on a few extra appointments each week. The "numbers" aspect of sales alone means that your company must increase its sales revenue.

Of course, there will be mishaps and miscommunications. This is especially true in the early stages of a telemarketing appointment program. Many problems can be avoided if you provide direct contact between your telemarketers and the outside salespeople. Your program will gradually be refined because your salespeople are relating what happened on the appointment to the telemarketers. This way, the telemarketers learn to give the salespeople what they want in terms of a qualified appointment. Also, your telemarketers act as a kind of unofficial assistant sales manager. They are interested in how your salespeople are doing because they receive a bonus when a sale is made. Therefore, they serve to remind and reinforce your salespeople regarding the next step of the sales process.

The telemarketing appointment program I designed for a major insurance broker resulted in $1 million in premiums sold in one year. This was the work of one telemarketer who set appointments for a staff of five insurance brokers. In addition, the telemarketer researched expiration dates of over 800 companies that had already renewed their insurance that particular year, meaning that the following year the insurance brokers would know exactly when to approach these prospects to offer quotes on their insurance products.

3. Selling. The "inside-outside" team approach is equally effective when both members of the team actually sell. There are several variations that you can use.

a. *Shared Accounts.* In this approach, the outside sales rep and the inside telemarketer both service the same accounts. The salesperson has a regular schedule for visiting them at predetermined intervals—once a month, once a quarter, or even once a year. The choice is yours. Between visits, the telemarketer maintains contact by calling the customer, which gives your customers the feeling they are being serviced properly because they hear from or see a representative of your company on a regular basis. Correspondingly, this system allows your outside sales reps to visit many more accounts than they would otherwise. Your inside group services your customer base, while your outside group continually expands it. The additional sales results can be astounding.

b. *Division of Accounts.* In this approach, your outside salespeople split accounts with your inside group. They also refer prospects and customers to each other. For example, your outside group can deal with larger companies that offer greater dollar sales potential. Because your outside reps will sell exclusively to those customers who exceed a certain minimum dollar amount of projected sales, whenever they encounter a prospect that falls below the minimum, they refer this company to your inside group. The outside rep receives a bonus based on the sales generated, which encourages compliance with the referral program. Because the outside sales reps are producing higher sales by spending more time with bigger accounts, it is to their advantage to refer smaller accounts to the inside staff.

By the same token, the inside sales staff is encouraged to refer larger accounts to their outside counterparts. Because it is difficult to retain a large account without occasionally visiting that account, it makes sense to the inside salesperson to refer an outside rep to service that account. To encourage compliance, give the inside salesperson a bonus or commission based on the sales that will be generated. In this way, a reciprocal relationship is fostered between your incoming and outgoing groups.

There are countless possibilities open to you in synergizing the various components of your marketing mix. To some extent, you may want to experiment to find which will work best for you. There is no question, though, that employing telemarketing in conjunction with direct mail, media advertising, and outside sales calls will result in sales revenue beyond what you might expect if you just used these other marketing components individually. That is synergy.

PART TWO

GETTING STARTED IN TELEMARKETING

5

The Entry-Level Approach

Most companies have more than one product or service. If you have one product or service only, you will have no problem deciding what your entry level approach will be. However, with several products and several variations of each product, the question comes up "What do you sell first?"

Your selection of an entry-level approach is a vital component of your telemarketing program. Your entry-level approach is the initial offer you make that allows you to establish a relationship with your prospect.

HOW TO CHOOSE AN ENTRY-LEVEL APPROACH

Whatever you have to sell, for your entry-level approach, choose the one item that is easiest to sell. Your choice may be based on which product serves the most universal need or is most widely recognized by end users.

Once you have chosen the product or service to sell, you must make it easy to buy. Remember, in an entry-level approach, our strategy is to create a relationship with the prospect. Our first objective is to attract a *new customer*. Then we can proceed to develop this customer into one who purchases frequently and in higher volume.

To create a relationship with a new customers, make the first sale easy on both of you. You can do this by offering a small introductory order at a discounted price. Offer to pay the freight if the order exceeds another level. In addition, offer other products free as a premium if another order level is reached.

Importer Turns Company Around

One of my clients, an importer and distributor in the automobile aftermarket industry, had a network of manufacturers' representatives who sold his product line around the country. Primarily the company sold automobile light bulbs, hose clamps, fuses, duct tape, and packaging tape to jobbers, who then sold them to service stations. The most popular item was the number 1157 bulb. This is the bulb that fits most American car taillights. If your automobile's taillight burns out and you take it into your neighborhood gas station or auto parts dealer, they will replace it with an 1157 taillight in most cases.

Although my client sold many other light bulbs for automobiles, we decided to stress the 1157 in our initial sales call. In addition, we offered to send all customers who bought $200 worth of bulbs a gross of automobile fuses.

My client had a list of 10,000 jobbers and wholesalers he wanted to contact. He designed and printed a four-page flyer that fit into a number 10 envelope, announcing the new telemarketing program and listing the entire product line along with special promotional prices on the 1157 bulb. In addition, he offered to pay the freight on any order over $100.

About a week after the flyers were sent, telemarketers began calling to follow up. They were instructed that the minimum sale was $50.

As a direct result of this approach, which stressed a sample order of 1157 light bulbs, the company attracted over 1000 new accounts with an average initial order of more than $100 each.

In the months ahead, these accounts were called and sent flyers at regular intervals, which led to additional sales. The company, once floundering due to poor sales coverage by its manufacturers' representatives, actually doubled its sales.

Video Company Boosts Sales

Another client sold video training to hospitals and schools. Its marketing approach had been to mail catalogues to a list of approximately 35,000 hospitals and schools, taking orders from customers by mail and phone. In addition, they could preview the training film or video and then decide whether or not they would keep it.

We designed an outgoing telemarketing program where five telemarketers called those hospitals and schools that had not ordered in the past two years. My client had over 1000 titles of programs to sell. We determined that our entry-level approach would be oriented towards promoting and selling the newest productions which were developed around seven packages of programs.

In support of our new telemarketing program, the company offered two key sales facilitators:

1) Buy five titles and get three more free.
2) Trade in a similar title and receive $75 as a trade-in allowance.

The first month of operation, we generated $60,000 in sales and $500,000 in previews. Over 10 percent resulted in additional sales. This program increased sales revenues over 50 percent the first year.

APPOINTMENT STRATEGIES

If your telemarketing program is being used to set up qualified appointments for outside sales representatives, your entry-level approach is extremely important. The traditional way to set appointments is to give only enough information to "sell" the appointment. You don't want to sell your product or service, in this case, by telephone. Remember, giving too much information may lead your prospect to think he or she knows enough to make a decision. On the first call, there is better than a 50 percent chance the decision will *not* be favorable. Therefore, in an appointment-setting program, your telemarketers should give only enough information to sell the next step.

There are two major strategies for setting appointments by telephone. Your entry level approach can then be interwoven with either of these strategies. The first is simply to call and ask for an appointment. The second is to call and offer to send more information. Let's examine both briefly:

1) Cold Call for Appointment

This works best when there is something new that your prospects are not aware of, or would like to learn more about. Such an approach might have been taken by a company selling cellular phones when they first appeared on the market. This approach also may be taken by companies that sell business machines, computers, or special services.

2) Cold Call for Literature

In this approach, the telemarketer introduces the company or product, qualifies the prospect, and offers to send additional information. When the prospect responds positively, the telemarketer goes on to say he or she will call after the literature has arrived to discuss it briefly. This is a more indirect approach because the second, or follow-up, call is made for the purpose of setting an appointment. Incidentally, this approach can be expanded and varied so that several calls are made and several mailings are sent before the appointment call.

When a series of phone calls and mailings preceed the request for an appointment, you naturally provide more information than when you simply cold call for an appointment, which is very advantageous to a company selling a complex product or service. It also allows your prospects to qualify themselves. If your prospect consents to an appointment after receiving detailed information about your company's products, you have a much better chance of success. This strategy is very effective with top executives of corporations and where the sales transactions will involve large sums. It also serves to build credibility, especially when the literature or brochures you send are impressive.

Selling Insurance. This latter method has been used very successfully to sell executive compensation packages that are funded by insurance programs. One of my clients had a single telemarketer call executives of closely held corporations and offer to send information on how they could defer income and taxes. After sending the literature, the telemarketer made a follow-up call and set appointments. This program generated an additional $75,000 in commissions for my client the first year. The second year his additional income jumped to $500,000 using this program.

KEY FACTORS IN YOUR DECISION

There is another set of factors to consider when deciding which of the two strategies to select. If you have an exceptionally capable staff of telemarketers, they can probably set appointments without needing to send additional information. On the other hand, if your telemarketers are merely competent, or if there is a great deal of competition for your prospect's time, it would behoove you simply to ask for permission to send some important information. This latter approach conveys a greater sense of professionalism.

Whether you use a one-call or a two-call approach for an appointment, you must "sell" to your prospect the value of making the appointment. You can do this by offering a free analysis of the company's existing situation, some other service, or even a free gift.

Free is still a magic word. One of my clients sells an automatic device that thoroughly cleans swimming pools. He developed a two-call approach: In the first call he offered to send information regarding cleaning the swimming pool more effectively, and at the same time asked whether the prospect used a pool service, an automatic pool cleaning device, or cleaned it themselves. Based on the information received, the telemarketers sent appropriate literature. About a week after the initial contact, the telemarketers then called to offer a demonstration of how this pool cleaner worked, which in effect was an offer to clean their pool for free. This approach was a stunning success—over 50 percent of the pool owners who received a free pool cleaning purchased the system.

Another client sells an extremely complex deferred compensation program to high-income executives. Here, too, we used the two-step approach very successfully. The initial call established contact and offered to send the executive the results of a survey of executive compensation at the top companies in California, along with a free 10-minute audio cassette. The second phone call, made about a week later, set the appointment. This extremely effective approach resulted in sales of millions of dollars of deferred compensation programs.

This program also has been used very successfully with only one call. The difference primarily is that the telemarketer setting appointments on the very first call is extremely talented and develops such excellent rapport that no follow-up call is necessary.

Another successful example of a single call for appointment program was one used by a computer company selling accounting systems to accountants to service their clients. They used a seminar approach. Accountants were called and invited to attend a free seminar to learn more about systems to serve their clients better *and* receive continuing education credits in their profession. This worked very well. Each week, the company held two seminars, with an average attendance of seven accountants. An average of three eventually became clients.

DEVELOP A UNIQUE APPROACH

Business is becoming increasingly competitive. To get the attention of someone who can buy from your company, you must be willing to develop a special approach. You can use an approach similar to those discussed or create one that better meet the needs of your company and prospects. The key to success is offering something your customer wants. Rather than orient it toward selling products and services, your approach is designed to get you in the door to begin a relationship with a customer. The entré can be simply an appointment or it can be a sample order. After your prospect develops a sense of your company's credibility you will sell more and different products and services.

If you are making appointments, you sell the appointment, not the product or service. If you are selling products or services by telephone, you sell a sample introductory order, not the large order you eventually want. That will come later—on the next call.

6

Target Marketing by Telephone

I came across the following in a book of old sayings: "To prepare for the future, examine the present. To understand the present, study the past." Although the person who penned this aphorism probably was not thinking about its marketing implications, it is extremely applicable to this chapter.

PROSPECT PROFILES

By examining current customers, you can construct a profile of their characteristics and seek new customers who match this profile. Begin by making a list of your *best* customers. Use the 20/80 principle to make your selection. By this I mean that *20 percent of your customers give you 80 percent of your business.* Examine your company's top 20 percent and expand your customer base in this direction.

What are your best customers' characteristics? If you sell to other businesses, how many people do they employ? What industries are they in? What is their average annual sales volume? Are they single or multiple location companies? Are they manufacturers, distributors, or retailers? Do they sell products or provide services?

If you sell to consumers, what characteristics do your best customers have in common? Are they blue collar workers, professionals, executives, or office workers? What is their average income range? Where do they live? What other important qualities are similar?

By analyzing the profiles of your customer base, especially those customers who do the most business with your company, you can begin to identify the prospects that will be most profitable to pursue. Why not seek new customers among those who potentially have the most to offer? Rather than seek new business randomly, identify customer profiles and then market to other companies or consumers that match those profiles.

TARGET MARKETING

Target marketing is the process of identifying companies or consumers who fit specific parameters or demographics, and then orienting your marketing process to those prospects. Once you identify the unique characteristics in your "best customer" profile, buy or rent a list of companies or consumers who fit those same specifications.

Although this concept of target marketing is simple and logical, it is amazing how few companies actually employ it. Most companies continue to market in the same old manner, with no real plan. For example, does *your* company have a marketing plan? If it does, you are decidedly in a minority. Although it is beyond the scope of this book to help you create a marketing plan, it would be worthwhile for you to do so as soon as possible, and include telemarketing as an important part of that plan.

Before you purchase your lists you need to take some time to analyze your existing customer profiles, including their SIC codes, annual revenue, number of employees, and buying history.

Since you intend to pursue those prospects that will be most profitable, understand what characteristics your most profitable customers have in common.

A client whose customers are hospitals that vary in size from 25 to 500 beds performed such an analysis and learned that their most profitable market was composed of hospitals with 150 to 300 beds. They targeted this market by securing a list of such hospitals and then began telemarketing to them. They increased their sales by 50 percent. Now they only market to hospitals with fewer than 150 beds when they are training new telephone sales people. This is a way to get new people started without any great risk of loss. After their salespeople become proficient, they switch them to the larger accounts where the greatest profit can result.

Once you have an understanding of the markets that offer the best potential, it is an easy matter to get an appropriate list. In every area there are innumerable list houses and list brokers that concentrate on providing accurate lists to their customers.

PROFILING PARAMETERS

Businesses are categorized by Standard Industrial Classification (SIC) codes, which identify the specific business activity they perform. For example, a company that distributes automotive products would be classified with the SIC code 5013. In addition, businesses are identified in terms of number of employees, annual dollar sales, home office, or branch. SIC listings can be found in *Dun's Marketing, Contacts Influential,* or your local Chamber of Commerce.

Incidentally, if the annual sales revenue is not available, you can make an accurate projection by taking the number of employees and multiplying by $50,000 for each employee. This will, by and large, put you in the right range.

LISTS AND DIRECTORIES

"List" is a generic term that refers to sequential listings of prospects, including their addresses and possibly other significant information. The term also refers to names and addresses presented in other formats, such as index cards and mailing labels. Because they do *not* automatically include telephone numbers, you must specifically request that phone numbers be furnished. A directory is a list that is printed in book form.

If your telemarketing program is computerized, you may request your lists on magnetic tape or diskettes. If you are not computerized, I recommend that you use the card format to give your telemarketers the sense that each card is important and unique. An alternate format is labels, which may be affixed to cards or prospect sheets, allowing your staff to make extensive notes regarding each call. Card and label formats permit easy filing for follow-up calls. Lists must generally be transferred to some other form for follow up.

Lists and directories vary in cost from a few cents per name to as much as $2 per name. As a rule, the more expensive the list, the better it is in terms of completeness and accuracy of information. Companies that provide lists may rent them, license their unlimited use for a specific period of time, or sell them outright. There is a great deal of variance in the permitted use of these lists. For example, most phone companies make cross-street directories available to the public on a quarterly rental basis. Computerized services may license the unlimited use of a floppy diskette containing leads—generally for a limited period of time. Other companies will sell directories with unlimited rights. Still others will sell leads for single use only. Also, lists that cover a specific field *exclusively*—such as doctors, people with high incomes, lawyers, architects, and so on—cost more to rent or buy. *Dun's Marketing* provides comprehensive information, but is not inexpensive. Other sources are chambers of commerce and numerous other list brokers and directories. Just look under Mailing Lists in your local *Yellow Pages*. You need to experiment to determine whose lists work best for you. However, it is a good idea to remember that any list is better than none. You'll be way ahead by doing telemarketing with a mediocre list, than not doing it at all. If you have any doubts about the list you want to use, order a trial or sample of names on that list and test it. If it proves accurate and you are generating good quality appointments and sales, then order some more. If not, go on to the next.

There are, of course, ample lists of consumers. They are classified in a variety of categories from investors in real estate to mail-order buyers and members of many professions. It is amazing just how many different kinds of lists are available.

COMPUTER MATCHING

Some list houses are extremely sophisticated in their use of computer power. For example, suppose you have a product that you believe would sell extremely well to those households who subscribe to both *Ladies' Home Journal* and *Playboy*. It is possible to get a computer tape of *Playboy* subscribers and match it against a tape of *Ladies' Home Journal* subscribers and produce a final output tape or list of only those who subscribe to both. This kind of targeting can give you impressive results.

Target marketing is diametrically opposite to the kind of nuisance phone calls that annoy most people, especially consumers, at home. Most companies who use telemarketing call at random, using reverse street directories or telephone directory white pages without knowing anything about the company or consumer being called. This is extremely wasteful and relies totally on the old adage that if you make enough calls, eventually you'll find someone who has an interest in what you're selling. It's far more effective to profile your market and obtain good lists that target that market. There is a greater initial investment when you procure good lists, but that investment is more than paid back in terms of the quality of leads and the savings of your telemarketers' time.

7

Creating a Telemarketing Environment

The concept of facilities planning for telemarketing is a very recent one, unheard of in the early days of the boiler room. Now, however, companies are becoming aware that investing in a proper environment will help increase the efficiency of the people who work in that environment.

Ergonomics, the study of adapting the environment, including furniture and equipment, to human beings, has now been applied to telemarketing. The result is an onslaught of new furniture, communications equipment, and computers all oriented toward telemarketing. Examples of what is available are provided in the following pages. There are configurations for every budget. It is possible to make do with what you have or use state-of-the-art modular furniture at a cost of up to $2500 per station.

YOUR MAJOR OBJECTIVE

To help you sort through the confusion of the choices now available, you must remember that the purpose of your telemarketing facility is to optimize your sales, so the physical layout of your telephone center should be designed with the emphasis on effective telemarketing. It should certainly be functional and attractive. The need for function is obvious; later we'll review some specific aspects of increasing your center's effectiveness.

What is not so obvious is the significance of making significant, your telemarketing environment pleasant and appealing. Telephone work, whether part or full time, is difficult and often demoralizing. An attractive phone room serves to counteract the negative side of telemarketing.

Ideally, your phone center should be designed to be as self-sufficient as possible. It should contain customer files and product information. Office equipment and supplies should be handy. The principle is to design the room to save time, increase productivity, and promote the comfort of your telemarketers.

ROOM LAYOUT

Good planning can save time and expense. Begin by measuring the dimensions of your phone room, and lay out those dimensions to scale on graph paper. There are numerous design possibilities from which you may select. The size and shape of your room, as well as the number of telemarketers, will certainly influence your decision. Whichever design you select should make it possible for your telemarketers to overhear each other, yet still have a sense of their own privacy.

For example, in the triple station system, each telephone sales representative's space is sufficient to support his or her efforts. The verticals of the partitions can be used to post information. There is desk space for follow-up work. Workers have their own areas, yet are able to overhear each other, which helps foster a sense of friendly competition. It also allows telemarketers to learn from one another by overhearing key phrases, and helps build a high level of energy in the room, energy that helps overcome individual rejection.

The amount of space a telemarketer requires also varies based on several other factors:

Is this a computer assisted telemarketing program?

Is this an incoming or outgoing program?

Is there a need for reference material?

How big is the potential sales volume?

Is this an appointment-setting or sales program?

Common sense will prevail. The greater the sales potential, the bigger your budget should be for the telemarketing furniture.

Another consideration is the location of the supervisor's desk. One functional design is a U-shaped room, where the telemarketers are arranged along three of the walls of the room, and the supervisor or manager is at the open "U" end of the room (see Figure 7-1). The supervisor's desk may be elevated if desired, to enable the supervisor to view each of the telemarketers clearly. This arrangement is effective in appointment setting, lead generating, and survey applications. It is also used when relatively inexpensive items are sold by telephone, such as newspaper subscriptions. Alternatives to this layout are shown in Figures 7-2 and 7-3.

Workable layouts for salespeople and customer service representatives may be single units, double units, or modules of three, four, and five. These can be clustered in various combinations, depending on the space available. See Figures 7-4–7-9.

FURNITURE

There is a wide spectrum of furniture available for telemarketing. You may expect a typical workstation to require an investment of $1000 to $1500. Variables of material and design determine the cost. If necessary, you can always begin with the traditional desk, chair, and phone; and then graduate to an environment that is designed specifically for your telemarketing requirements.

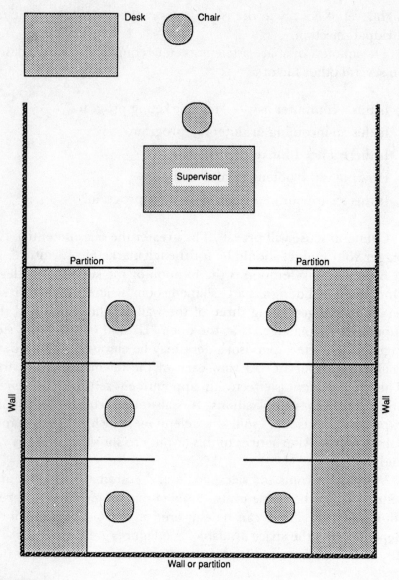

FIGURE 7-1

TELEPHONE SYSTEM

Your choice of the proper telephone equipment is certainly among the most important decisions you make. With the deregulation of AT&T, hundreds of independent phone companies have been created. There's a wide variety from which to choose. Quality differs greatly.

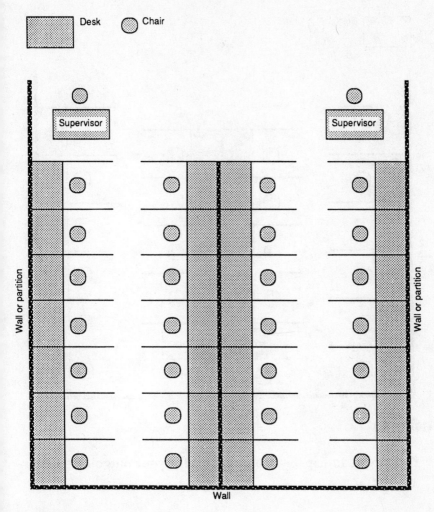

FIGURE 7-2

Generally, the independent companies offer advanced features at lower costs than AT&T. You must, however, be aware of service and reliability. This is not to say that the competitive equipment is not high quality. Rather, there is a great deal of variance and cost should not be your only consideration.

Regardless of which company you select to furnish your telephone equipment, you should make the following decisions:

1. How much growth do you foresee?

2. Do your people need to communicate with other departments?

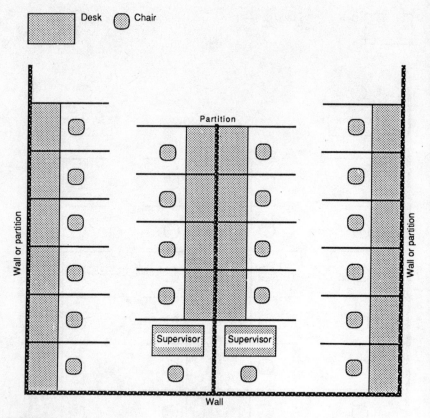

FIGURE 7-3

3. Do you anticipate incoming calls for your outgoing telemarketers?

The answers to these questions will determine the number of
lines and the station configurations. For example, if you expect
your telemarketers to receive incoming calls as well as make outgoing calls, you must have sufficient lines to handle this activity.
Your telemarketers also should have a phone system that will allow them to put one line on hold and use another line. Modern
technology offers a variety of methods to accomplish this. You can
have multibutton telephone instruments or instruments with no
buttons that allow multiple lines, hold capability, and conference
calling. Whatever system you choose will depend on the application. Good planning is very important here.

The number of lines you need will depend the number of telemarketers, the amount of paper work, and whether you are

FIGURE 7-4

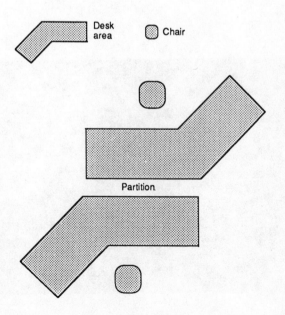

Desk area   Chair

Partition

FIGURE 7-5

85

Desk Area | Chair

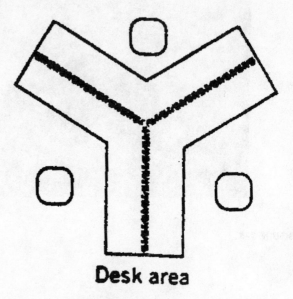

Desk area

FIGURE 7-6

FIGURE 7-7

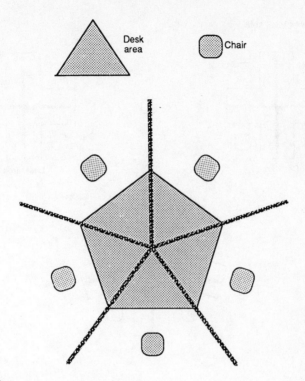

FIGURE 7-8

computerized. In general, if there are five or fewer telemarketers, you should you have one line available for each. If you do not use computer assistance and there is some paperwork required, you may use five lines for every six or seven telemarketers, because all lines will not be needed by all the telemarketers at any one time.

On the other hand, if there is little paperwork and you have an efficient computer-assisted telemarketing program, each of your telemarketers will be spending most of his or her time on the phone and will require an available line at all times.

For an inbound telemarketing operation, you will of course require one line and instrument for every telephone service representative. If you have more than five incoming representatives, you should install either a call sequencer or an automatic call distribution (ACD). The latter automatically distributes incoming calls on a preselected basis. It can distribute the calls to those telephone representatives who have been idle the longest, while an-

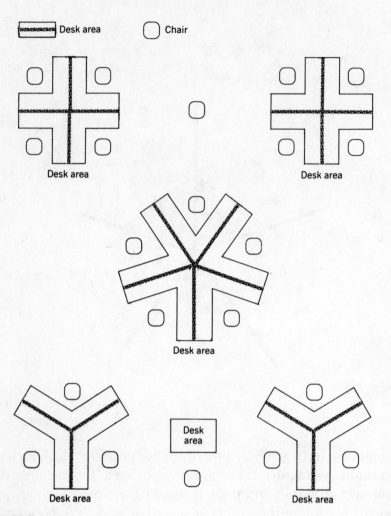

FIGURE 7-9

swering and queuing calls during busy periods. It also can play recorded messages. If the delays are too long, the ACD transfers them to a secondary group and even provides management with reports on the call activity. Automatic call distributors also can be used to send more calls to the more experienced operators and fewer calls to those with less experience.

The call sequencer is a simpler, less expensive version of the automatic call distributor. With it, operators make decisions regarding the longest idle calls. This system also furnishes management with basic reports and may make recorded announcements to callers in overload situations.

In many telephone rooms, headsets are mandatory. This is especially true in incoming phone centers. Headsets allow greater comfort for the phone representative, are more efficient in that the operator need not hang up or pick up the telephone continuously, and are especially useful in computerized operations where the operator has both hands free to key information. Another important benefit of using headsets is that the noise level of the phone room is lower. It may take some adjustment on the part of your telemarketers, but headsets are generally appreciated by the majority of the people who spend long hours on the telephone. There was a time when people found them uncomfortable, but design improvements have removed the discomfort. Even executives who spend a good deal of time on the phone find they prefer a headset.

SPECIAL EQUIPMENT

You should furnish your phone room with a device that allows a supervisor or group of telemarketers to overhear both ends of the conversation. This is a very powerful training tool as well as a monitoring technique. There are several alternatives, either mechanical or electronic. For example, each phone may be wired with an external speaker that will allow the group to overhear the conversation. Or it may simply contain an external jack allowing the supervisorto plug in his headset and listen to or even participate in the conversation.

1. *Advanced phone systems* allow a supervisor to monitor any conversation in the room from his or her own station by simply dialing the proper code. Choose the method most practicable in your situation.

Some phone rooms are configured so that each individual telephone representative has a 1-line instrument and the supervisor's telephone set contains all the lines. In this way the supervisor can depress any button and overhear the conversation taking place.

Many phone rooms utilize such equipment to help close the sale or set an appointment. A telemarketer having difficulty raises his or her hand, whereupon the supervisor picks up and listens in on the conversation, perhaps even taking over the call and completing it successfully. In phone room parlance, this is called a turnover, or *TO*.

2. *Least-cost routing* is a system that automatically determines which telephone service is most economical to complete the number being dialed. This is a valuable option when there is a great deal of long-distance calling, but is not necessary in a small phone room, or one where most calls are local. A least-cost routing system will select from regular Bell system lines, WATS lines, and services such as Sprint, MCI, and so on.

3. *Foreign exchange lines* are lines outside your central office area, and offer cost savings, if you make a good many calls to a specific section of the city that requires a toll call. Instead of incurring toll charges, you pay a fixed fee for the foreign exchange line and every call made using that line is a local call. A traffic study can determine whether it is economical to use foreign exchange lines.

4. *Station message detail recording,* using a device that keeps track of the calls made on each individual station and provides reports to management on the usage, can be used in conjunction with an automatic call distributor. This helps increase effectiveness and deter personal phone calls by virtue of computer printouts reporting which calls were made by which telemarketer, length of each call, and charges.

5. *The telephone record control* is a device that makes a tape recording of both sides of a telephone conversation. It starts when the telemarketer begins to dial and stops when the telemarketer hangs up. This is an excellent tool for training and for monitoring performance.

6. *Facsimile machines* are also finding their way into telephone centers. This device transmits printed information over telephone lines to other locations for an exact copy. This is useful when a phone room is used to generate appointments, for example, for a number of remote locations. When appointments are set, they are

transmitted electronically at high speeds to the remote center where they are distributed to salespeople. This method of transmission speeds response and cuts down on errors.

A phone room will most likely not require all these options. Once you have determined your objectives, it is wise to use all the proper equipment that will help you realize those objectives. An investment in a modern facility will pay for itself in increased effectiveness and reduced employee turnover.

PART THREE

BUILDING A TELEMARKETING STAFF

8

How to Recruit and Hire Telemarketers

During the past seven years, I have designed, developed, and implemented more than 100 telemarketing programs. As a result of this experience, I can state categorically that the most important ingredient in a successful outgoing telemarketing program is the telemarketer. The quality and ability of the people who make the phone calls are the deciding factors in the degree of success or failure of the program.

To put these comments in perspective, the programs I get involved with usually are specialized, rather than mass marketing, approaches. In the latter, which depend mostly on quantity not quality, such as magazine renewals, credit card applications to preapproved potential applicants, and other such high-volume marketing programs, individual excellence is relatively insignificant. It is largely a numbers game.

Programs I have been involved in, and which I trust are similar to yours, have the following characteristics:

1. Company image is important.
2. The market is targeted and specific.
3. Vital information must be communicated.
4. The caller must appear knowledgeable.
5. There is relative difficulty in setting the appointment or completing the sale.

In short, when the telemarketing program requires complex communication, or the ability to get through to key people and maintain their interest and attention, the essential success factor is the quality of the person on the phone—the telemarketer.

Computers, electronics, and stocks and bonds are some examples of industries that require complex communications. These industries demand that a high caliber, intelligent, knowledgeable message be conveyed. Now this does not mean that all telemarketers have all these qualities. It simply means that they must communicate them. Skilled telephone sales people have the ability, with just enough data—perhaps only a page or two—to express articulately the information necessary to make a sale or set a qualified appointment.

In the same way, industries like insurance, real estate, and business machines require extremely personable individuals who are adept at establishing rapport and probing and qualifying prospects. These telemarketers must be able to make strong presentations, handle objections, and respond with alternate closing statements and questions that result in appointments with qualified buyers.

Many times, the prospect who initially believes he has no need must be made aware of a need. This is no easy task.

Most prospects for sales in these industries do not think of themselves as having a need. They don't want to spend their time discussing insurance, for example. They think they have addressed all their needs. In order to be successful at setting qualified appointments, or selling products and services in these industries, the telemarketers must be very skilled in interpersonal communication.

As most managers know, starting out with a good employee makes training a lot easier. Telemarketing is no different. If you can start out with an articulate, motivated, persuasive person, it will be a lot easier to train him or her to be more successful and effective.

QUALITIES TO LISTEN FOR

Before you can hire the right employees, you must know what attributes they ought to possess. The key word is *listening*. You're not going to spend a good deal of time *looking at* potential employees, because neither will your prospects. In all likelihood, they will never meet them. Therefore, the most important quality is how they sound on the telephone.

How do their voices sound? Are they pleasant to listen to? Reasonably enthusiastic? Can they modulate, giving variety to their expression? Is grammar and diction correct? Do they convey confidence? Is there an overall air of optimism, or is there a negative attitude conveyed? Do they listen in the interview, or step on your words? Do they vary the pace of their conversations to make them more interesting? Do they have a sense of humor? Are their voices deep, grating, or high? Do they speak loudly enough?

In short, what is your overall impression of your candidates' abilities to speak on the telephone?

Obviously, you're listening for someone to whom other people would enjoy talking. The question you must ask yourself is, "Do I like talking to this person?" If you don't, chances are most other people won't either.

Realize that the perfect telephone voice does not exist. So even though we are listening for all these qualities, it is not possible to find them all in one human being. And if you did, he or she would be in the wrong profession and should be an actor or politician. Although a telemarketer may not necessarily have the perfect set of vocal tools, that person can compensate for a deficiency in one area with an abundance in another.

I prefer people who ask me questions, people who probe to qualify me or my company. My reasoning is: If they probe when they talk to me, they'll do the same when they talk to my client's prospects, which is what I want.

Persistence is another vital component in a telemarketer's tool chest. Anyone who earns a living on the phone receives countless refusals. How quickly does a person give up? How much effort will he or she make? I love to hear stories of how a telemarketer called someone 5 or 10 times or more before setting an appointment or making a sale. This shows me persistence.

More about the importance of humor: A good sense of humor is possibly the single most important characteristic possessed by a telephone salesperson. Humor can relax the prospect and make it easier to listen to the presentation. Humor can help handle an objection and put it in its proper perspective. With humor, there is room to go back and close again after one attempt fails. A person who uses humor naturally, effectively, and appropriately is very hard to deny.

WHAT NOT TO LOOK FOR

The first thing not to look for is a stunning appearance. How attractive, impeccably groomed, and well dressed the candidate is does not matter for telephone selling. You should seek an appearance acceptable to the social environment of the office. The attitude and culture of your company may emphasize that the telemarketer's appearance fit in with the overall appearance of the other people who work there. In that case, be sure that the applicant has no dramaticaly undesirable characteristics that would make it difficult for the other people in the office to feel comfortable. You certainly don't want to disrupt the work others are doing. However, some companies go so far as to have separate areas for their telemarketers. They literally segregate them from the rest of the company. In such an environment, the telemarketers' appearance matters not at all.

Interestingly, one of the best telemarketers I ever hired had about the worst appearance you can imagine. She was a woman in her late 50s, dressed in old raggedy clothes, and bore a marked resemblance to those bag ladies we see on the streets in any major city. She was overweight, her skin was blotched, and her hands trembled.

I met Jane when she answered an ad I ran for a telephone solicitor to set appointments for a computer company. She sounded great on the telephone. Although her voice was very deep and could easily have been mistaken for that of a man, her overall presentation was very effective. You can imagine the surprise and embarrassment when this bedraggled woman entered the modern office of my computer company client. Before I had much of a chance to talk to her, the vice-president of the company beckoned me aside and told me in no uncertain terms, "Get her out of here!"

Although I knew she wasn't destined to work there, I felt I owed her the courtesy of an interview, since she had made the appointment. While talking to her, an idea began to form. I thought, "Why not have her work for me?" I really liked the way she communicated on the telephone. I told her I would call her later and follow up on some ideas I had. I began to realize that although she would be very effective as a telephone solicitor, I didn't want her in my office, either. She was about as out of place in an office environment as a punk rocker at a debutante ball.

The solution was to have her call from her own home. I gave her a presentation and leads with which to set appointments. She called me at the end of each day, asked for changes in my schedule, and gave me the names and addresses of the appointments she had made. Most of our contact was by phone and mail. One day I dropped off some leads to her. To my great surprise, she was living at a sort of halfway house. It was not especially pleasant there, but she had installed a telephone in her room and worked at it every day.

To complete this digression, I must tell you that many of the appointments she set for me resulted in extremely profitable business. As a matter of fact, two of my best clients—leaders in the insurance industry—came from appointments which she set.

Another facet of the candidate's history that I don't pay much attention to is frequency of job changes. Whereas in other careers job hopping is certainly undesirable, in telemarketing I've learned to be tolerant of it. My rationale is that most companies give very poor training to their telemarketing personnel. It is also true that many companies engaged in one form of telemarketing or another have in the past exploited their people, not showing a concern for their long-term well being.

Telemarketing is a newly emerging industry and many disreputable practices have occurred, so I find it quite natural that the experience people I interview have not stayed very long where conditions have been undesirable. I believe if you select good people, train them well, give them a decent working environment, and compensate them fairly, they will stay with you. Some of the people I hired more than four years ago are still with the same company.

One last important question remains: "Should I hire an experienced person only, or should I hire someone who has no experience?" This is a controversial point. Some people only hire experienced people who have a long history of working on the telephone. Others believe that all the good telemarketers—those with the desire, experience, skills, and abilities—are already working and are earning a good income. Therefore, the only experienced salespeople they expect to interview are those who have not been very successful. Unfortunately there is a great deal of truth to this.

The very best people, in general, are working somewhere now, and want to change. Why should they? Chances are that if your ad attracts people who have experience, they will be those whose experience has been bad. That is to say, they will not be the top achievers in the industry. It is also true that experienced people who are not among the top achievers in the industry will also very likely have bad habits that are difficult to correct, so some consultants advocate hiring the inexperienced with good basic skills and the ability to learn. Unfortunately, those who fit into this category do not generally have any interest in being telemarketers.

My own solution to this problem is to be open to both experienced and inexperienced people. I have had great success, and some failures, with both. Fortunately, one of the advantages of telemarketing is that results are quickly assessed. If you have a good phone person, you will know literally in a day or two. If not, you will know that also.

HOW TO RECRUIT

Although there is a variety of ways you can recruit good people, the most effective is classified advertising. Before we discuss the writing and placement of the ad, let's briefly review some other methods of recruiting.

1. Referrals

Other people will tell you about good telemarketers. Your friends or your current employees may know some individuals who sound impressive. I have found that another's idea of what constitutes a good telemarketer is often different from mine, but they are certainly worth a phone call.

2. Solicitors Who Call You

Occasionally, you receive a telemarketing call from someone who really impresses you. Perhaps they are selling an entertainment package, or some advertising, or office supplies. If you really are impressed with their overall professionalism or telephone demeanor, talk to them about your opportunity. These occurrences are usually rare, but in time they will happen to just about anyone; and when that happens to you, make the most of it.

3. Bulletin Boards

You can place your ad on a public bulletin board, or opportunity board, like those found at supermarkets, community centers, and colleges. Students are often interested in part-time work, and are a good source of talent. With students, however, the risk is that their tenure will be short. Exams will come up, changes will take place in their schedule, or they graduate and are gone.

WRITING YOUR AD

Before I write an ad, I look through the classified section of the major newspaper in the area of my client's business to determine a normal range of hourly wage. Whatever that norm is, I like to exceed it by at least 50 cents to a dollar per hour. This way, I know that my ad will attract more people than the others, and in that group I will have a better chance of selecting from the best available candidates. Now you may say, "Why pay an extra 50 cents to a dollar an hour? Isn't that more than you need to? That's not good business."

On the contrary, by paying people a little more than the norm you can find those who are worth it. The number of qualified prospects or the amount of closed sales such people will bring to your company will more than compensate for the few dollars extra you pay them. I believe in having the best possible field from which to select. Pay more, and you will attract more and better people. In that group will be the few you want. Otherwise, you will never meet them.

The heading of your ad should read "Part Time," "Telephone Sales," "Telephone Solicitor," or "Telephone Appointment Secretary." Any of these is effective. Make your ad stand out, by running a bigger ad than others, or using double-size capital letters, or bold type to get attention. You should also give the salary early in the ads.

TELEPHONE SOLICITOR—INSURANCE	TELEPHONE SALES—COMPUTER
Earn $5/hr. + $5/appt. + bonus	$250 base salary + commiss.
Set appts. for outside agents	Sell training videos/films
Excellent training and work conditions. 9 A.M.–2 P.M.	Excellent training and work conditions. 6 A.M.–Noon.
L.A. Call Stan (213). . . .	Chino. Call Stan (714). . . .

Notice that in both ads, the industry is clearly spelled out. I let them know what business it is. Also in both cases the earnings are clear and specific. Telephone soliciting tends to be a part-time or hourly job, so I state the amount they can expect to earn per hour, plus the dollars they will receive for every appointment they set (that is kept), plus a bonus. In sales, I expect people to work longer periods of time and be more concerned with their dollars per hour than with their weekly rates, so I give them a specific figure of $250 per week, or whatever is appropriate to the industry and the caliber of people we need. Generally, this will let people know they are not going to be exploited. They will receive a base while in training and, once trained, there are commissions to be made.

In the solicitor ad, applicants realize their job is to set appointments for outside agents, and they will receive excellent training. Since these ads are for my clients, I know the training will be excellent, because I will be giving it. In addition, the conditions will be excellent because, in most cases, I've also designed, developed, and will implement the program.

At this point, I ask them to call me or one of my associates: "Call Stan" makes it easy for people to approach you and your company. The name also serves as a call identifier for your receptionist. It saves time. In some cases, especially if I know the newspaper covers a large geographical territory, I will designate the specific town or county where the program is to take place. This will prevent a lot of calls from people who live too far away to commute to our location.

When there is a rigid calling schedule, I also include the hours: "mornings only" or "afternoons only," for example. Again, this deters calls from people who are unavailable when we need them. Usually the programs I design are flexible. They are engineered to attract the most able people, and to allow them to perform their work at times that are mutually convenient.

My purpose in this type of advertising is always to attract a large pool of potentially qualified applicants, which means I also will be attracting a number of nonqualified applicants. That's all right; they'll be weeded out. I want the best possible selection I can get. Don't you?

Once I have written my ad, I place it in the Sunday edition of the most widely read newspaper in town. As a rule, I find that just one ad placed on one Sunday will give me more than enough applicants to fill my job requirements.

Remember, most of the consulting work I do is for small and

medium-sized companies. Therefore, the projects I initiate usually begin with a small number of people. This makes the program easier to control, monitor, and adjust as necessary. It also makes it more successful in the long run, because it is easier to expand a small program that is working efficiently, rather than cutting back on a non-productive bigger one.

HOW TO FIELD YOUR AD RESPONSES

When I first began placing ads for my clients, I made a point to handle the responses personally. On Mondays, I or an associate had to be in my office or my client's office for an extended period of time, waiting to receive phone calls from job applicants. Naturally it was very inconvenient. But how else could I screen the job applicants and make accurate assessments of whether I should interview them?

I received my answer in a rather surprising way. One day, early in my career, a crisis arose with a major client. It happened on a Monday I had set aside to field all the phone calls from an ad I had placed. I had no secretary, and I worked from my apartment. It was too late to arrange for anyone else to answer the phone for me. All I could do was turn on my answering machine, get to the troubled client's office, resolve the situation there as quickly as possible, and return. Hopefully, I wouldn't miss too many calls while gone.

It is strange how sometimes an adverse situation can inadvertently provide a solution, to an old problem. The situation at my client's office took several hours to resolve. I hurried back to my apartment/office as quickly as I could. I hoped there would be just a few responses by this time, but just as I opened the door, I could hear the last few words of someone leaving a message, and the hum of my machine as it shut off. "I missed another one," I said to myself. "Too bad."

Quickly, I went to the answering machine. I saw that there had been 11 messages recorded in my absence, so I shrugged my shoulders and pressed the rewind button. My only hope was that some of the people had actually left their names and telephone numbers.

I pressed the play button and, to my great surprise, eight of the people *had* left their names, numbers, and a short message. But far more important was the realization that even those who left no message, just a name and number, were communicating a great deal to me. Simply by the quality of their voice, I could make a decision whether or not I wanted to talk further with them. This would save me a great deal of time. I found that of eight calls where a message was left, I could screen out five that were undesirable because of their diction, their accent, or the overall quality of their voices.

Revelation! From now on, I would no longer be confined to my phone on a Monday morning following a Sunday ad. It was much better, more productive, and effective to allow those who responded to screen themselves by leaving messages for me. Possibly I had missed some good people, but maybe not. If they didn't want to leave a message, they would call again or not. If not, I wouldn't worry about it because I would have sufficient interest from those who did leave messages. From then on I made my answering machine my first level of screening.

Generally, I get more than 20 responses to each ad, and, as a rule, I can eliminate approximately 12 or 13 of those, making my selection from the seven or eight remaining. Remember, all I want from any one ad on any one Sunday is from one to five good people. That's the maximum number I want to select, hire, and train at any one time.

FOLLOWING UP

What do you do next? You now have a group of people who have responded to your ad. You've eliminated those not qualified. What then? Of course, you call them, but what will you say? What will you ask?

When I call people back, I have a telephone presentation or a script for the way I would like the conversation to proceed. To create this presentation, I use the same techniques and principles

I use to train the people I hire. Chapter 9 will go into greater detail about how to train your people, including specific techniques to use.

For now, let's consider not how I make the call, but what information I want to gather. Certainly at this point I want to probe further to determine whether Steve, the person I'm speaking to, is the one I want to hire. Therefore, I'll ask him questions that will allow him to speak to me at greater length. I want to hear how he handles himself on the telephone. Is he easy to talk to? Is he pleasant? Does he answer my question to the point? Or does he digress in a way that is unproductive? Does he have a sense of humor? Can he get me to laugh? If he does, he will very likely get his prospects to laugh as well.

One question I am sure to ask is if he's currently working in the telemarketing field. If the answer is yes, it means that he has at least sold someone else the idea that he is worth employing. On the downside, it could mean that he's not doing well and wants to escape. I'll ask him what he likes about his job, and what he would like to improve or change. Then I'll ask him to approach me just as he would if he were selling me his product or service, or setting an appointment.

I'll roleplay with him, raising objections, and evaluate how he handles them. Is he persistent or does he give up? Does he sound natural and conversational, or stilted as if he were reading? Of course, everyone hates talking to telephone solicitors who sound as if they're reading a script. The best telemarketers usually have a way of taking the information and transfering it to their own style. They communicate as if they were talking to a good friend.

If he's not working currently, I'll ask him about his last job. What was he doing? What did he like about it? What would he have improved or changed? I'm not really interested in the specific content of his answers to these questions. What I want is to determine his attitude. Overall, is he more positive or negative?

At this point I will reveal a little more about the specific job I have, explaining the objective—either to set appointments, make sales, or conduct surveys. I'll tell him how many hours I expect him to work and discuss how many appointments, sales, or surveys I expect him to achieve. Then I'll ask him if he thinks he can handle it.

Since the questions I ask do not have the objective of getting specific answers, I'm able to concentrate on the overall impression I receive. How does this person conduct himself using the tool called the telephone?

IMPERFECT IS ALL RIGHT

Occasionally I will hire people who have some blatantly negative qualities for telephoning. However, their other qualities are so impressive I judge that they will be successful with good training. Usually, I have been correct. One such person is Holly. Holly is a woman in her early 40s who worked much of her life as a full-charge bookkeeper for a variety of companies. She wanted to make a change, saw one of my ads in the Los Angeles area, and responded. Holly has a very pronounced New York accent. In L.A., that is a negative.

Holly also has a sparkling personality that shines through the telephone lines. My client was an entertainment company that produced blackjack and poker tournaments at Las Vegas and Atlantic City hotel casinos. They sent tens of thousands of direct mail pieces to subscribers to gambling journals, as well as to previously registered hotel guests. My client realized it could multiply its response by conducting a telephone follow-up campaign after the initial mailing.

My job was to assemble a complete telemarketing program, including hiring people, creating a presentation, and training and coaching them. The telemarketers objective was to make reservations for the next blackjack tournament scheduled in Las Vegas. My ad had attracted a large number of capable applicants, applicants with successful track records and good communication skills.

Holly had no previous experience in telemarketing. What she did have was a quality of warmth that was contagious. She genuinely enjoyed people and had a desire to do something new. She sold me on giving her the opportunity, and had the second highest sales in the group of seven. An interesting footnote to the story is that the person who later won the blackjack tournament was one of Holly's customers. Holly, with a great deal of persistence and sales skill, was finally successful in convincing her reluctant prospect to give it a try. That person won more than $50,000 as a result of Holly's persuasive abilities. So, neophytes can do very well with proper training.

Another example is John, a young man with a distinct Armenian accent who recently immigrated to the United States and discovered L.A. He answered an ad for a program selling cassettes to consumers. The client is a noted real estate entrepreneur who has made a fortune buying and selling real estate. He appears on television often, and gives seminars teaching people how to buy real estate with no money down. Every time he appears, more than 400 people call to order his products or get more information; and about half the calls result in orders. The rest are considered to be good leads, which are sent to an outbound telephone center for follow-up.

When I first spoke with John, I was impressed with his tremendous desire to do this work. Even though he had a pronounced accent, his manner was pleasant and he had a drive to succeed. Generally, a foreign accent is not a plus on the telephone. Exceptions are English and French accents, which, for some reason, are attractive to the American ear. Other accents usually create more distance between the telemarketer and the prospect.

My hunch was John's excellent drive would motivate him to be persuasive on the telephone. He received the same training as the others in the program, except that I urged him to take the presentation home and practice it, and encouraged him to work on speaking more clearly. His first 4-hour shift proved disappointing. Others in the group had converted as many as nine inquiries into sales. Their customers were people who, for one reason or another, were hesitant to order when they first called. After learning that the program was completely guaranteed, and they had 15 days in which to receive their money back if they weren't satisfied, many of those agreed to order.

John received only one order. I had a talk with him and explained that he needed to put more effort into his work, to spend more time at home practicing the presentation and learning to handle the objections he would receive. I explained that if he couldn't improve, I would have to let him go at the end of the week. He understood and thanked me for being direct with him. The next day he came back determined to succeed. He progressed every day, until at the end of the week he was leading the entire group. In spite of his inexperience, in spite of his foreign accent, his desire and determination made him successful.

CHOOSE BETTER WITH PRACTICE

Of course, you want to make the right choices, and the information in this chapter will help you considerably. As you get more and more experience, you will develop a knack for selecting the right people. Don't be afraid to make any mistakes. Go ahead and choose and you'll find out quickly enough if your choice is correct. If not, you can always replace the person you selected. Give it your attention and you'll continuously improve your ability to select those who can be good telemarketers.

If you want further assistance, there are tests available to help you determine if the applicant has good potential for your particular position. One such test has been created by John Alden Associates in Holden, Maine. The test is given to the existing telemarketers in the company, and their scores are matched with their performances. When potential recruits takes the tests, their scores are compared with the existing scores of the current staff and a determination made as to their potential for success.

These tests measure the ability of applicants to exert influence on other people, based on assertiveness and persuasiveness. They also test such things as responsiveness, steadiness, thoroughness, and verbal skills.

Frankly, I have never used such tests myself, but I have no reason to doubt that they can be helpful. If you are just beginning to create a telemarketing program, they probably would be a valuable aid in helping you get started. If nothing else, the results would either support your decisions or dispute them. Either way, you would have information from which you could learn and grow.

APPLICATIONS AND REFERENCES

If your company uses written applications for employment, by all means have your telemarketing applicants complete them. Again, I use the application to get an overall picture of the applicant, and as a guide for the interview. It gives us something to talk about when we meet. Always bear in mind that the nature of telemarketing fosters a great deal of "job-hopping," so don't be concerned with the frequency of job changes. If your product is worthwhile, your compensation program is fair, and you provide good training, you will retain your employees.

It is usually not the most productive use of time to check a telemarketer's references. Everyone has someone who will give a good reference. One would have to be very stupid to list a bad reference. If you do check references, be sure to ask a question toward the end of your conversation like, "Well, you've told me a lot of good things about . Where would you say he (she) could use some improvement?" The answer to this question usually gives some indication of your candidate's real nature.

There is one reference that is worth checking: a credit reference. The credit report is usually correct and cannot be fabricated, giving you an indication of the person's financial status. Depending on the caliber of the position you are offering, this may or may not be significant. When hiring a telemarketing manager or director, a credit reference is probably worthwhile.

9

Designing Your Compensation Program

How you compensate your telemarketers will affect the success of your program. If you pay too little, you attract a low caliber of people who won't perform well. The better people you attract will become discouraged early by their measly earnings and will quit. If you pay them too much, they will reach a comfort level.where they produce enough to satisfy themselves, but not enough to meet your company's requirements.

Therefore, you should pay your people a combination of salary plus commission and bonus. A variation on this approach is a draw or advance against commission and incentives, including trips, jewelry, stereos, and other attractive awards.

Each telemarketing application, be it sales, appointment setting, lead generating or surveys, requires a compensation program unique to it. Each application must also consider the following factors:

How well known is your company?

How well known are your products or services?

How difficult is it to get through to the decisionmakers?

Following are general guidelines that will allow you to establish a compensation program to meet the minimum expectations of telemarketers:

1. Surveys—$5–$10 per hour.

2. Qualifying leads—$5–$10 per hour.

3. Setting appointments—$10–$15 per hour.

4. Selling products or services—$15–$20 plus per hour.

The above ranges are, respectively, what telemarketers who handle those particular applications excpect to earn from their salary, commissions, and bonuses. In general, you should not pay them solely by salary. Some companies pay a salary plus a bonus when a sale is made from the appointment. This is somewhat unfair, because the telemarketer's compensation is dependent upon the closing ability of the sales representative.

However you decide to create your compensation package, you should structure a plan that will allow your telemarketers to reach the maximum amounts listed above, based on their successful performance. Let's examine appropriate compensation arrangements in relation to four specific applications.

Surveys

As mentioned earlier, I consider surveying to be the least productive use of telemarketing. There may be occasions where a survey program is worthwhile. Generally, it is more desirable to use your telemarketers' time to qualify leads, set appointments, or actually sell by telephone. People who are surveyed find it easy to give information when there is no threat of being asked to buy. Although much of the information may be accurate, the best way to determine if they are prospects is to set an appointment with them or actually sell. Many companies that depend on the results of a survey find some shocking realities when they actually begin marketing based on the survey results.

At any rate, you can pay your telemarketing surveyors the following schedule:

Salary—minimum wage to $7 per hour.

Commission—$.50–$1.50 for each completed survey.

Bonus—$5–$25 per week

If it is important to project a good image of your company while taking this survey, you will want high-caliber people—those who command up to $7 per hour. The hourly wage also depends on your company's location. In a major city like Los Angeles, Chicago, or New York, you must pay the upper end of the scale. In a smaller city or town, you can pay minimum wage or slightly more. Companies in larger cities paying minimum wage attract lower caliber people whose work is relatively ineffective.

You can expect surveyors to complete a maximum of five surveys per hour. This maximum will only be achieved when your surveys are brief and the respondents are reached easily, and those reached easily will rarely be a company's decision makers.

If the survey must be taken with decision makers, you may expect one to three completed surveys per hour. Again, this depends on a variety of factors, including the customers' interest in your industry, the amount of phone calls that respondents receive, and the benefit you offer your respondents for participating in the survey.

Incidentally, you can increase the number of responses by offering some sort of inexpensive gift—a copy of the results of the survey, a special report relating to your industry, or a token gift. Another tactic for increasing responses is to send a printed survey questionnaire with a cover letter and a 1-dollar bill. The letter may offer the dollar for the recipient's favorite charity, in the hope he or she will take a few minutes to respond to your survey. This doesn't necessarily motivate a great many written responses; but when the telemarketer calls, it usually makes it easier to complete the survey.

Some managers question the worth of paying a commission for

each completed survey, believing that this encourages falsifying information for higher earnings. Yes, there is always that possibility, but hopefully, your judicious selection of personnel will prevent it. You can, of course, choose not to pay a commission for each survey but offer a higher salary or give your people a bonus after the successful completion of the project. You can also spot check their information by making phone calls to a random selection of the respondents, asking if you can verify the information you have received.

Recently, I conducted a 100-hour test program for a client who wanted surveys taken to determine the interest of California companies in health maintenance organizations. We paid the telemarketers $7.00 per hour and a $50 bonus each upon the successful completion of the program. This allowed the two telemarketers to be reasonably comfortable about their salary and gave them an incentive to be proficient, accurate, and thorough. The program was very successful.

Qualifying Leads

A lead-qualifying program is similar to a survey program in that information gathering is its primary function. There is no attempt to sell anything, or even to set an appointment. The only objective is gathering data. The principal difference is that in a surveying program information is sought regarding the marketability of a product or service; in a lead-generating or profiling program, information is sought regarding the qualifying characteristics of the company as a potential prospect. This is a more active approach to marketing. The degree of proficiency required by your telemarketers is about the same as that of telephone surveyors.

Therefore, you can compensate your telemarketers who generate leads in the same manner as is indicated for surveyors, with one exception—you can pay a bonus for every lead that is converted to a sale. This encourages your telemarketers to provide more accurate information, while being as persistent as possible in gathering that information.

The bonus you pay for a lead that becomes a sale can be as small as $5 or as much as $500. It all depends on the kind of products or services you sell, the cost, and the difficulty of getting good leads.

Setting Appointments

A good appointment-setting program is invaluable for most companies. Indeed, in many sales situations, getting in front of a prospect who is willing to listen is half the battle in making the sale. Telemarketers who possess the ability to set appointments for outside salespeople are extremely valuable. This is especially true for companies who sell "big ticket" products and services. You can compensate your appointment setters according to the following:

Salary—$5–$10 per hour.

Commission—$5–$10 per good appointment.

Bonus—$10–$500 per each sale.

The more difficult the nature of the appointment-setting process, the more you need to pay your telemarketer. For example, setting appointments with chief executive officers of corporations, doctors, or attorneys, you will need to pay toward the upper end of the scale. These decision makers are bombarded by calls, making it difficult to get through to them, difficult to obtain their initial interest, and difficult to get an appointment with them. The people capable of setting appointments on this level are often worth their weight in gold. Because of this, it is worthwhile to give them a bonus for setting each good appointment. A good appointment is one where the decision maker is present and knows what the sales representative is coming to sell.

One of my clients who sells deferred compensation programs to executives regularly pays a $500 bonus to his telemarketer when he makes a major sale. My client, Bill MacDonald, has earned as much as a $500,000 commission on one sale that resulted from a telemarketing appointment.

The number of good appointments a telemarketer can set varies depending upon the city, the company, the market, and the interest level in the product or service. Generally, it is very difficult to set appointments with doctors and attorneys. It is also difficult to set appointments *for* insurance agents. On the other hand, it would be relatively easy to set appointments for representatives from major corporations like IBM, Xerox, and ITT. If you have a brand new product or service that offers exciting benefits, it will also be a relatively easy task to set an appointment for your company's representative.

As a rule, you can probably expect no more than one or two appointments an hour at the most, to as few as one appointment every four or five hours. This of course depends on a combination of the factors already mentioned.

One of the more successful telemarketers I have known works in insurance sales, setting appointments with the chief executive officers in a variety of industries. He receives a salary of $10 an hour and $10 an appointment, plus a bonus of 1 percent of the agent's commission. He earns $1500 to $2000 a month setting appointments part time. His employer sells insurance programs to affluent individuals, earns a great deal more, and is delighted with the program. Depending on the size of the sale and the accompanying commission to the salesperson, you should compensate your appointment setter with a minimum of $10 per hour to as much as 10 percent of the salesperson's commission. This of course depends on a number of considerations. Some companies get their salespeople involved to the extent of sharing the cost of the telemarketers' salaries, commissions, and bonuses. In these cases, the company may pay the telemarketer's salary, while the sales people pay for each appointment. When a sale is made, the salesperson and the company each contribute a bonus for the telephone solicitor. There is a great deal of latitude and flexibility in creating a compensation package for telemarketers who set appointments. Ideally, you should structure it to allow your telemarketers to earn $10 to $15 per hour. This way you attract and maintain personnel who give you the quality and the quantity of appointments you need.

Salespeople

Proper compensation is nowhere more important than with your inside sales staff. The telemarketers who sell products and services are the people who generate the company's cash flow and should be remunerated fairly. The better your compensation program for your salespeople, the more your company will flourish. There is a great deal of flexibility possible here. You can pay people commissions, salary plus commission, or draw against commission. Some companies pay salaries and bonuses, with no commissions. It really depends on the individual characteristics and combinations of market, company, and products or services.

Some telemarketers are content to eke out a few dollars per hour, while others earn six figures annually. How you pay your salespeople is dependent on a great many factors—not the least of which is your gross margin.

Companies pay their telemarketers commissions of 5 to 20 percent or more based on the nature of the products or services involved. Companies that sell office supplies, advertising specialties, or speculative investments such as oil and gas leases pay commissions of 20 percent or more. These are, of course, very difficult to sell. On the other hand, well known companies that sell low risk, familiar products and services pay commissions as low as 5 percent. The following schedule may be useful in providing some guidelines:

Salary—$5–$12 per hour.

Commission—5–15%.

Bonus—$10–$200 for reaching established goals.

An alternative approach is one where instead of paying a salary you provide a draw against commissions, which is especially useful where a sales cycle is several weeks or longer. In instances where information must be sent and follow-up calls made, it is helpful to pay your salespeople a draw to help them get through the first few weeks or even months of waiting for commissions. In these cases the following schedule applies:

Draw—$1,000–$2,000 per month.

Commission—5–20% per sale.

Bonus—$50–$500 based on reaching established goals.

Red Mottley, a top executive at NCR, once said, "Nothing happens till something gets sold." The salesperson is a vital component of today's business, and paying that person carefully and fairly insures your company's continued success. However, you are in business to make a profit, and a good rule of thumb is to assign 20 percent of your gross income to cover the cost of sales. This means that all of your telemarketing sales cost, including salespeople, phone costs, support personnel, percentage of overhead, and so on, should equal 20 percent of your sales revenue. In many cases you can afford to pay your sales staff between 7 and 12 percent of the sales they generate.

Although it is true that many telemarketers are content to earn approximately $20 per hour, if you can maintain your profit margins and pay them more, your company will gain. Why? Because you will attract and retain professionals who will continue to generate additional revenue for your company.

Incoming Telemarketers

There are two primary functions handled by incoming telephone people: order taking and customer service. In smaller companies, often both functions are handled by the same employee.

Order-taking personnel can be a critical source of additional profits, especially when they are trained to upsell and cross sell. In addition to taking orders, they can often add 10 to 20 percent in sales revenues by asking for additional orders. Order takers, however, are not motivated to sell when they receive no bonus or commission. Companies can increase revenues substantially by reviewing their compensation practices in this area.

One good approach is to total the sales from orders taken by your incoming telemarketing staff and use this figure as a base or norm. You can then pay a bonus of 5 percent or more of all sales revenue in excess of this established base. This can be figured on a monthly basis.

Some companies even pay their incoming telemarketers on a straight commission basis. I don't recommend this. Instead, it is preferable to pay them a salary plus a bonus for increased sales.

A salary varies of course with the location of your company, and the nature of your products and services.

Order takers earn salaries from $1000 to $3000 per month. Too often, companies are shortsighted in this area, and offer no commissions or bonuses, because they believe there is no way of determining what the customer planned to order and how much the order increased due to the telemarketer's sales skill. This is certainly true. Still, it is to the company's advantage to establish a normal sales month for each order taker, and then pay a bonus whenever that month is exceeded.

Customer service people who trace shipments, answer questions, and handle complaints contribute primarily to customer retention. It is very difficult to assess their contribution of additional sales revenue. Generally, they should be paid a salary, possibly with an additional bonus, based on the overall sales of the company. This can be as small as $100 to $200, but will be repaid in heightened morale and continuing dedication.

10

How to Train and Coach Telemarketers

Once you have hired your telephone staff, the next step is to train them properly for success. A good, organized training program can greatly increase the telemarketing bottom line; a poor one will only delay the results you want. Invest your management time and talent to create and develop a training program for new employees, with a follow-up program for existing employees.

We'll begin by discussing training for new employees; this program can be divided later into modules for follow-up training.

MAKE IT EASY FOR THEM

When people start a new job, they're always somewhat nervous about their ability to perform well, so begin by making them comfortable and easing them into the more difficult tasks. If you have an employee orientation program, have them go through that first. If your facility is large enough, give them the grand tour. Show them where your products are manufactured, if production is on site. Describe the responsibilities of every member of your staff; show them the restrooms and recreational areas; tell them about the coffee. Help them to feel at home as quickly as possible.

If your company has a written employee manual, have them read it and review any other important company literature such as brochures, data sheets, and catalogs.

Be clear about company rules and regulations. Is smoking permitted? Where? Let employees know exactly what is expected of them in terms of dress codes, personal calls, and conversing with other employees during working hours.

It is a good idea to introduce them to some of the key people in the organization. Make them feel as if they are a part of your company, not just visitors. If you have an old employee who is especially warm, friendly, and hospitable, get that person involved with orientation, to make the new telephone staff feel even more at home.

After the orientation tour, it is a good idea to take your group into a conference room or some other private place where you can speak to them together without interruption. Begin with product or service information. One of the great sales masters, J. Douglas Edwards, advocates giving new salespeople only enough information for them to have enough confidence and enthusiasm in your product or service to begin to sell it. This is a good rule of thumb for telemarketing programs as well.

Review the company's product brochures with your telemarketers. Stress the highlights, the important features, and benefits of your company's products. Review the potential uses and why your prospects need your products and services. Help your telemarketers appreciate the cost-effectiveness of doing business with your company. If you have important competition, brief your telemarketers on the relative strengths and weaknesses of your competitors.

No product or service is perfect. Let your trainees know where your company's weaknesses are, where your products may not compare favorably with the competition. Then be sure to help them realize why all the positive qualities of your company, including the many benefits of your products and services, more than compensate for the few weaknesses.

This briefing allows your new employees to gain confidence in what they are selling. It prepares them to handle jolts to their confidence that come from prospects' objections such as the lower cost of your competitors' product lines, their delivery, or quality. Be sure your telemarketers know what the major strengths and weaknesses are of your competitors as well as your own company.

Make a list of the features and benefits that sell your product or service. Include your length of time in business if it is more than 10 years—otherwise don't mention it. List all the qualities that make your company and product desirable. If your price is favorable, include that. If not, justify it with superior quality, service, or delivery. Make certain your trainees know what results customers can expect as a result of investing in your company's products and/or services.

List the major questions and objections that have been raised about your company and products, and provide the best answers to these questions that you can. This should all be typed or printed, and every telemarketer should be given a copy.

While some telemarketers, especially those with greater verbal skills, may require less product information to get started, most feel more confident if they have can put their hands on information that will allow them to answer most questions that may be asked. Prepare as much as you can. Distribute a typed or printed primer titled "Here's How to Handle Objections." Include as many as you can.

I usually try, depending on the complexity of the products involved, to get the telemarketers on the telephone by the first day. Sometimes this isn't realistic, but it is desirable to have your telemarketing people begin calling as soon as possible. Certainly no more than two days should pass, in most cases, before your people actually start telephoning. With this in mind, allow approximately a half day to orient your new people to the company and product. The remainder of the first day should be dedicated to basic telephone training, review of the presentation, including questions, objections, and answers, and, if possible, making preliminary phone calls.

INITIAL TELEPHONE TRAINING

Once your telemarketers have an understanding of your company's business, its market, and its competition, the next step is a definite understanding of their purpose. We assume everyone must know this, but we are often wrong. Surveys have shown that many employees really do not know the major objective they need to accomplish. They do not understand their essential purpose automatically, so it is very important to spell out exactly what work they perform and why. What are the priorities? What are the primary and secondary objectives?

For example, if you are using telemarketing to make sales, the primary objective is to close the sale. On the other hand, if you are using telemarketing to set qualified appointments, the primary objective is to get a definite appointment with a qualified prospect.

The telemarketers should also know what their secondary objective is. A secondary objective is one they accomplish if they cannot attain their primary objective. A secondary objective might be to get a commitment from a buyer to seek approval from his or her management, or it might be to get a commitment from a buyer to review the catalog and place an order at a future time. A secondary objective might be to have a prospect review written information about your company and agree to discuss it again in a week.

Whatever the appropriate objectives for your particular program, be sure your telemarketers have a clear understanding of what they are there to accomplish.

BASIC TELEPHONE TRAINING

It is always worthwhile to remind your new team of fundamental telephone techniques they should already know but possibly forget to use regularly. Basic information includes:

1. Speak directly into the mouthpiece.
2. Use good diction.

3. Use correct grammar.

4. Avoid slang and colloquialisms.

5. Sound natural.

6. Avoid sounding as if you are reading.

7. Smile into the phone as you speak.

8. Vary your speed.

9. Modulate your voice.

10. Use enthusiasm.

11. Be sincere.

Let's review these basics in detail to help you train your staff effectively.

1. *Speak directly into the mouthpiece.* It's important to speak directly into the mouthpiece when you talk to people on the telephone to assure that they hear you. If you don't speak directly into the mouthpiece, you run the risk of either annoying the person you're speaking to, or of not being heard. Many people won't admit they haven't heard you or don't understand what you said. Rather, they will politely wait for you to finish and then say they are not interested. Speaking directly into the telephone mouthpiece also compensates for an overly soft voice. No one likes to say repeatedly, "What was that please?" or, "I can't hear you." By speaking directly into the mouthpiece you sound more professional. Incidentally, men should lower their chins when they speak, if they want to add a deeper resonant quality to their voices. If you happen to have an extremely loud voice, then—and only then—you may hold the mouthpiece away from your mouth while you speak.

2. *Use good diction.* By good diction, I mean pronouncing words clearly and correctly. This not only makes it easier for your prospect to understand you, it also communicates that you are a knowledgeable, reasonably intelligent person. Good diction conveys professionalism. Lazy pronunciation and garbled words may lead the prospect to think your company and product are equally lacking in quality.

3. *Use correct grammar.* Correct grammar is an equally important indication of quality. A person who doesn't use good grammar is either uneducated, lazy, or stupid. None of these qualities makes a good impression. Because a prospect cannot see you, he or she judges you by what you say. To maximize your impression, speak properly.

4. *Avoid slang and colloquialisms.* Slang will detract from your sense of professionalism. Using good English promotes the idea that you are a well educated, articulate, competent individual, with no ulterior motive in this conversation. Remember, many people are skeptical, if not absolutely suspicious, of telephone offers. You want your telemarketers to do everything they can to communicate to your prospects that they are high-caliber individuals.

5. *Sound natural.* Sound as if you are talking to your best friend. This means that your language shouldn't be formal or stilted in any way. This doesn't mean you should be too familiar with people, just be yourself. Use language that you feel comfortable with and speak in a manner normal for you. By being yourself, you will be more effective and won't trigger a nonverbal message that you are making a sales presentation.

6. *Avoid sounding as if you're reading.* Sound conversational, not as if you are reading a scripted presentation or answers to questions and objections. If you sound too much as if you are reading a presentation, one technique is to say "uh" and "um" intentionally.

7. *Smile into the telephone as you speak.* When you smile, personal warmth is transmitted electronically via the telephone line into the ears of the person you are speaking to. Prospects can't see you, but they can sense your smile. If you have any doubt about this, just shut your eyes and have someone speak to you. First have him or her smile while speaking, then speak without smiling. You'll sense the difference very quickly. A useful tool for reminding people to smile into the telephone is a small mirror mounted to the wall they face. Seeing themselves in the mirror reminds them to smile. You can even mount the word *smile* at the top or bottom of the little mirror. It is amazing how this subtle difference can add to the positive response you want to achieve.

8. *Vary the speed of your conversation.* It's much more interesting to listen to someone whose rate of speech is varied rather than constant. To do this, speak slightly slower when you are talking about something that is important and speed up somewhat when you mention something less important or more obvious to your prospect. Pause at the end of an important phrase to allow your listener more time to absorb what you have said. Certainly, you should pause at the end of a question.

9. *Modulate your voice rather than speak in a monotone.* By raising and lowering your pitch on the telephone, you make it much easier for people to listen to you. Be careful of ending your sentences. Many people allow their voice to go up as they end their sentence. For example: "I'm with the ABC company." By raising their pitch on "company" they imply doubt or question. It is preferable to end your sentences by dropping your voice on the last word. This suggests confidence and strength. A monotone presentation will not keep the attention and interest of the buyer.

10. *Use enthusiasm.* Enthusiasm, a vital component of any good telemarketer's bag of tricks, can be the deciding factor in setting qualified appointments or closing sales. Enthusiasm conveys conviction and is contagious. This doesn't mean that you need to shout into the phone while pounding your fist on the table. You can communicate enthusiasm in a variety of ways, but you must begin by being genuinely sold on what you're doing. Your voice will convey your inner enthusiasm to the other person. Allow your positive emotions to be expressed and your effectiveness will increase.

11. *Be sincere.* Unless you are a great actor or actress, your lack of personal sincerity will come across to the other person on the telephone. Don't say something unless you mean it. One way that typical telephone solicitors demonstrate their lack of sincerity is by asking, "How are you?" when they call a stranger, never waiting for the answer to their question. If they do get an answer, they demonstrate very quickly how little they care about the other person by launching into their presentation without a pause. Encourage your people to be sincere in what they're saying or asking. There is an old joke about this: "Be sincere, whether you mean it or not." Remember that is only a joke.

After presenting these 11 basics, it is a good idea to ask your people to contribute. Asking them if they have any other ideas or suggestions to add to this list is a good way for them to loosen up and start participating.

Encourage an informal, participative, open atmosphere for your meeting. Allow your people to feel free to share what they have learned. Allowing them to speak will make it easier for you to receive information later. You need not worry that your group will get out of hand. Because you have already discussed most of the basics at length, their additional contributions should not take much time. Whatever else they add will probably be worth listening to.

Should the group digress too much, or get involved in an otherwise unproductive discussion, you can always interrupt and say something like, "That's a very good point and we'll make time to discuss that later in our advanced training; but for now, let's cover some more of the basic information we need to make this program work." Finally, distribute your scripts or telechart. (A telechart is a key phrase presentation, rather than a word-for-word lengthier script.) You should also distribute a separate feature/benefit page, a question-and-answer page, and an objection-and-answer page.

FIVE IMPORTANT STEPS IN TRAINING

I have found that using the following five-step approach to training allows you to work effectively with both individuals and groups, however diverse they are in learning ability. First let's outline the five steps, and then examine them in greater detail.

1. Lecture
2. Example
3. Participation
4. Role Playing
5. Feedback

1. Lecture

In this phase, simply show and tell people something you want them to learn. You talk about the information you want conveyed to your audience. For instance, if you wanted to discuss the importance of not sounding "canned," begin by stressing the necessity of speaking naturally. Point out that no one likes talking to someone who seems to be reading from a script. Ask them to remember occasions when they were called by someone obviously reading from a script and ask them how they felt at those times.

2. Example

Next, give a specific example, reading from a script, of what it sounds like to speak naturally. You might also read the script, by way of contrast, in a stilted, unnatural way. So far, you have only talked about the subject and given an example to reinforce your point.

3. Participation

Next, ask individual members in the group to read a line or two of the presentation, speaking as naturally as possible. If any individuals have a problem here, ask some of the others to give further examples—sounding both natural and as if they were reading.

4. Role Playing

After everyone has an opportunity to participate in front of the group, separate them into groups of twos or threes, and instruct them to roleplay with each other, practicing a natural-sounding presentation. Throughout the roleplaying exercise, they should alternate partners until everyone has a chance to roleplay with everyone else. If working with a very large group, you do not need to have everyone work with everyone else. Four or five different partners are generally sufficient.

5. Feedback

After roleplaying in groups, each individual should roleplay with you (or your designated instructor) in front of the group, one at a time. After each individual's presentation, give positive feedback emphasizing all the good points about it. Then ask for positive comments from the group. At this point, you want only positive feedback in order to encourage and reinforce each trainee.

After your positive comments and those of the group, it is appropriate to say, "There is one thing I would like you to work on." Here, you can point to an area of improvement, being sure to limit it to just one because it is easier for people to improve one area at a time. After working with a group for a while, you can then turn to the group and ask *them* what one area of improvement they can target for the individual in front of the room. However, don't do this initially, because the early feedback should be as positive and supportive as possible. After a group has worked with you for a while, they know what you expect of them and won't turn the feedback session into a crucifixion. It is meant to be a friendly, positive, supportive session to help each other improve.

Using this method of training not only accomplishes the desired results quickly, but also makes it fun for the trainees and enhances their morale. It also builds a spirit of teamwork, and a sense of camaraderie among your telemarketers. They realize quickly they are not being judged so much as helped, making training a lot easier and more fun for everybody.

AFTER TRAINING

Once your people have reviewed the fundamentals of telephone calling, and have become familiar with the presentation, including answers to questions and objections, they are ready to begin calling on the telephone. If *you* are particularly effective on the phone, I recommend you begin by making the first call and allowing the group to listen to you on the phone. Using an external speaker, to allow the group to hear both sides of the conversation, is helpful.

I find that making the first several calls myself helps set new telemarketers at ease. After each call, I review the positive elements in it and ask the group what they thought I did well and what else I might have done. This further instills a cooperative attitude among the individuals and the group. This technique is not for everyone, though. You do need to have confidence about your telephone ability and not get your ego involved to the point where you are afraid of criticism.

After I make the first call in front of the trainees, I then ask the person I think has shown the most ability to make the second call. After the call is over, I first ask that person, and then the group, what was good about the call and what could be improved. Encouraging people to make these calls while others listen is an excellent way of teaching. They literally learn from each other. Occasionally, one or more of your people may be inhibited about speaking in public like this. Encourage them to do it anyway, stressing that it's an important learning experience.

If you prefer not to demonstrate the calling procedure, your next step is to have everyone go to their telephones and begin. You can then move from conversation to conversation, coaching on an individual basis. Some trainers, at this point, prefer to let their trainees get their feet wet without any coaching. They simply sit at their desks, taking in the general flow of conversation and making notes about additional training they will give particular individuals.

Time and experience will allow you to determine your best approach. Make your people realize you are not there to spy on them, but simply to help them improve. Since they are just beginning to make phone calls, their desire to be effective is highest right now. They all want very much to succeed and make a good impression.

Do everything you can to support them. If you hear someone make a blatant mistake, allow him or her to finish the conversation, then praise the good things about the presentation before mentioning the area needing improvement. Don't destroy your trainees' motivation by being overly critical. Telemarketing is difficult. It is rife with refusal, which people tend to interpret as rejection. Be supportive and instructive.

Another tool you can utilize as part of your training is the tape recorder. Encourage your people to tape their conversations and listen to them. There are devices that allow you to record both sides of the conversation directly from the telephone. Your legal department can inform you of any restrictions on the use of such devices for training purposes.

Very few people will be enthusiastic about recording their conversations and listening to their voices, but encourage it because listening to one's own conversation is a great way to improve. It reveals what one is doing properly and what one needs to adjust.

Using this method will enable most people to recognize what they could have done and said, for a different outcome, how they could have handled an objection better, or answered a question to bring the prospect closer to "yes." It becomes much more apparent when they listen to themselves speak. They realize whether they were listening well and relating to the other person or simply saying what they wanted to say, regardless who they were talking to and what that person's interests were.

The first week that your people are on the phone should be considered part of their training. The manager should hold brief staff meetings during the day, stressing techniques, skills, or portions of the presentation that need reinforcement. Allow your telemarketers to learn and grow from their own and each others' experiences.

After the first week, hold a follow-up session in which you ask them what they think they are doing particularly well and what areas need improvement. Next ask them about the presentation. What parts are effective? What parts should be changed? Then, turn to the questions and objections. Does the material provided work? Can they handle all the objections they receive? Can they answer all the questions they are asked? What improvements can they suggest?

You can also use their feedback to adjust your telemarketing program. Take advantage of their experience to help refine your approach.

ERRORS TO AVOID

When you monitor your telemarketing staff, be aware of the following mistakes and work to correct them as quickly as possible.

1. Sounds Like Reading

Instruct your people to sound as natural as possible. If they can't sound natural with the script you provided them, rewrite it or have them rewrite it to sound more natural. Another approach is to use a key-word presentation rather than a word-for-word script, which is a list of important phrases in the proper order. Allow the individual to use discretion in creating the conversation, being sure to touch on every key phrase.

2. Speaks Too Fast

When someone speaks rapidly on the telephone, especially someone who is attempting to set up an appointment or sell something, the listener associates that with pressure. Generally, those who speak rapidly are only doing so because they are afraid they will be cut off before being allowed to finish, and they deliver their spiel as quickly as possible. The effort to complete the presentation in this way only results in an irritated prospect who hangs up anyway. Be sure your people learn to control their rate of speech.

3. Insincerity

Listeners are quick to identify insincerity. One of the ways telephone salespeople telegraph a lack of genuine interest is by asking people, "How are you today?" and then not waiting for an answer, or ignoring the response given. Asking these questions is all right, but only if you are genuinely interested in the answer you get and respond to that answer. Otherwise it is better not to ask. It is preferable to get to the point of your call. An exception is if you are calling long distance. After stating where your call is from, a friendly, "How is the weather over there?" or other such pleasantry can relax the other person, and set the stage for an affable conversation.

4. Insufficient Probe

Most telephone salespeople do not ask enough questions, do not receive enough relevant information, and then proceed too quickly to the presentation. The more information your telemarketer gathers, the easier it is to identify how your products and services relate to the needs and interests of the people they are calling. The probe is probably the most vital element in the entire sales presentation. Constantly emphasize the need to ask more relevant questions.

5. Lack of Feature/Benefits

All too often, telemarketers do not give enough reasons to buy a product or meet a sales representative. Your prospect will agree to buy or see a salesperson only if it is to his or her advantage to do so. Be sure your presentation contains sufficient feature/benefits information to attract your prospects. For example: "Our new widget is attractively priced at five dollars a dozen, and you can sell it for twelve dollars a dozen, which is still two dollars less a dozen than your competition charges. So it will be easier to sell and quite profitable. Isn't a profit of seven dollars a dozen attractive?"

6. Poor Listening

Telemarketers, intent on giving their presentation, often miss opportunities handed to them by their prospects. For example, if a prospect expresses a great need for prompt delivery, your telemarketer should not continue to discuss price, quality, or service, but reinforce your company's prompt delivery—even describing instances of how appreciative your customers have been because you've met their delivery requirements or in certain instances delivered sooner than required. Proper listening and relating can make the difference. It is a good idea to keep your telechart, or key word script, in sight so that you can react in a flexible manner to opportunities that result from good listening.

7. Quits on Objection

Because telemarketers encounter more refusal in one day than outside salespeople get in a month, they sometimes will not overcome objections. You must remind your telemarketers that objections are potential buying opportunities and prepare them with drills on handling objections. Allow them to role-play with each other until handling every major objection is second nature.

8. Too Much Talk

Telemarketers have a tendency to go on and on talking or selling without getting any feedback, when they should allow the prospect to give a reaction to the ideas they are communicating. Be sure your people are trained to seek feedback. This can be as simple as, "Our products have a shelf life of over three years. Is that long enough?"

9. Lack of Confidence

Confidence is based upon knowledge and success. Give your people all the product information they need to make them comfortable on the telephone. Have data sheets, questions, answers, and feature/benefits statements all prepared and at their disposal. Make sure they know how the products and services have benefited others. Give them the feel of success by allowing them to roleplay, answer questions, handle objections, and close the sale.

10. Lack of Enthusiasm

Enthusiasm is based on genuine conviction. Get your telemarketing staff involved with the company and your products and services. Give them, whenever possible, the experience of what your products and services can do. This develops genuine enthusiasm for your company. If your people sound like they're just going through the motions when giving their presentation, take them aside and ask them if they believe in the capabilities of your products and services. Give them as much experience as possible with the value that your company provides. Remind them that their enthusiasm is contagious.

11. One or No Close

A survey of top salespeople who earn in the six figures asked the question, "How many times do you ask for the order in one call?" The average answer was seven times. Think of it, top salespeople find seven different ways to ask for an order. Most others barely ask once, and rarely more than three times. Develop alternate closes, and train your people to use them. The fewer times they close, the fewer sales they make.

12. No Postclose

The postclose seals the agreement and paves the way for future customer satisfaction. It also helps eliminate buyer's remorse, and can even be used to get referrals. What often happens, however, is that the telemarketer is so excited about getting a yes that he or she gets off the phone without sealing that agreement and avoiding a possible future cancellation. Be sure to remind your telemarketers that what happens after the close is an important part of the entire sales process. They must review the terms of the agreement with the buyer and emphasize how satisfied the buyer will be once he or she begins using your company's product or service. This is also an ideal time to ask for a referral.

FOLLOW-UP TRAINING

Provide training reviews at least once a week. Have your telemarketers work on one skill at a time. Give an award to the person who masters that particular skill best. Encourage your telemarketing team to develop their level of proficiency. Help them develop a sense of pride in their professionalism.

The moment of truth for your telemarketing program comes when your telemarketers pick up the telephone and begin to call. All your efforts to develop your strategy, identify markets, create a telemarketing environment, and train a staff contribute to the success of your program. The remainder of this chapter helps you further by providing specific examples of materials for you to furnish you people.

Certainly you will want to give your telemarketers a manual that contains information regarding the company, its products, and services. It should also contain policies and procedures as well as an organizational chart depicting your company's structure. In addition, you may insert catalogue sheets or brochures that give specific data regarding each product as well as the telephone presentation script with typical questions and answers. A section containing a directory of key people in the company and their respective departments and areas of expertise is also a good idea.

LEADS

Leads can be furnished in a variety of formats; but the most popular are lists such as your own computer printouts, 3″ × 5″ cards such as *Dun's Marketing* or *Contacts Influential* cards, and customer ledger cards.

Of course, if you have a computer-assisted program, you may input leads automatically onto floppy diskettes, magnetic tape, or hard disk.

You can also create lead cards by generating computer labels and affixing them to 5″ × 8″ cards, or whatever size card is convenient. In general, cards are preferable to lists and can be handled easily. There is room to write notes on the front and back and they can be filed conveniently for call backs. When you use lists, more transferring of information is usually required. Although cards are generally more expensive to buy than lists, the cost is offset by the time and convenience. (See Figure A-1).

You also must design a systematic filing system for your people to use. If your telemarketers must create their own system, some will be organized and efficient while the less organized will become bogged down and ineffective. In telemarketing, it is vital to keep track of your prospects and follow up on a timely basis. One such method of assuring timely follow up is the tickler file. This is a file organized by the dates of the month. If you use 3" × 5" cards in your file, it should contain a series of index tabs numbered from 1 to 31, one for each day of the month. If a prospect asks your telemarketer to call back around the 25th of the month, your telemarketer will simply file that card behind tab number 25.

The files should also contain dividers labeled with the names of each month, so when a prospect asks to be called back in November, the telemarketer files that card after the November tab. If you use file folders instead of cards, you can arrange the same system using a Pendaflex file. In this case the dividers are labeled from 1 to 31, and January to December. The hanging files are a good alternative to the card files, because they offer the added benefit of allowing you to include previous orders and other relevant information all in the same place.

The Appendix contains a sample manual you can use as a model to create your own. Depending on the size of your company and the scope of its telemarketing, you may want to expand upon the contents of your manual, or condense it. Use it as a guide to achieve the results you want.

11

Advanced Telephone Techniques

After your people have been calling for several weeks, they will be ready for additional training. By this time, they will have garnered a good deal of experience. They will have made sales or appointments and also will have dealt with much refusal. This is an excellent time to give them extra training, because they will appreciate the help. They will be aware now of the specific problems they encounter and will know where help is needed.

Although the reasons for both "yes" and "no" answers seem equally elusive to most telemarketers, let's review some of the major reasons that prospects say, "No!"

WHY THE SALE IS NOT MADE

There are five major reasons why your telemarketer will not close the sale or make the appointment: (1) The prospect does not trust the telemarketer; (2) The prospect does not feel a need for the product or service; (3) The prospect does not believe the telemarketer has a solution; (4) The prospect has no sense of urgency; and (5) The prospect has no money.

1. "I Don't Trust You"

Although this statement is rarely, if ever, expressed out loud, it is one of the major reasons that the sale is not made. The public at large views salespeople with general distrust. Unfortunately, this reputation is not all undeserved, considering the history of the used-car dealer and others. On the telephone there is added skepticism, because the potential buyer cannot see you or touch your product. Plus, there can be a great deal of suspicion on your prospect's part concerning your intentions.

2. "I Don't Need You"

Very often your prospect does not realize he has a need for your product or services. Again, this is heightened by the fact that many telephone sales operations do not carefully identify target markets. They call people virtually at random. Many people being telephoned are not potential customers of that company in the first place. Still, there are many bona fide prospects for your company's products and services who do not understand they have a need that you can fill. With proper training, your telemarketers can help their prospects develop an awareness of a need for your products or services.

3. "You're Not the Answer"

A prospect may trust you and even recognize a need, and yet not buy from you because he or she does not believe your product is the answer to those needs. The problem has been acknowledged, but the belief that you can provide the solution is not there yet. Help your telemarketers communicate more clearly and directly so prospects understand how your company has the answer they need.

4. "There's No Rush"

Your prospect may trust and respect you, acknowledge a need, and accept that you have the answer to this need, and still not buy from you because of a lack of a sense of urgency: "What's the point of buying now?" With good training and the right offer, your people can create a sense of urgency that will provoke action now.

5. "I Have No Money"

After every other major objection is handled, the last hurdle is the money objection. Even though the prospect feels a definite sense of urgency, understands you have the solution, acknowledges a need, and trusts you, there simply may be a lack of financial wherewithal to buy. Your telemarketer can even develop skills and a sense of purpose to help them overcome the last financial objection.

The advanced telephone techniques we'll discuss now will overcome the five major reasons for not buying, assuming that your product or service does truly meet the needs of your prospect. If your products or services do not meet the needs of your prospect, then instruct your telemarketers to find another prospect. There are plenty of potential users of your company's product line. Don't have your staff waste time selling to people who can't benefit from what you have.

When communicating by telephone, as opposed to communicating face to face, you are unable to call upon all your good qualities. Your appearance is irrelevant. Your smile is invisible. Your strong handshake is not felt. You have your voice, your brain, and your ears. You interact by speaking, hearing, and thinking. Because you do not have the advantage of some of your other attributes, you must heighten and develop the full use of your telephone qualities. The best telephone communicators do, much as the blind compensate for their lack of vision by developing an acute sense of hearing.

Let's focus more closely on voice, which includes what you say, how you say it, and the order in which you say it. What you say is the content of your presentation—the meaning, the ideas. How you say it is your choice of language, your rate of speech, your enthusiasm, and the tone of your voice. The order you use is the structure of your communication. We begin our discussion of advanced telephone techniques by giving you an overview of an effective structure to increase your positive responses. I call this the structure of the sale.

THE STRUCTURE OF THE SALE

If you were offered a treasure map that directed you to a stash of $100,000, you would be sure to follow it very carefully, I am sure. By following the structure below, a good telemarketer will increase annual earnings by a minimum of $5000. This will be the result of just two additional sales per week, with an average commission of only $50 per sale. In a 20-year career, that will become an extra $100,000.

1. *Preparation:* Plan and program your outcome.
2. *Approach:* Get favorable attention, rapport, respect, and trust.
3. *Probe:* Identify needs and person; create awareness of needs.
4. *Presentation:* Create Solution in terms of prospect; use benefits to create desire to buy; get feedback and agreement.
5. *Close:* Induce action.
6. *Postclose:* Anchor the agreement; eliminate buyer's remorse.

This structure allows you to go through your communications process in the most logical manner I know. Let's review it in greater detail.

1. Preparation: Plan and Program Your Outcome

There are both subjective and objective elements in your planning and both are equally important.

Objective planning includes knowing as much about your prospect as possible before the call. You want answers to the following questions: How big is the company? How often do they buy? How long have they been in business?

Depending on the complexity and volume of the potential sale, you will want your people to do a proportionate amount of preparation. This also includes preparing answers to questions and objections and reviewing them before each call. In short, they must be as armed with facts as possible to make the phone call successful.

Subjective preparation includes getting your people "psyched" for the call. To do this, have them shut their eyes and take a few deep breaths. Tell them to forget the last call; it has nothing to do with the next one. Remind them that their cause is just—your products and services are truly beneficial. They are indeed doing your customers a service. Have them remember all the good they have done in the past. Have them recall phone conversations where they have overcome resistance and ended by making the sale. This sort of subjective preparation helps them generate more confidence. They should even go so far as to visualize the outcome they want. Have them see themselves making the sale. They can even imagine getting resistance and hear themselves handling that resistance and turning the phone call into a sale or a qualified appointment.

2. *Approach:* Get Favorable Attention, Rapport, Respect, and Trust

In a telephone approach, your staff must learn to be direct; otherwise they provoke distrust. "What is this all about?" is what the person on the other end of the phone is thinking, even if those exact words don't come out. Remember that "I don't trust you" is the first reason for not making the sale.

In a good approach, the telemarketer will identify himself or herself and company directly and come quickly to the point. a rapport-building and/or an attention-getting phrase to arouse interest on the part of the buyer comes next. For example:

CALLER: Good morning, John Jones. This is Fred Field, of the ABC Company. I understand you just opened a new branch office downtown. Is that true?

PROSPECT: That's right.

CALLER: Well, I'm calling because, since you just opened a new office, I imagine you would like to bring in sales as quickly as possible. Am I right?

PROSPECT: Of course.

CALLER: Well, I specialize in helping companies increase their sales, through telemarketing and sales training. I've had tremendous results helping companies increase their sales 20 to 50 percent or more.

The foregoing dialogue demonstrates a direct but attention-getting approach, to quickly arouse the interest of your prospect.

3. Probe: Identify Needs and Person; and Create Awareness of Need

This is really where the sale is made. If you can glean enough information, you will have all the tools you need to close the sale. Every company has unique requirements that must be satisfied. Everyone is different. Every person has his or her own hidden criteria for buying. It is only by identifying and understanding what those requirements and criteria are that you then can fulfill them. A good probe gives you enough information either to close the sale, set an appointment, or plan for a follow up. An example of a probe that identifies some needs, and creates greater awareness of those needs in the prospect's mind, follows:

CALLER: How many salespeople do you have?

PROSPECT: Five.

CALLER: How many appointments do they set each week?

PROSPECT: About six or seven each. That's not too many, I suppose.

CALLER: How many appointments would you like them to have?

PROSPECT: They should have two or three a day, at least.

CALLER: How many more sales would they make if they had 12 appointments a week?

PROSPECT: Oh, they'd probably almost double their sales.

CALLER: If I could show you how to get them two or three appointments a day, would it be worth discussing?

PROSPECT: Absolutely.

The above illustrates an effective probe that identified needs and helped the prospect become aware of those needs. We'll go into greater detail in Chapters 11 and 12 regarding how to create systematically an awareness of need in the mind of the prospect.

4. Presentation: Relate Solution in Terms of the Prospect, Using Benefits To Create Desire To Buy

The main purpose of this part of the phone call is to motivate your prospect to want your product or service, or to want to meet with a representative of your company. Once you have succeeded in establishing rapport with your prospect and have asked sufficient questions to gather important information, it is relatively simple to adapt your presentation to satisfy your prospect's interests. By doing this properly, by presenting key benefits that relate to your prospect's major needs, you create a desire in your prospect's mind to own your product, use your service, or to pursue the subject further by meeting a representative of your company. For example:

CALLER: My company, Fidel Communications, has been implementing successful telemarketing programs for the last six years, so we do have some experience in the field, right?

PROSPECT: It sounds like it.

CALLER: We've worked in a variety of industries, including yours, and our communications principles are fully tested, so we won't be experimenting with you. That means we won't be wasting your time or money. I'm sure you don't want to be a guinea pig, right?

PROSPECT: No, we don't want to pay for your education.

CALLER: The bottom line is we can help your salespeople receive enough appointments every week to increase their sales. Isn't that what you and they want?

PROSPECT: If you can do that, that's exactly what we want.

5. Close: Induce Action

The purpose of the close is to help your prospect move in your direction. You must help the prospect make a commitment either to buy to set an appointment, or to review information and discuss it with you later. Nothing happens unless your prospect acts. The best time to close is when your prospect's enthusiasm is at its height. After that, interest will wane. At this point, summarize briefly your prospects major interests and agreed-upon product benefits. Then ask for what you want. For example:

CALLER: Well, since you definitely want more appointments for your salespeople, and we're experienced in doing just that, let's arrange a brief introductory meeting where we can pursue this a bit further. What's better for you—mornings or afternoons?

PROSPECT: Oh—afternoons are better.

6. Postclose: Anchor the Agreement and Eliminate Buyer's Remorse

The value of a postclose is that it summarizes the agreement made, clarifies the details, and prevents cancellation or change of mind. Ideally, the telemarketer puts the prospect in the future, happy with the appointment or the sale.

CALLER: Since afternoons are better, suppose I drop by next Tuesday; or is Wednesday better?

PROSPECT: Wednesday around two would be better.

CALLER: Fine, let me confirm your address. Are you still at 2525 West Tenth Street?

PROSPECT: Right, suite 1210.

CALLER: Fine, John Jones be there next Wednesday afternoon at two, suite 1210, 2525 West Tenth Street; and when you meet him and see what he has to show you, I know you'll feel the time is well spent. Thank you, good-bye.

PROSPECT: Good-bye.

The foregoing is a systematic approach to persuasive communications. Rarely will your telemarketer be allowed simply to go on without interruption and make the sale or appointment. Usually, the prospect asks a question, raises an objection, or digresses. That's fine, because the telemarketer simply uses this structure as a general guide to making the sale.

If taken off track by the prospect, the telemarketer simply falls into step with the prospect's digression, question, or objection, and then when it's appropriate returns to the point in the structure where he or she left off. If necessary, the telemarketer can always backtrack or begin the process again.

Imagine taking a trip from L.A. to New York. You have your map and you've planned a direct route to your destination. Along the way, perhaps you decide to take a side trip. After you've reached your new destination, you check your map and head back to your point of departure, or what appears to be the best possible route to get back on your main road. In the same manner, this structure is a map towards making the sale. If you find your prospect is not cooperating fully in the probe, that's an indication that you have not achieved the rapport or trust you need in your approach. So back up, digress, get more friendly, or use another approach to reestablish your credentials or credibility. Then you may proceed to the probe again. If you find your prospect is objecting all through your presentation, this is an indication that you have not gathered enough data, or engendered the prospect's trust or respect. Or, the prospect may be nervous about having to make a decision. You must learn to use your "map." Recycle through your structure. You may use a fresh approach or begin probing some more.

Train your telemarketing staff always to be aware of where they are in the structure of the sale. This allows them to make a smooth presentation without belaboring the point or spending too little time in a vital area. With practice and experience they can become adept at reaching each part of this structure its appropriate time.

Choose Your Words Well

If a man speaks to a woman and says, "When I look at you, time stands still," that means one thing. If he says instead, "You have a face that could stop a clock," that means something quite different. Our language is very powerful. Be sure to raise the awareness of your telemarketing staff so their language is always promoting their objective and not delaying it.

Words To Use	Words Not To Use
own it	buy it
opportunity	deal
agreement	contract
drop by	set an appointment

Some words raise the anxiety level of your prospects, others are more neutral. We always want our prospects to be as free from fear as possible. Other words that your people should use in their presentations are *you, profit, love, benefit, safe, secure, control, power, easy, simple, guaranteed, new, free.* "*Cost-effective*" is a good term to use with businesspeople, as is *bottom line.*

Don't underestimate the power of language. The choice of words is an important ingredient of the overall presentation. The right words can make the difference between almost making the sale, or setting an appointment, and barely making the sale or setting the appointment. It's better to just make it than to just miss it, isn't it?

Studies in communication reveal that *how* we say something is even more important than *what* we say. Have you ever wondered what is the correct tempo of speech to use on the telephone? What is the right level of enthusiasm? What is the proper tone of voice? These are the *how* elements of telephone communication. Their impact is more subtle than *what* we communicate.

MATCH AND GUIDE

This is a principle of communication that can be used in a variety of ways to foster improved rapport and guide the prospect to a positive decision. It is based on the fact that most human beings like to be around people who are like themselves. We are more comfortable with those who think the way we think, dress the way we dress, and live the way we live. Here's what I mean: Suppose you went to a party dressed in a business suit, while nearly everyone else was dressed informally in jeans, slacks, and casual shirts. One other person in the room is dressed in a business suit. Assuming you were unacquainted with all the other guests, to whom would you be most likely to find yourself talking? Wouldn't it be the other person dressed in the business suit?

Most people communicate most easily with those they are most alike. The same is true on the telephone. Therefore, what we want to convey on the phone is that we are like the person we are speaking to. We are trustworthy, competent, and worthy of respect—just as he or she is. Let's examine some ways we can transmit a sense of "being-like-you" on the phone.

1. Rate of Speech

How quickly or slowly we speak can either attract or repel the person to whom we're speaking. If your listener is a cautious, conservative, slow-talking person, and you speak at the rate of 10 words per second, what will the listener's reaction be? Won't you come across as a fast-talking salesman, unworthy of trust? We associate pressure with a rapid rate of speech. Train your people to match their own rate of speech to the rate of the person they're talking to. If they speak to some one who talks very slowly, they should start out speaking very slowly too. Then, they can speed up gradually, making sure the listener's conversation keeps pace.

On the other hand, if your listener is fast-talking, fast-thinking person, in a hurry, and you speak very, very slowly, what reaction will you get? Won't I the other person find you slow-witted, dull, or boring? He or she will want to get off the phone as quickly as possible. "Match and guide" means you start out using the same rate of speech as your prospect, and then adjusting as necessary. By speaking at the same rate as your prospect, you subtly convey that you are similar: fast talking and in a hurry; or slow talking and cautious. This promotes greater rapport and enables you to get your message out to more people who will give you the attention that you want.

2. Tone of Voice

In the same mode, the tone of voice your people use on the phone can incite receptivity, antagonism, or indifference on the part of the person spoken to. This means you must train your telemarketers to be sensitive to the tone of voice their prospects use. If their prospects have a friendly tone, your telemarketers should have a friendly tone. If your prospects have a suspicious tone of voice, your telemarketers should have a suspicious tone at first. If your prospects have an abrupt, hurried tone, so should your telemarketers. It's important to train them never to be overtly hostile or angry with their prospect. They should merely reflect the same tone of voice their prospects use. By matching the other persons' tone, you earn their respect. Why? Because you are just like they are. Remind your telemarketers to *guide* their prospects gradually in the direction they want to take them. This means your telemarketers should ultimately lead their prospects to use a friendly tone, one conducive to reaching agreement.

3. Key Words

Every industry has its own key words, its own special vocabulary. Unfortunately, most people are not familiar with the key words that your company may use. Therefore, do not use your special language, but instead use the special language of the people who buy from you. Use their key words, not yours. If you have a very technical product or service, don't use your technical language unless you are speaking to someone who understands your technology. Instead, use your prospect's key words, to show familiarity with that company's needs and problems.

4. Favorite Sense Language

We all think we're speaking the same language—English. Actually, there are three favorite languages that people use: seeing, hearing, and feeling.

Seers are prone to say things like, "I see what you mean." "That looks good." "It's clear to me." *Hearers* like to say, "I hear you." "Sounds good." "I can tune into that." *Feelers* like to express themselves thus: "I'm comfortable with it." "Feels good." "I want to weigh that in my mind." Each of these separate types has a favorite way of making sense out of the communications the receive. The seers translate a good deal of the data they encounter into pictures (mental images). Therefore, when you identify someone as a Seer, speak to him or her in visual language. Give the Seer a picture of what you're saying. Describe what your product looks like or describe the visual benefits your service provides.

When speaking to a hearer, be as hearing oriented as possible. Your language should include words like, talk, discuss, music. Let your hearer use his or her favorite language to make sense of your proposal.

When speaking to a feeler, use feeling words or sensation oriented language. Your presentation should include terms like, love, warm, tough, and so forth.

Here's an example of how you can describe the same thing in three different ways. Let's take a day in the country:

To the seer: It was a bright clear day with white billowing clouds sailing slowly across the light blue sky.

To the hearer: Away from the city noises all I heard was the music of the local birds and the whisper of the wind.

To the feeler: It was comfortably warm and I had a pleasant sensation in my body as I walked through the countryside.

In the same way, your people can learn to adjust their presentation to the language of their prospects. In my training seminars, I teach *flexibility*. Learn to adjust to the communications needs of others. Develop flexibility of language, and you increase your rapport.

Remember that many people are hybrids; they may have two favorite languages. Such an individual might say, "I want to look at it and see how I feel." That is a seer who is also a feeler. You could answer such a person this way, "Let me show you some more, and after you look at it perhaps you will feel like going ahead with it." Some of the problems people encounter are the result of not speaking the same language. A man may return home and say to his wife, "This place *looks* a mess." His wife will respond, "Yes, but it *feels* so comfortable." Here we have a seer communicating to a feeler. Both are using their own languages. Train your people to be aware of the other person's favorite sense language.

Early in my career as a telemarketing specialist, I called a manager of a franchised employment agency. No matter how hard I tried, she wouldn't agree to meet me. Finally, I heard her say, "You haven't *told* me why I should *talk* to you." Suddenly I realized she was a hearer. I quickly switched gears and said, "If I could *tell* you how to get your *message* across to more people, would you want to *talk* about it?" She answered, "Let me get my book." She didn't want to see me, but she would talk to me in person. After meeting and *speaking* to her for an hour, we agreed that her people would benefit from telephone training. We certainly would not have made this mutually beneficial agreement if I hadn't known about favorite sense languages. And now *you* know it, too.

You can train your people in language flexibility by having them take a statement about your company, product, or service, and then translate that statement into the three other sense languages to create a seer statement, a hearer statement, and a feeler statement. Have everyone begin by writing a statement that they could make about your company product, or service. Then ask them to translate that into a second, seer statement. After they have done this, have each read his or her original statement and then the seer statement. After everyone has finished, ask them to translate it into a hearer statement. Again have everyone read the original statement and the translation. Repeat the process for the feelers statement. It soon becomes apparent to everyone that the seer, hearer, and feeler statements are much more powerful than the original statement that each person started with.

SAY IT/ASK IT

This technique allows you to keep control of the sales presentation. The principle here is to ask a question after you make a statement, or at least after you make a series of statements. End with a question. Most people in sales mistakenly think that controlling a conversation means doing all the talking. Who really controls the conversation: the person who makes the last statement, or the person who asks the last question?

You actually control more effectively by asking rather than by telling. Most people resent being told what to do or what is good for them. Yet, almost everyone likes being asked to tell what they think. Take advantage of this by instructing your people to ask a question after they speak. For example, "I've helped companies increase their sales by as much as 40 percent. Would a 40 percent increase be exciting to you?" Or, "I can get you single-sided or double-sided floppy diskettes. Which do you use?"

By saying something and then asking something, you not only control the conversation, you get valuable feedback from your prospect. Isn't that true? Your telemarketers learn by asking whether they need to say more about a subject or benefit or if they should go on to discuss the next one. Can you see how that would make their presentations more effective? You may have discovered that I have been using this technique throughout this book. Have you?

You can train your people to use the say it/ask it technique by having them write down typical statements they make during their everyday telemarketing. Have them read aloud their statements individually, and then ask them to write an appropriate question after that statement. Then give everyone a chance to say it/ask it. You can also use this tool to answer questions. It's especially useful when someone has called your company to find out more about your products or services. Has this ever happened to you or your telemarketers? You're asked a question. You answer it. You're asked another question. You answer it. You're asked another question. You answer it. Then the person says, "Thank you very much. You've given me a great deal of information. I'll think about it and get back to you. Goodbye." You're left feeling used, abused, and abandoned.

When you're asked a question, answer it, then ask another question back. This does two things. One, you get feedback about whether your answer was sufficient or effective in promoting your company. Two, when your prospect answers your question he or she, in effect, is continuing to be sold on what you are offering. Three, it prevents the prospect from controlling the conversation and simply gathering information.

ACTION QUESTIONS

This technique allows you to use a question as a springboard to complete the sale or appointment. Whenever possible, answer a question with another question that brings your prospect closer to the action you desire.

Remember that your telemarketers are not in the business of providing information to your prospects. Their objective is to close sales on the telephone, or set appointments, or provide another related marketing function. When providing information brings your prospect closer to a decision, by all means provide information. The objective, however, is not simply to provide information. The objective is always to bring about action. Here are some examples of how to answer questions with questions in a manner that brings the prospect closer to making a buying decision.

PROSPECT: Can I get delivery next week?

CALLER: If I can get you delivery by next week, can we go ahead with the order today?

PROSPECT: What happens if I'm not happy with your product?

CALLER: What would you like to happen in that case?

PROSPECT: Have you worked with companies like mine before?

CALLER: Would you prefer to work with someone with experience in your industry?

The natural tendency, when asked a question, is to answer. A telemarketers have an above-average desire to answer questions and provide information, because they think it brings them closer to the sale. It is important to train your telemarketers to use action questions instead. Notice how much more powerful the above action questions are, in terms of bringing the questioner closer to action. Let's take the question, "Can I get delivery next week?" Suppose the answer were yes. All that does is allow the person who asked the question to say, "Thank you, I'll think about it. Goodbye."

It is much more effective to ask instead, "If I can get you delivery by next week, can we go ahead with the order today?" This forces your prospect to be sincere. If delivery by next week is important, shouldn't he or she give you a positive answer now?

You can train your staff to use action questions by having them first write some of the typical questions that encounter in their daily work. Then have them use their own intelligence to construct action questions to answer the questions raised. Sometimes an action question isn't appropriate. In cases like these, just use the say it/ask it technique to answer the questions. For example, suppose the answer to the question, "Have you worked with companies like mine before?" were "No." If the telemarketer were to say, "Do you want to work with someone with experience in your industry?" and the answer was "Yes," the telemarketer would have a problem. Another approach is simply to say, "No, I haven't. By working with new industries, I can take a fresh approach to an old problem, rather than be stuck in a rut handling problems in the same way. Would a fresh approach be important to you?" This way I can answer the question and guide the conversation in the direction I would like it to go.

At this point you may begin to appreciate how valuable it is for your telemarketing group to possess as many sales skills as possible, and to be able to choose the right skill at the right time. This is why your weekly follow-up training is so important. It helps instill these techniques in your telemarketers. With repetition and practice, the training becomes a habit.

ANSWERING OBJECTIONS

The ability to answer objections is what distinguishes super telephone achievers from the merely mediocre. The simple way to answer an objection is to use the following structure:

> I understand . . . (repeat objection), and still . . . (give.. reason for appointment or purchase).

Here's how this works. When asked for an appointment to review the company's group insurance, your prospect may say, "I'm happy with my agent." Train your staff to respond, "I understand that you're happy with your agent, and still we do have some new programs to offer you that will certainly give you some good cost comparisons, as well as some new options. Don't you owe it to yourself to know what else is available to you?" Another example is a sales situation: "That's too much money." The response can be, "I understand you feel it's too much money, but the quality and reliability you get makes this a great buy for the money. Aren't quality and reliability important to you?"

When unskilled telemarketers are faced with an objection, they either give up totally or get defensive and upset. Neither of these tactics brings a positive result. The better way is to empathize with your prospect by saying, "I understand . . ." This also communicates to your prospect that you've actually been listening and have heard his or her reaction to your presentation.

A variation on this approach is to say, "I can certainly appreciate that. And still . . ." (give reason for appointment or purchase.) This method is similar to the first except that instead of repeating or paraphrasing your prospect's objection you simply acknowledge it with conviction. "I can certainly appreciate that," conveys to your prospect that you understand the way he or she feels. Of course, it's very important that this be said with sincerity and not in a perfunctory manner. A different technique for handling this objection is called "the judo approach." Essentially you use your prospect's objections to help him or her realize it is to his or her advantage to grant an appointment or to buy. In the example where the prospect says, "I'm happy with my agent," here's how you can use the "judo approach": The telemarketer's response is, "I'm glad to hear you're happy with your current agent. How long have you worked with that agent?" Your prospect may answer, "Oh, about five years." The telemarketer's response is, "Well, that is a long time. What are some of the things that you like about your agent?" The prospect responds, "He (she) gives me very good service, and his (her) prices are very good." The telemarketer answers, "Well, before you began working with your current agent, did you have another one?"

Let's suppose your prospect answers, "Yes." Then the telemarketer's next question should be, "What made you decide to change agents?" The prospect then might say, "Because I wasn't getting the service I wanted and the prices were high." The telemarketer then responds, "So you changed agents in order to get better service and prices; is that correct?" The prospect's answer is, "Yes." The telemarketer now can close by saying, "Well, since you changed agents in order to get better service and prices, wouldn't it be to your advantage to change again, if you could get even better service at a lower price?" By using the information that your prospect gives you in this manner, your telemarketer is effectively utilizing the "judo approach."

You may be thinking, "What if the prospect answered 'No' when was asked if he or she had worked with another agent before finding the present one?" In that case, the telemarketer can use the following variation, "Since you've only used one agent in the past five years, and you like him (her) because of good service and low prices, isn't it to your advantage to find out if you could get even better service and prices?" It's important to remind your telemarketer that these approaches will not work 100 percent of the time. They will certainly work some of the time. And they will certainly not work 100 percent of the time if they are not used. Encourage your telemarketers to use these approaches and not merely accept the objections they receive.

One of the most common occurences is the "put off." Here, the prospects stalls or puts off a request for an appointment or sale. An effective way to handle this type of objection is "the compliant approach." Here's how you use it:

A. Begin to comply.
B. Ask two questions.
C. Give a benefit.
D. Close again.

Let's look at an example: The caller has asked for an appointment and has been put off with the request to send something in the mail.

CALLER: "I'll be glad to. Is your address still 1825 West Tenth Street? Fine. I'll get that out to you right away. By the way, are you married?"

PROSPECT: "Yes."

CALLER: Do you have any children?"

PROSPECT: "Two."

CALLER: (sounding enthusiastic), "It sounds like this would really be to your advantage. Let me suggest this. Our agent will be in your area next week. Let's have her drop by, shake your hand, and leave the information with you. That way she can answer any questions you might have. And, it won't take more than 5 or 10 minutes, fair enough?

Encourage your telemarketers to practice using these objection-handling techniques and their success rate will increase dramatically.

Another objection handling technique is called, "the validation approach." With this approach, the telemarketer takes the objection, turns it into an objective and then helps his prospect reach that objective. This approach can be separated into the following six steps:

A. Rephrase the objection and question form.

B. Question further if necessary.

C. Find objective and confirm.

D. Offer solution.

E. Get agreement.

Here is an example of how a telemarketer can use this approach to get an appointment.

PROSPECT: I spend too much on insurance already.

CALLER: Are you saying you spend too much on insurance now?

PROSPECT: That's right. I'm insurance poor.

CALLER: What percent of your income are you spending on insurance?

PROSPECT: Twenty-five percent and that's more than I want to.

CALLER: Why do you spend that much?

PROSPECT: I need the coverage, but I prefer it not to cost so much.

CALLER: So what you really would like is to spend less on

your insurance and still get the same or better coverage. Is that right?

PROSPECT: Absolutely.

CALLER: That's exactly what we specialize in. If we can cut down on your insurance premiums without affecting your coverage, wouldn't it be worth investing a half hour of your time?

PROSPECT: I guess so.

This approach can also be used to sell a product by telephone. Notice how the same principles work in the following example.

PROSPECT: That's too much money.

CALLER: Are you saying that's too expensive?

PROSPECT: Yes it is.

CALLER: How much money were you planning to invest?"

PROSPECT: About seven hundred fifty dollars.

CALLER: So what you really want is to buy this product and pay no more than seven hundred fifty dollars. Is that right?

PROSPECT: That's right.

CALLER: So if I can get you what you want, and see to it that you only spend seven hundred fifty dollars, can we go ahead with it today?

PROSPECT: Fine.

CALLER: I have another model that gives you the features you need without any extras and is only seven hundred fifty dollars. So I'll send that out to you today. That's what you want, right?

The key to the validation technique is to question further and determine the your prospect's underlying objective. Often, the objection is a key to the objective. The trained telemarketer can investigate the objection further, and then turn it into an objective. Once there is an agreement on an objective, then the telemarketer can relate how the product or service meets that objective.

The last resort for handling objections is the "direct question." You simply confront your prospect in the following manner: Why is . . . . (repeat objection) more important than . . . . . (give benefit)? Here is an example:

PROSPECT: That's more money than I wanted to spend.

CALLER: Why is the fact that it's more money than you wanted to spend more important than the years of maintenance-free service you'll enjoy?

PROSPECT: I never do business on the telephone.

CALLER: Why is the fact that you've never done business on the phone before more important than this outstanding opportunity today?

PROSPECT: I'm very busy now.

CALLER: Why is being very busy now more important than the thousands of dollars you can earn as a result of meeting me?

PROSPECT: I'm not in the market for anything now.

CALLER: Why is not being in the market for anything now more important than taking advantage of a tremendous opportunity that can cut your expenses enormously?

The preceding techniques will give your telemarketing staff a wide range of tools with which to handle objections. You must, however, keep training and drilling them in all these techniques. Otherwise, they have a tendency to let their skills slide.

"I'M NOT INTERESTED"

One of the most common early responses to a telemarketer's call is, "I'm not interested." Because this particular objection occurs so frequently, special attention is warranted here. Very often when people are called, whether at home or in the office, it is not a opportune time. People are not just sitting there waiting for you to call. They are doing something important to them. So when they are called by a stranger, their first reaction is often, "I'll end this so I can get back to what I'm doing." With this in mind, train your telemarketers not to take the "not interested" objection so seriously. Here are some approaches that can be used. All they require is some courage and perhaps a sense of humor.

"I'm not interested."

"Of course you're not interested. Otherwise you'd have called me. At this point, you don't know enough about it to be interested. But once you learn more, I'm sure you'll be interested. . . ."

"I'm not interested."

"Of course you'll be interested, once you get enough information. And that's why I'm calling. . . ."

"I'm not interested."

"Have you ever been 'not interested' in something at first, especially something that you first heard about on the telephone; but the more you learned about it, the more your interest grew until you were glad that you got to hear more. That's happened to you, hasn't it?"

"Yes."

"Well this is like that. . . ."

Your weekly training drills should include handling the "not interested's." Your telemarketers will take great pride in turning around a prospect who starts out with strong objections, and then ends up buying your products, or agreeing to keep an appointment. One caution should be observed here. It is not to anyone's benefit to sell products to customers who don't need them, or set appointments with prospects who won't benefit from your offer. These techniques should be employed in conjunction with the other components of a telemarketing program, including identifying target lists. When your telemarketers find a qualified prospect, they should do everything they can to work with that prospect. A prospect is someone who wants or needs your product or service, and can pay for it. Prospects may not always be aware they have a need. Yet they still may be prospects if the need exists. The salesperson's job is to help create awareness of that need. Chapter 11 will discuss a series of techniques that will help your telemarketers create a greater awareness of needs. First we'll explore techniques for gathering information.

HOW TO ASK QUESTIONS

There are three primary ways of asking questions:

A. Open-ended questions
B. Closed-ended questions
C. Question-mark questions

Open-ended questions allow unlimited expression. They should be used by your telemarketers to encourage the flow of conversation. Some examples are:

"What are your long term objectives?"

"What do you like about your current suppliers?"

"What would you like to change or improve?"

The above questions give your prospects the freedom to answer at length, which defines a question as open-ended.

Closed-ended questions limit the answer. Your prospect or customer is directed to answer the question with a few words. Some examples are:

"How many salesmen do you have?"

"When did you review your equipment last?"

"Do you buy the computer ribbons for your company?"

These questions limit the answer to, "Yes, Twenty five, March 25, 1984, and Yes." They are used to guide the direction and focus of the conversation.

Question-mark questions keep the conversation flowing. This is an easy tool to use to engage your prospect in conversation and is also useful to get greater depth of information regarding a subject. This technique requires that the telemarketer repeat the last phrase that his prospect has uttered with a questioning tone. For example, consider the following:

"I'm very busy."	"Very busy?"
"I just bought."	"Just bought?"
"I'm happy with my current supplier."	"Your current supplier?"

This technique allows your telemarketers to clarify or expand their knowledge of their prospect's condition. It also allows them to keep the conversation going when they have a doubt or question regarding what to do next. They simply repeat the last few words of their prospect's comments in a questioning tone. The prospect then speaks at greater length regarding the subject. Now let's examine how your telemarketers can develop an awareness of need on the part of your prospects.

THE SLIP-IN TECHNIQUE

The SLIP-IN technique should be used only when the telemarketer has established such good rapport with the prospect that the prospect is willing to go through an extensive list of questions. It is inadvisable to use the SLIP-IN technique with a prospect who is in a hurry.

Conceptually, the purpose of this technique is to create an awareness in their prospects that they have a more serious problem than they thought. With the prospects' awareness of a serious problem comes a potential for action. If there is no problem, there is no urgency to act. It's much like having a painful toothache. When the pain is unbearable, you visit your dentist. So the object of the SLIP-IN technique is to show the prospects that they have a problem serious enough to warrant their immediate attention. "SLIP-IN" is an acronym for the following:

1) S. *Situation.* The telemarketer begins by asking fact questions regarding the prospect's specific situation. These are generally nonthreatening questions so that the prospect is not averse to answering them. As a telemarketing specialist, I might ask, "How many salespeople do you have? How many appointments do they have every week? How many sales do they make every week?"

2) L. *Like.* These are questions regarding what the prospect likes about the situation. Again these are generally nonthreatening questions that allow the prospect to expand on the positive. "Like" questions I might ask are: "What do you like about your salespeople's performance? What are some of your best successes? What do you like about how your salespeople are doing?"

3) I. *Improve.* These questions relate to what improvements or changes your prospect would like to make. Because your prospect has just told you what he or she likes, it is now easy for the prospect to tell you what he or she would like to change or improve. This is an important area for your telemarketers. What could be improved or changed is the weakness that your company has the potential to strengthen. This is the beginning of finding the need. Some "improve" questions are: "What would you like to improve or change regarding their performance? How many more appointments would you like them to have each week? How many more sales would you like them to make each week?"

4) P. *Problems.* These questions develop a greater awareness the prospect's part regarding a problem. Asked properly, these questions will also raise a feeling of discomfort in your prospect. Remember, this is good. Your prospect won't feel a need to act unless he or she recognizes a problem. Some "problem" questions I might ask are: "What difficulties does that cause? Is that a problem for you?"

5) I. *Indirect Results.* These questions concern the ramifications of the existing problem. Here, we want the prospect to have a greater awareness of the effects of the particular problem. These questions should make your prospect even more uncomfortable, creating a sense of urgency. Some questions I might ask are: "How does that affect your earnings? How does that affect the cash flow of your company? How does that affect the budget that's allocated to you?"

6) N. *Need.* These questions seek the acknowledgment that an important need exists. It is at this point that the prospect reaches an awareness of a need. "Need" questions I might ask are: "Would you say then that you do need to do something about the situation? How useful would it be to you to have a solution to this problem? If I can help you find a solution to this problem, would it be important to you?"

By taking your prospects through this series of questions, your telemarketer then establishes the existence of a need and paves the way for receiving an attentive ear to his or her presentation. The greater the awareness of need, the greater the urgency to act. After completing the SLIP-IN steps, it is desirable to summarize what you have learned in that process. Your telemarketer can do this simply by paraphrasing the important information received. To learn to be more effective, the telemarketer should certainly take notes as he or she asks the SLIP-IN series of questions.

BENEFIT BUILDERS

What do you do when you receive a positive statement from a prospect? What is the best response when a prospect tells you: "Oh, I've heard of your company," or "Your president has a good reputation," or "Oh, that sounds good." What most telemarketers do is ignore these positive comments. They are so intent on continuing with their presentation that they literally pay no heed to the positive feedback that they have received.

Instead, they should use their prospects' positive remarks as a steppingstone to reveal additional benefits. After all, the prospect has said something good about your company, its product or service. The telemarketer should reinforce and add to these comments. Remember, the more benefits your prospects find, the easier for them to say yes. Therefore, when prospects acknowledge benefits by expressing positives, telemarketers should seize the opportunity to move the sale along.

There are two methods for building benefits. The first is simply to ask a "binder" question when you hear a positive. For example, suppose the telemarketer hears the comment: "That price sounds fair." Your telemarketer simply can ask, "Doesn't it?" Or, told, "Your president has an excellent reputation," the telemarketer need simply bind that comment with the two-word question, "Hasn't she?" By asking a binder question, your telemarketer reinforces the positive by getting the prospect to reflect on what might have been simply a glib comment. Very often people will say something complimentary without realizing the full significance of what it is they said. By responding to these compliments with a question, you guide them into reflecting on what they have just said, allowing them to grasp the full significance of the benefit they have stated.

Another method of building benefits is to use the "tag-on" method. The telemarketer tags an additional benefit to the one just mentioned by the prospect. The best way to do this is to use the following three-step approach:

1. Acknowledge

2. Tag-on

3. Get agreement

It works this way: Your telemarketer hears a positive comment and acknowledges the comment by giving support to the prospect. Then he or she tags on or adds another benefit. Finally the telemarketer asks a question seeking agreement, such as, "That price sounds fair." Or, "You're right. The price is fair. And not only that but the quality is excellent. And that's certainly just as important, isn't it?"

Suppose a customer says, "I like your fast delivery." The telemarketer should respond with, "Thank you. It *is* excellent, and in addition to that we allow you 30 days to return your merchandise for any reason whatsoever. Doesn't that make you feel better?"

The second method of tagging on an extra benefit to the initial one is very effective in building up the prospect's confidence in your product, company, or service. Prospects decide to buy or agree to an appointment because of the benefits they expect to receive—not the costs, risks, or liabilities involved. So your telemarketer demonstrating that the sum of benefits is greater than the sum of costs clinches closing the sale or getting the appointment.

LISTENING

Listening better is something that everyone can learn to do. Most of us are so intent on what we have to say that we don't listen effectively. By listening effectively, we are able to present *our* thoughts and ideas in a much more useful manner. We should listen better to be more effective in achieving the outcome we want. Have you ever wanted to say something, but politely waited for the other speaker to finish before you said what you wanted? This is what prospects do. Isn't it better, therefore, to be the one who waits for the other person to finish speaking? If the other person is given the chance to finish speaking, he or she is more likely to listen to what you have to say. Persuasive communication involves attentive listening. You never can get enough practice at good listening skills. Time and again we neglect this in favor of expressing ourselves. One of the best ways to motivate your people to listen better is to remind them continually that by listening better they will be able to speak better and sell better, which is what they really want, isn't it?

Good listening involves maintaining a calm state of mind and simultaneously being open to the other person's ideas while being aware of your principal objective. You maintain a calm state of mind so you can think clearly. You're open to the other person so you can truly listen to what he or she says without attacking or defending. You maintain an awareness of the objective of your call so you can guide your prospect in the direction you'd like to go.

Train your staff to be continuously on the alert for a prospect's statement that leads to a potential problem, need, desire, or solution. This is where sales are made. By listening for the needs, wants, desires, and solutions of the prospect, you are obtaining information that you can connect to your presentation. This same information helps you make the sale. Lack of this kind of information forestalls your closing. The act of effective listening can be broken down into four separate components.

1. Select What Relates

When we speak to people regarding business situations, they give us a variety of information. Some of it is relevant to our purpose and much of it is not. Astute telemarketers learn to discriminate, choosing that which will help them close the sale or make the appointment. Let's suppose I am selling a training program for salespeople. I speak to Ed, the sales manager, who tells me the following: "Well, Stan, you'd better check back with me in a couple of months when I have a new budget. Right now my sales aren't what they need to be, and my secretary is out of town so I'm really swamped." Of the above, what do I want to select: The fact that his budget will be available in a few months, that his sales aren't what they should be, or his secretary is out of town and he is swamped? Obviously what relates to my objective is that his sales aren't what they should be.

2. Acknowledge and Reinforce What Relates

Once an item for further discussion has been pinpointed, the next step is to encourage the prospect to speak more on that subject. The best thing to do this is acknowledge that key phrase simply by repeating it. For example, Stan can say, "Your sales aren't what they should be?" By acknowledging one part of a person's comments the person will continue to speak about that particular topic. Many salespeople waste time and get their prospect off a productive track by acknowledging and supporting parts of a conversation that are not going to make it easy to sell. For example, if the Stan were to say, "You don't have a budget?" that will simply reinforce in Ed's mind that he has no money. And that will not promote the sale, will it? A more effective comment would be, "I'm sorry your sales are down. How low are they?"

3. Summarize

Next, you repeat or paraphrase in an empathizing manner so your prospect realizes you have understood what he has said; and in so doing you help your prospect understand that you know what he is talking about. An example of summarizing is, "Let's see if I've understood you. Your sales are down 25 percent, you've lost two of your best salespeople in the last three months, and your competition is beating your price by 10 percent, so you're very concerned about this year's projections. Is that right?"

In this way your listening is both passive and active. You are allowing your prospect to communicate to you and you are registering what is said. In addition you are also guiding him in a direction that is productive for you.

4. Guide

Here is where you gently guide your prospect in the direction you choose. This step can be used with the other three or alone. An example of how to use the guiding step is as follows:

"Since your sales are down, Stan, and you are concerned about this year's projections, and I do have some new sales and marketing ideas that definitely can help you increase your business, it certainly seems important for you to make some time for a brief meeting, doesn't it?"

TIME IS ON YOUR SIDE

In the training I provide, I emphasize repetition, practice, and effort on the part of the telemarketers. I point out to them that if they have the awareness of new skills, and they work at using those skills, in time they will become proficient at them. People go on for extended lengths of time without progressing because they have no information, which forces them to repeat continuously only what they know and get the same kinds of results. With new information, and genuine effort to assimilate and use it, they must in time become more adept at what they do. Time is on their side.

This should be very encouraging to your telemarketers. It boosts their morale. It gives them increased hope. The logic is quite acceptable. In the past, they recognize they reached a certain level of performance. They were stuck at that level. Now with new information and effort, they can reach a higher level. This means more job satisfaction, more self worth, and more money.

12

The Psychology of Selling

Instruction in advanced telephone techniques would not be complete without including a discussion of the psychological aspects of telephone selling. Additional knowledge regarding their prospects from a psychological point of view can only help make their telephone calling more effective. In addition, knowledge of their own psychological attitudes, predispositions and behaviors will help them deal with stress, rejection and success.

Dr. Joseph Murphy, celebrated author and minister of Divine Science, once told me there were four primary motivations for man. He said, "Every person wants better health, sufficient wealth, satisfactory love, and true personal expression." He said that every goal or achievement that people reach can be traced back to one of these four. For example, people who seek fame or recognition really seek a form of love.

Whether or not you agree with the simplicity of the above four, you probably can accept that they are strong motivators for many people. In general, most people respond favorably to such benefits as:

More power

More control

Saving money

Greater security

Excellent quality

More approval.

When selling to businesses, people responsible for making decisions respond well to such "dangling carrots" as:

More output

Less effort

Increased profits

More sales revenue

Less cost

BUYERS AND SELLERS

Although each of us is unique, philosophers and scientists have tried since the beginning of recorded history to understand what makes human beings operate the way we do. People have been trying to classify, categorize, and comprehend other people with varied success from the dawn of civilization.

In telephone selling, such information regarding human motivation and decision making is extremely valuable. If you know how someone thinks, and you know what they want, you have a reasonably good chance of relating what you have in an effective manner. This translates into making the sale, setting the appointment, or completing the survey.

The sales process is also complicated by the psychology, motivations, and *modus operandi* of the telemarketer. Human dynamics is operating during every sales call. So we have two variables: the buyer and the seller. Each of these people has his own knowledge, skills, interests, motivations, problems, ideals, and attitudes. When you consider how different the two may be, it is a wonder that communication takes place at all. Yet it does. Because in spite of all our differences, there are some universal traits. We all want the four basics: health, wealth, love, and expression. All of us pursue happiness in our own way.

According to the works of psychologist Carl Jung there is a basis for classifying people according to how they function. Jung identified unique models of behavior, which he called "archetypes." These included the "father," the "mother," the "hero," the "amazon," the "wise man," and others. These archetypes exist in everyone's unconscious mind, and are models for all our behavior.

At times, we want to be adventurous, take risks, save the day: be the "hero;" at other times, we want to be responsible, do what is best for our family: be the "father" or the "mother." We incorporate the various archetypes into our lives and function according to the major models, or combination of models, that we have chosen. Jung stresses that these models are not generally conscious, but largely are unconscious. Most people do not recognize what motivates them. Yet, all have a behavioral example for living their lives—even if they are not aware of it.

COMPONENTS OF BEHAVIOR

Jung identified several types of behavior that are opposite in nature. These include the following:

1. Extroversion versus introversion
2. Thinking versus feeling
3. Sensation versus intuition

Individuals function by favoring various combinations of these types. Everyone has a mixture of these ingredients. Who we are and how we behave is definitely based on our own particular combination of these polarities. To understand them better, and how they apply to the sales process, let's examine them in some detail.

1. Extroversion Versus Introversion

The extrovert is someone primarily oriented to the world outside, whereas the introvert is primarily oriented to the world within him or her.

The extrovert is acutely aware of external objects, including people and environments, and is comfortable relating to whatever is outside. So, the extrovert likes being with other people in pleasant surroundings and will choose situations that foster those opportunities.

The introvert, on the other hand, is acutely aware of the world within—the subjective world of thoughts and feelings. He or she is more comfortable relating to ideas, and is more apt to spend time alone, reading or developing a solitary skill.

Thinking Versus Feeling

Whether extroverted or introverted in their preferences, it is by thinking or feeling that people make *judgments* about their world. Those who think tend to relate logically the components of their world. For example, the thinking person may say, "If you install a personal computer and a printer in your sales department, you will then have a tool to send out more correspondence more quickly." The thinker uses an orderly process of "cause and effect" to put facts together.

On the other hand, those who feel relate the elements of their world by association rather than logical connection. The feeling person may say, "You will feel so efficient if you have a computer and printer in your sales department." Feeling people also tend to be oriented toward relationships based on emotional values rather than logical principles.

Sensation Versus Intuition

The way we *perceive* reality or take in knowledge is another polarity. The sensation-oriented person is attentive to facts or details that are directly perceived by the five senses. This person will be aware of concrete information about people or environments—the size, shape, colors, sounds, scents and tastes. On the phone, the sensation-oriented will note that someone has a deep voice, uses proper English, and positive expressions.

The intuition-oriented person is more apt to overlook individual facts or details in favor of grasping the whole. He or she may speak to someone and intuit an overall idea that the person on the other end of the line is successful, without being aware of the individual details or qualities that make up this impression.

The old saying, "I can't see the forest for the trees," is an illustration of the differences between those who are sensation oriented versus those who are intuition oriented. Sensation people will perceive individual details or "trees," while the Intuition people will perceive the "forest" or whole, without being aware of the details.

If we accept that people are either extroverts or introverts, that they make judgements primarily based on either thinking or feeling, and they perceive reality from either sensation or intuition, then there are eight different combinations possible for categorizing people psychologically.

In addition, this is complicated further by the knowledge that one is also sometimes functioning as a "hero," or as a "father" or as any of the other archetypes that Jung discovered. So, at different times a person will be more adventurous or more cautious, or more flamboyant or responsible, and so on. There may be as many as 64 different combinations, or psychological types. For practical purposes, that is too many to be applied easily to the purpose of enhancing our telemarketing.

EIGHT MAJOR TYPES OF PROSPECTS

For the sake of ease of applying these precepts to improve our objectives, let's look just at the combinations derived from the various polarities, ignoring the influence of the archetypes, while being aware that the archetypes do color just how extreme one's behavior is, at any particular time.

These combinations are derived by treating everyone as either an extrovert or an introvert, who also favors either thinking or feeling, or is sensation oriented or intuition oriented. I've represented the different possibilities on two charts. (See Figures 12-1 and 12-2). You may identify someone's psychological type from the combination of the vertical and horizontal lines on the chart.

I have given each of these types a double name to convey both the positive and the negative aspects of each one. It is worthwhile to remember that these categories are not black and white. Humans run the full gamut of possibilities and at different times favor different behaviors and different combinations of behaviors. What follows, however, are useful tools for understanding people's predispositions so that you may communicate more effectively with them.

The King/Tyrant

These prospects are a combination of the extroverted and thinking polarities. They want to stay in control of their lives, be the masters of their fates. As such, they are most comfortable with objective facts, rather than vague generalities. King/tyrants tend to be materialistic and conventional. They deal with people in an extremely rational manner, so much so that others may find them cold and unfeeling. Because they are so rational, they are generally very structured in their communication. They tend to use words very precisely and are not tolerant of those who are not equally careful in their choice of language. They are strong leaders, excellent at planning and making intelligent decisions.

They tend, however, to deny their emotional sides, and may not be aware that some of their behavior is indeed irrational. Their "blind spots" are in those situations that demand feeling, like showing affection or complimenting someone on a job well done.

Extremes of this type are downright tyrannical in their relationships with others. Their slogan: "My way or the highway." They can be totally insensitive to the feelings of those around them.

When communicating with the king/tyrant, you should not be overly warm in your approach. Stick with the facts and demon-

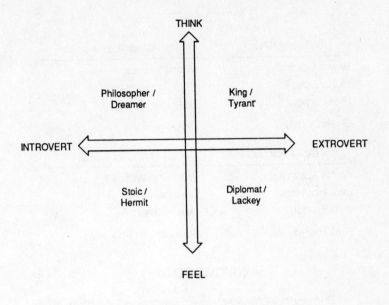

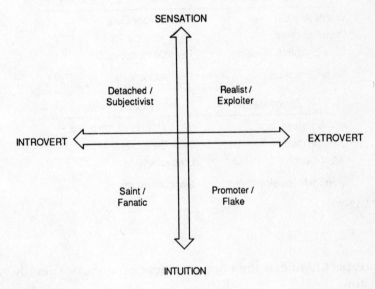

FIGURE 12-1

strate your strong sense of logic. Present benefits that foster additional control, greater power. Be specific in your presentation. Use facts rather than generalities. Don't be overly enthusiastic or make emotional appeals. Organize your presentation in a logical manner. Use words carefully. Don't exaggerate. After you've won

4 EXTROVERTED TYPES

King/Tyrant	Realist/Explorer
Wants Control	Wants Success
Likes Facts	Likes Excitement
Uses Logic	Uses Five Senses
Gives Details	Give Quality

Diplomat/Lackey	Promoter/Flake
Wants Approval	Wants Innovation
Likes Harmony	Likes Being First
Uses Humor	Uses Intuition
Give Friendship	Give Bottom Line

4 INTROVERTED TYPES

Philosopher/Dreamer	Detached/Subjective
Wants Wisdom	Wants Tranquility
Likes Theories	Likes Abstractions
Uses Creative Thinking	Uses Dissassociation
Give Concepts	Give Questions

Stoic/Hermit	Saint/Fanatic
Wants Inner Control	Wants World Betterment
Likes Simplicity	Likes Essences
Uses Restraint	Uses Ideals
Give Self-Development	Give Universals

FIGURE 12-2

their respect, you can then begin to develop a more friendly relationship.

Diplomat/Lackey

These prospects are extroverts who are feeling-oriented. The major concern is in maintaining friendly relationships. They want those around them to get along with each other and are most uncomfortable with the prospect of unpleasant disagreements. They want people to like and approve of them—recognize they are nice. Therefore, they are very sensitive to the needs and interests of others. They do what they can to preserve harmony and are careful not to offend. They generally have developed a strong sense of humor and are adept at using it to remove tensions. They are excellent in social situations: being a host, offering personal compliments, and voicing approval.

In their desire to please everyone, however, they may be too compromising and overly yielding to others. They may make light of a situation when being serious is more appropriate. Since they are so concerned with propriety they are unlikely ever to reach a conclusion that they feel is improper.

Those who go to extremes become subservient to everyone around them. They are so compromising they have no values of their own, but, like a slender tree, bend with every breeze. They are virtually unable to say "No" to anyone, but are equally unable to accomplish very much.

To deal effectively with diplomat/lackey prospects, be warm and friendly. Establish a personal relationship. Demonstrate that you like and approve of them. Show them how they will win more recognition and approval from others, as well as yourself, by accepting your offer. Sell them on the increased harmony that will result from action now. When they offer verbal assent, which is most likely, gently urge them to commit now. Otherwise, they will also say "Yes" to those who dissuade them later.

Philosopher/Dreamer

These are the introverted thinker types, are the theorists who prefer to deal with concepts and generalizations rather than individual details or facts. They are more concerned with understanding the principles that govern events than the events themselves. Abstractions are favored over individual facts. In fact, they prefer not to be interrupted with facts. As Oscar Wilde once wrote, "Nothing that ever actually occurs is of the slightest importance." They love to discuss ideas, especially new and original ones.

Extremes in this group may fall in love with their theories, regardless of their relationship to reality. Their ideas may be too original, in the sense that no one else can understand them. In addition, they may value their lofty speculations above the feelings of those around them. Conversely, their own emotions may be immature or oversentimental. They also tend to be poor judges of others.

In your communications with philosopher/dreamers, it is best to deal on a conceptual or abstract level. Avoid giving detailed illustrations. Present them with original, or at least interesting, ideas. Be as complex as you like. They will understand.

Stoic/Hermit

These prospects combine introversion with making feeling judgments. They seek greater control of themselves, coupled with inner peace or serenity. They often place a shield or wall around their emotions. Because they keep their feelings inside and do not express them easily, they may appear to be devoid of feelings. This is not so. Actually, their feelings are quite intense, but they are mostly kept within. As a result, this type can really be very shy, though others regard them as remote or aloof. Because their feelings run deep, they are capable of dramatic or even courageous acts.

On the downside, they can be quite moody and uncommunicative. They are likely to keep others at a distance and not develop close relationships. As a result, they are not good judges of others. In addition, they tend to be simplistic in their thinking. They are not good at subtleties and generally are very rigid in their beliefs.

Those who are extremes of this type may separate themselves from others to the point of being hermits. Under stress. they can become hysterical or almost paranoid, believing there are plots against them. These extreme types are even capable of developing counterplots against their competitors.

When communicating with the stoic/hermit, use simple, direct statements in favor of being too fancy or picturesque in your language. Offer benefits that appeal to their personal self-development, inner peace, and satisfaction. Do not attempt to establish personal relationships quickly. Be careful how you compliment them. Although they want to be liked by others, they may also become distrusting.

Realist/Exploiter

These prospects are extrovert who are sensation oriented. They are total realists interested only in external objects and concrete facts. They may be either very down-to-earth and unassuming, or sensualists in constant pursuit of stimulation and excitement. They are capable of being good managers who stay in touch with the basic realities of their positions and environments. Another variation of this type is the playboy going from one sensual adventure to another. Because they are so aware of reality, their senses may become refined to the point that they are excellent judges of quality.

In their major focus on the facts, or sensual satisfaction, they may be indifferent to the feelings or needs of others. They may be so concerned with their own desires that they lose sight of the desires of anyone else.

Extremes of this type become exploiters. Other people become only a means of achieving their desired ends. They may even develop an indifference bordering on brutality. Some may then also project their fears onto other people and become quite suspicious, even paranoid.

To communicate most effectively with the realist/exploiter, be very fact-oriented and realistic in your conversation. Talk benefits that relate to quality of experience. To the realists who are down-to-earth, talk about how they'll be more successful by using your product or service. If you're talking to sensualists, appeal to the satisfaction they will derive that is sense-oriented. They, or their companies will look better, sound better, feel better, and so on. Tell them how they will receive more pleasure, joy, fun from your product or service.

Promoter/Flake

These prospects are the extroverted intuitive types. They are at the vanguard of their fields, always looking for something new and exciting. They love being the first and are willing to take great risks to support their beliefs. They are excellent at discovering trends or grasping the future possibilities of current events. They are "bottom line" people in a hurry to get to the end result, rather than dwell on the details. This is the Mike Todd-type who, on the verge of bankruptcy, produces a successful film that turns his life around, and in the process invents a new film technique.

Because they are so intuitive and directed to the end result, they tend to neglect concrete details which may ultimately prevent them from completing their projects. Their lack of interest in individual facts may give them incomplete information that prevents their success. They also have a tendency to get bored easily with whatever is too old or familiar. They may not complete projects that take too long.

Extremes of this type have one idea after another. Like bees going from flower to flower, they buzz about but never finish, and sometimes never start, anything. They are continuously pursuing the new and losing interest in the old.

You can communicate more effectively with the promoter/flake by stressing what is new and innovative about your product or service. Let them know they'll be the first on the block to have it. Stress the end result or bottom line concerning what you have to offer. Don't be afraid to mention the risks involved, if there are any. Remember, they like taking chances. Stress benefits related to the future, being ahead of competition, feeling the excitement of winning, or being first.

Detached/Subjective

These prospects are introverts who are sensation-oriented. Their realities are based on what they make of the world from the five senses, yet they have a way of rearranging this information to suit themselves. They are adept at maintaining distance between themselves and others. When they speak, they are generally matter-or-fact rather than enthusiastic about their subjects. They appears to be emotionally detached and objective about life, but actually possess a great deal of subjectivity that colors their beliefs and reactions. This person is very good at solving problems and creative abstract thinking.

As a result of their introversion, however, they are not particularly good at communicating the results of their thinking to others. They tends to devalue what is outside, and in discussing their beliefs they project take-it-or-leave-it attitude.

Extreme subjectives react to reality in a way that bears little relation to what is actually taking place. Their interpretations are totally subjective and are based on their own mental constructions, which have nothing to do with the facts.

When speaking to a detached/subjective, don't expect any kind of enthusiastic response to your presentation; and it is best not to be very enthusiastic yourself. Ask what potential problems will arise without your product or service, then present your product or service as a possible solution to that problem. Ask them if they can suggest other solutions your product or service might provide to a similar problem. In short, get them involved intellectually, and then they will get involved emotionally.

Saint/Fanatic

These prospects are introverts who are intuition-oriented. They are concerned with the betterment of humanity. They are spiritual in terms of being tuned in to what Jung called, "the collective unconscious." They relate to ideas and essences, rather than concrete facts. Generally, they are very religious or mystical in their beliefs. They are quick to grasp the whole of an idea in an intuitive flash, especially if the idea is in any way related to the realm of the psychic or spiritual world. They are adept at understanding inner relationships.

This type neglects what is real or concrete. While dwelling on an idea to save humanity, they may burn the toast. They tend to ignore actual circumstances and minimize physical limitations. Their tendency is to stay in the realm of their spiritual visions, and let someone else take action.

Extremes of this type are the crackpots or fanatics who pay virtually no attention to the realities of this world, but dwell on the "true world of the spirit."

When you communicate with the saint/fanatic, stress how your product or service will help not just your prospect, but the whole world—or at least the community. Don't stress individual details, but dwell on the big picture relating to your product or service.

SELLING TO THE EIGHT TYPES

The golden rule is, "Do unto others as you would have them do unto you." Unfortunately other people do not necessarily want to be treated the same way you do. The "platinum" rule is, "Do unto others the way they would be done unto." In other words, treat people the way they want to be treated. Sell people the way they like to be sold.

To see how this works, let's examine selling a product to each of the eight psychological types. Let's remember that these types are useful *guidelines* and that most people will behave differently at different times, although everyone does have favored modes of behavior. This will give you a greater understanding of how to appeal to people who share that psychological type.

Let us suppose that my company product line is video training. The features/benefits of my company and product line include the following:

High standards for production

Reputation for integrity

High quality

Innovative technology

Leader in the field

Produce the most new videos each year

Systematic approach to learning

Detailed information

Continous support

Entertaining

Simple, direct information

Easy to learn

Modular formats

Inspirational themes

Universal concepts

Conceptual understanding

Consistent with modern philosophy of training

Develops employees' potential

Fosters better communication

Right- and left-brain-oriented

Appeals to logic and intuition

So, if I were selling these video training cassettes to a king/ tyrant prospect, I would discuss the systematic approach we take to every video. I would give detailed information regarding the planning and production of each training tape, and I would talk about the increased control over his or her business that these tapes would provide. I would demonstrate the increased security he or she would feel as well. The king/tyrant finds that a rational approach, coupled with assurances of safety, is very compelling.

If I were selling to a diplomat/lackey prospect, I would talk about how entertaining these videos are, how easy they are to learn from, and how we provide modular formats allowing greater flexibility. His or her employees will enjoy watching them. A diplomat/lackey prospect seeks improved harmony in his or her organization, wants people to like and approve of him or her. Therefore, these appeals are virtually irresistible.

If I were selling to a philosopher/dreamer, I would discuss the overall concepts of video training. I would review the principles of how they work and include the available theories on the subject in my presentation. I would explain that the training is conceptual, not just factual—the videos represent a philosophy of how to train people. His or her staff will understand the theory behind the training as well as simple details of what to do. These appeals to concepts and theories would be most acceptable to the philosopher/dreamer.

If I were selling to a stoic/hermit, I would show him or her how the videos would allow employees to be better trained without disrupting his or her tranquility. The information is simple and direct, presented in a dignified manner. Employees will develop more inner strength and calm in their work. They will be less likely to interrupt with questions or disturbances. They'll have better control over their emotions and the office will have a more peaceful atmosphere. The stoic/hermit is likely to respond positively to this approach offering serenity and calm.

If I were selling to a realist/exploiter, I would provide concrete facts that back up my company's reputation for excellence, our high standards, and our high quality products. I would talk about our continuous support. The net effect of the training will be more production at less cost. I would ask him or her to imagine seeing and hearing the videos and feeling good about how it would contribute to his or her success. This would appeal to the realist/exploiter's orientation to sensation.

If I were selling to a promoter/flake, I would say that my company is the leader in the field. It produces the most new videos every year. It also utilizes the most innovative technology, putting it at the leading edge of the industry. No other company in the promoter's industry has dared to use this program. After working with my video training program, he or she will be way ahead of competition, and be acknowledged as an explorer in that industry. The promoter/flake will find this presentation of uniqueness and being first most appealing.

If I were selling to a detached/subjectivist, I would stress that video training offers a solution to the problems of helping employees acquire greater skills and expertise regarding their work. In addition, they will learn methods of creative problem solving. The programs will also help them communicate better with each other. The detached/subjectivist will respond positively to the creative solutions appeal.

If I were selling to a saint/fanatic, I would relate how my video training program is both left- and right-brain-oriented. It appeals to the intuitive nature of people, and helps them tune in to their deeper unconscious selves. It will help employees develop better skills that will allow them to reach their full potential, spiritually as well as materially. I would further explain how the whole company would be better off as a result of the training received. The saint/fanatic is attracted to benefits that offer realized potential and spiritual well being.

You can see how a king/tyrant, for example, would not be at all moved by the same benefits as a diplomat/lackey. It's important to help your telemarketers realize that they must treat everyone differently. If they treat everyone the same, they're treating most people incorrectly. Figure 12-2 summarizes the eight psychological types and the differing sales approach each requires.

TO WHOM ARE YOU SPEAKING?

Once you realize how important it is to tailor your presentation toward your prospects, you naturally want to be able to identify specifically who they are. To which psychological type are you speaking?

An easy way to find out is to ask. Of course, the prospect doesn't know your terminology, but does know what he or she wants. So you can ask an open-ended question like, "There's a lot I can tell you about our product, but to save time what would you most like to learn about?" The answer to your question will give you an indication of what type the prospect is.

If open-ended questioning doesn't give you the information you want, ask some close-ended questions like, "Do you want to know about controlling your costs, or helping your people develop?" Or, "What about receiving better quality, or quickly taking advantage of a great opportunity?" Or, "Are you interested in the details concerning how our products work, or would you prefer an overview of the concepts?"

The answer you receive indicates who your prospect is and what he or she needs to know to make a decision. At this point, your life is a lot easier; just tell the prospect what he or she wants to know, and you are on your way to closing the sale.

YOUR TELEMARKETERS' PSYCHOLOGICAL TYPES

Like your prospects, your telemarketers run the whole gamut of psychological types. As such, they have the same kinds of strengths and weaknesses. The king/tyrant telemarketer, for example, may give a very logical and structured presentation, but may be too dominant or controlling. Prospects may not believe he or she has their best interests in mind.

The diplomat/lackey is very good at establishing rapport with prospects, but tends to be put off easily by sales resistance, not wanting to risk being disliked.

The philosopher/dreamer is excellent at communicating the overall concepts or principles of your product or service, but may not relate them to the specific situation or need of the prospect.

The stoic/hermit may have excellent work habits and be capable of spending long hours on the phone, but may not be as assertive or personable as you would like.

The realist/exploiter may be very strong and persuasive on the phone, but may not be as conscientious about satisfying the real needs of the prospects. He or she may make a sale but lose a customer.

The promoter/flake is very creative in taking advantage of every possible sales opportunity, but often lacks follow-through ability and persistence. He or she becomes easily bored.

The detached/subjectivist is excellent at solving a prospect's problem, but not necessarily persuasive enough to sell the solution. He or she may project an air of not really caring.

The saint/fanatic is very concerned about the satisfaction of the prospect, but may neglect to care about the profitability of your company.

Telemarketers need to become more aware of their own predispositions as well as those of their prospects. This awareness will help them develop an understanding of the psychology of the sale. This in turn will enable them to relate better to the full variety of psychological types with whom they speak each day. They will, in fact, develop the flexibility to deal with virtually anyone.

By raising your telemarketers' awareness of their own motivation and the motivation of their prospects, you go a long way toward helping them increase their effectiveness and your profitability. Telemarketing is, after all, a people process. People sell and people buy. If you can help your telemarketers understand their own psychological nature, as well as that of their buyers, you help them make their jobs a lot easier and more productive.

PART FOUR

STATE-OF-THE-ART TELEMARKETING

13

Computerizing Your Operation

This chapter will probably make many people nervous at first, but by the end of the chapter hopefully they will realize their initial apprehension has shifted gradually into a desire for action. An initial case of nerves is natural. After all, the whole subject of telemarketing is a new one. Your reason for reading this book is either to learn how to create a telemarketing program for your company, or to improve and augment the telemarketing program you already have. In most cases, the subject is new.

Combining telemarketing with computer automation increases the complexity. Computers remain an inscrutable mystery to most people, including executives. There has been a great deal of resistance to understanding and using computers. Although this resistance has declined with the advent of the personal computer, the thought of working with two relative unknowns at the same time certainly can make a top executive justifiably jumpy.

As this chapter unfolds, more and more information will support your decision to use some form of computer-assisted tele-marketing. Within the next three to five years, you will very likely have some sort of computer-assisted program anyway. If you have any doubts, consider your current business equipment. Very likely, you already have one or more of the following business machines:

Electronic typewriters

Word processors

Personal Computers

Minicomputers

Main frame computer.

Chances are you did not run out and buy the above equipment as soon as it was announced. Time passed before you realized the equipment was cost effective and improved your productivity. When that happened, you made the investment. In the same way, you will in time realize that an automated or computer-assisted telemarketing system is a necessity. When that happens, you will invest in the appropriate software and hardware. This chapter is presented to help accelerate that process.

In addition, it will help you make a selection of the appropriate hardware and software that you need.

COMPUTER DIALERS

When most people hear the phrase *computer-assisted telemarketing*, their first reaction is, "No, not those computer-dialed calls that play a recorded message." Right. This chapter is not primarily about computerized calling equipment that automatically dials a stream of numbers and transmits the same prerecorded message. Although in the main this chapter will deal with much more so-phisticated uses of modern computerization, there is a value to this simpler, more basic automatic calling equipment, so we shall quickly address this facet of modern telemarketing before we pass on to the major uses of computer-assisted programs.

First of all, computerized callers are those machines that call preselected numbers automatically. When someone answers, a tape player transmits a message. It is usually equipped with a second tape which is programmed to record the answering party's responses. If the party hangs up abruptly before the presentation is completed, the system is programmed to rewind and go on to the next call.

These machines are occasionally used in conjunction with a human operator, who initially speaks to the answering party and then asks for permission to play a recorded message. In these cases the recorded messages are sometimes given by a celebrity or a major executive of a company. At the end of the recorded message portion of the call, the human representative returns to the line to complete the call.

Although there is a great deal of annoyance in response to these machines, they can be effective for certain specific applications. They have the capacity to make a large number of phone calls in a very efficient manner. As soon as one call is completed, the next one is dialed. Since marketing is a numbers game, these machines can certainly reach a great many people.

In a multilevel marketing company, one recorded message can be sent to every distributor in the system. Political announcements to registered voters can be made effectively. Whenever the same message must be given to a large number of individuals, a computerized calling system must be considered. It reduces the boring, repetitive work considerably. Other similar uses are:

Special promotions

Product announcements

Customer service reminders

Advertising goods and services

Boost meeting attendance

The above types of calls can be made without any need for recording the answering party's responses. They perform a valid function of broadcasting one message to a large universe of people.

When response is necessary, computerized calling can also be effective in generating qualified leads. Success is increased when there is some sort of free offer given. For example, solar energy companies used this method to announce there was a government financing program available to homeowners for installing solar energy systems in their homes. A free gift was offered if they were interested in learning more about the program. Then the home-owner had the opportunity to leave his or her phone number for more information. Those who expressed an interest were then called back and an appointment scheduled.

The best way to use this kind of equipment for prospecting is to be direct and announce a benefit early in the conversation. If your benefit is strong enough, you can ask one to three qualifying questions and close with an offer to provide more information and possibly something free. Finally, ask for the person's name and phone number.

Although most people will find this kind of call unappealing, interested parties will respond, making this method a form of self-screening. Used properly and professionally, it will provide qualified leads that will result in sales. It is probably best used in consumer marketing rather than in business-to-business.

Let us go on to the main thrust of this chapter, computer-assisted telemarketing. The difference between computer-assisted telemarketing and computerized calling is analogous to the difference between a 747 and a Piper Cub. We're in a new generation here.

WHY AUTOMATE?

The reason for automating your telemarketing operation is the same as your reasons for automating other facets of your business operations: You can achieve greater productivity more cost effectively, with less human stress. A computerized telemarketing program will allow your telemarketers to handle more accounts with greater success, which will result in increased revunes. By auto-mating, you also reduce the employee burnouts due often to re-petitive tasks that are uncreative and fatiguing, like dialing the phone a hundred times a day.

Before we delve into the topic of using computers cost effec-tively, let's put this whole marketing function into perspective. Companies make sales to either new customers or existing cus-tomers. So much attention and effort is given to the acquisition of new customers that existing customers often are neglected. There is so much pressure on salespeople to bring in new business that those customers who have given them business before are often forgotten.

For decades, salespeople have used phrases like "pipeline," or "hopper," meaning a systematic flow of prospects whom they can contact. The understanding is that with enough prospects flowing through their pipeline or being put into their hopper, some cus-tomers will emerge. In other words, a salesperson will sell a cer-tain percentage of his or her prospects. Therefore, it helps to have a growing number of prospects to convert to buyers.

A computer-assisted telemarketing program enables your tele-marketing staff to have the highest number of new prospects pos-sible while simultaneously working with your existing customer base to maximize sales.

IDEALS VERSUS REALITY

To appreciate computer assistance fully, let's examine ideal tele-marketing people and then compare them with real human beings who do the work. The ideal telemarketers prepare for every contact by having their presentations in front of them, com-plete with answers to questions and objections as well as other support material. They send preapproach letters to new pros-pects before calling. They follow up their phone calls by sending thank-you letters or other letters appropriate to each call. They keep commitments to call prospects again on the agreed-upon fu-ture date. They honor their promises to send relevant data sheets or literature. They call their existing customers at regular intervals to obtain additional orders. They correspond with these customers as well, telling them about special promotions. They upsell to take allow customers to advantage of quantity discounts. They cross sell by offering prospects products or services related to what they already buy. They use all the appropriate answers to objections and questions. They are aware of customers' credit ratings to avoid wasting time selling to customers who won't pay. They are aware of inventory so they don't make delivery promises that can't be kept. They always give complete presentations explaining the benefits of the products. They won't attempt to use shortcuts, or otherwise omit relevant features/benefits.

By now you've realized these ideal people exist only in dreams. Reality is that most telemarketers are so pressured to make their time count that they rarely do all the things they should be doing. And when they do, they are not as thorough or as consistent as we would like them to be. Most telemarketers know that sending a thank-you letter is certainly the right thing to do, when you have just taken an order. Most telemarketers know that a letter should be sent to confirm an appointment. Most telemarketers know they should call back prospects when they said they would. Yet, these things rarely happen. And when they do, it is in an inconsistent and incomplete fashion. This is why computer-assisted telemarketing exists. By using current state-of-the-art hardware and software, it's now possible to approach the ideal in terms of what you want your telemarketer to do.

There is now computer hardware and software for companies of every size, from a one-person telemarketing operation to a large company with hundreds of operators. Equipment and programs are available for both outgoing and incoming telemarketing. They range in expense from as little as $2500 for a total system, to hundreds of thousands of dollars. Software for a simple personal computer is available for as little as $500.

MAJOR FUNCTIONS

Computer-assisted telemarketing systems do the following:

Database management
Word processing
Calendaring
Automatic dialing
Screen prompting
File accessing
Report generating

1. Database Management

A data base is simply a collection of information. A primary function of any computer-assisted telemarketing program is the management of data relevant to your market. You can handle a large volume of relevant customer and prospect information using this resource. The various fields of information you'll want to retain in your database files are:

Customer name/address/phone number
Contact/title
Credit rating
Sales/year to date
Gross profit year to date/percentage/dollars
Date last ordered
Frequency of orders
Products or services ordered
Lead source
Sales representative
Time zone/geographical territory
Company size/# of employees/sales revenue

The ability to review this information prior to calling is a tremendous asset for your telemarketers. They have everything right in front of them, all the data they need to make the sale or arrange a follow-up contact in the most professional manner. This information will also be invaluable to your company in management reports, which will be discussed a little later. Data base management allows you to select whatever parameters relate to your needs. For example, you might decide to market a new product initially to those customers who have 100 employees or more. These will be sorted for mailings and phone calls. You may also decide to sort your all or part of data base in zip code order to send large mailings that qualify for special bulk-mail postal rates.

2. Word Processing

With the integrated software available today, your telemarketers can conclude a phone call, press the button, and set in motion the proper follow-up written communication. When a call is made, there are only five possible outcomes. Your prospect or customer will say any of the following: "Yes," "No," "Call me back," "Send me literature," or "I am not in to talk to you." Regardless of which response your telemarketers receive, they can press a button and initiate the appropriate follow up. If the call is to an existing customer who ordered, an order is filled out automatically and a thank you-letter can be included. If the customer did not order, a follow-up letter is sent that includes information on the product and a future date that the telemarketer will be calling.

If the prospect or customer asks for additional information, a cover letter can be sent with it, mentioning a follow-up day when the customer will be called back. If the customer or prospect is not in, an I've-been-trying-to-reach-you letter can be sent. This letter will ask the prospect or customer to call at a specified time. Even if the prospect or customer doesn't call, this paves the way for better acceptance the next time the telemarketer calls. In the next section on calendaring, we'll examine additional methods of automated follow-up.

Other word-processing capabilities with the software currently available are mass letters, personalized letters, and customized letters. Mass letters are those to the entire data base, or a special segment of the data base. Personalized letters include the name of your prospect or customer in the body of the letter. These letters also can contain variable fields to refer to specific interests.

Customized letters may embody the same information as mass letters but also refer to specific details that relate only to the addressee. In addition, the word-processing functions allow you to print addresses on labels or envelopes.

You can program an automatic series of letters to be sent at preselected intervals. Another feature of some of these programs is the ability to use "trickle drop" mailings, which means that instead of sending out your entire mailing at one time, you can send it out in segments. If you have 20,000 prospects to contact, you can choose to send out 5000 letters per month to allow your telemarketers to follow up your mailing in the most effective manner without too much time lapsing between the mail and telephone contact.

The value of an automatic series of letters is to create an awareness in your prospect of your company. When your telemarketer calls, it won't be a cold call, but rather a warm call, making it easier for the telemarketer to get through and establish rapport.

3. Calendering Functions

This facet of your computer-assisted telemarketing program allows your telemarketers to keep their commitments and insures that viable prospects and customers are contacted regularly. We said earlier that there are only five possible outcomes to a phone call: (1) *No contact,* (2) *Yes,* (3) *No,* (4) Call back, or (5) Send literature. The telemarketer tells the system the outcome of each call then gives it a next-contact date. When that date arrives, the system prompts the telemarketer to contact this prospect or customer.

In addition, the system may contain certain other marketing prompts. For example, the name and number of any customer who hasn't ordered in six months should be listed on a computer printout or brought up on a telemarketer's screen. A great deal of flexibility is possible. The most beneficial aspect of calendering is to offset the effects of staff turnover and vacations. The objective is always to be sure that nothing worthwhile falls through the cracks. By using a computer-assisted system, you prevent much of the time and sales losses due to human error, memory lapse, and inconstancy.

4. Automatic Dialing

This is the most obvious enhancement of computerization. Numbers are dialed for the telemarketer by the computer. The Tele-Marketer simply presses a button when ready for the next call, and it is dialed automatically by the system. This ensures that the number will be dialed properly and also saves a good deal of time spent searching the record to find the phone number. Thus, another tedious and time-consuming part of the telemarketing process is eliminated. By removing the boring and repetitive elements of telemarketing, we not only save time but we save stress on the telemarketer. There is no doubt that the automatic dialing feature of the system will allow your telemarketer to make many more phone calls, which in turn will lead to more appointments and sales.

5. Screen Prompting

Screen prompting is the use of the video display terminal to guide telemarketers in the content of their presentations. The script or telechart is displayed on the telemarketers' screens and they simply read it or refer to it as they go through the presentations. Key questions are listed as well as space for their answers. Alternate choices or branches are also indicated. If the telemarketer receives a particular response, he or she may go to Branch A. If he receives another response, he or she may go to Branch B, and so on.

It is not difficult to program a system to give every major response an appropriate branch. The advantage of this is it equips all telemarketers with the information they need to make sales, set appointments, or conduct surveys. What this does for your company is make your telemarketers more proficient.

Although some companies already use these, "if . . . , then . . . ," branches, they are in printed form. As a result, the telemarketers do not use them. After awhile, presentations and answers to questions and objections are buried under a pile of other paper or they are hidden in a drawer. Screen prompting assures they will be in front of the telemarketers' eyes. There is then a higher probability that they will be used. The negative facet of screen prompting is that it requires input from the telemarketer. Good telemarketers are usually people-oriented, rather than systems-oriented. Initially, they may resist using the computer terminal. However, once they experience the benefits of time savings, reduced stress, and immediate access to help, they will make the adjustment.

6. File Accessing

File accessing allows your telemarketers to gather information from other relevant files. For example, if a customer asks about delivery for a specific product, the telemarketer can simply access the inventory file to determine if the product is on hand. Another file telemarketers may need to access is accounts receivable. When an order is taken, your telemarketer can check the accounts receivable file to make sure the customer has not exceeded his credit limit, or to determine when the last check was received. Remember, your telemarketers are paid based on the sales revenue they generate. responsible for. It is also possible with some systems to update inventory and accounts receivable files automatically when an order is taken, which means a great savings of bookkeeping time. You also may want to generate a packing slip automatically with each order. With some systems, this is all possible.

7. Report Generating

This function of your telemarketing software keeps you in greater control of your operation. You can receive a whole variety of reports that relate to your staff's productivity: how many calls are made per telemarketer, per hour; how much time is spent on each call; how much time is spent off the phone; number and amount of sales per telemarketer; dollar amount of sales per phone call; number of sales and sales dollar volume per hour; how many calls a telemarketer makes to get one order. You can use this valuable information to fine-tune and control your telemarketing program.

FOUR APPROACHES TO AUTOMATION

There are four different systematic approaches to automating your telemarketing program. They run the gamut from one personal computer to a number of terminals connected to a microcomputer. The ensuing discussion highlights some key advantages and disadvantages.

1. One Personal Computer, One Telemarketer

This is the entry approach to computer-assisted telemarketing. You begin with one telemarketing person and one personal computer. The telemarketer uses the personal computer through all phases of telemarketing work. He or she uses the automatic-dialing function to call prospects, accesses and updates the database during and after the call, uses the calendar function to insure keeping commitments to call back, activates the word processing function to send a follow-up letter, and throughout the call the script-prompting function has helped him or her make an effective presentation. Finally, there is the ability to use the fulfillment functions to print an order and/or packing slip. Management has a record of all this for later summary via the report-generating function.

When there is one telemarketer and one personal computer, the initial investment is minimal. There is just the hardware and software. Depending on the size of the database, however, a system using floppy diskettes may not be adequate. An extensive database calls for a hard-disk system, which increases your costs to some extent. The major disadvantage of either starter system is that it is not as fast or powerful as a minicomputer. Still, it is considerably faster and more effective than a nonautomated system.

2. One Personal Computer, Multiple Telemarketers

In this approach, several telemarketers are supported by one personal computer. This means that they do not use automatic dialing or screen prompting, but they can take advantage of many of the other functions. With this system, computer printouts are distributed to the telemarketers containing names, numbers and other relevant information from the prospect and customer database. The printout, in effect, conveys, to the telemarketers all the information they would receive if they had terminals on their desks. The telemarketers make their calls manually, read from a printed script or presentation, and then indicate the response directly on the computer printouts. At the end of each shift, the printouts are returned to a sales support clerk, who then keys all the data into the personal computer. Whatever forms, letters, or orders are needed are then generated automatically. The major advantage of this approach is its cost-effectiveness.

By utilizing one personal computer in this manner, you are offering your telemarketers a great deal of support at minimal cost. The major disadvantages is that you are not taking full advantage of the system's capabilities. They don't utilize the auto-dialing or screen-prompting functions. In addition, you pay for the time and labor of a sales support clerk or secretary to update all the information and administer the follow-up. Still this approach is an ideal way to get started in automating your telemarketing program without a great deal of financial investment.

3. Multiple PCs, Multiple Telemarketers

In this system every telemarketer has a personal computer and each individual uses all the advantages of the system enumerated previously. This system is cost-effective for up to four or five telemarketers. Each telemarketer has a database that is not connected to the database of any other telemarketer. This means gathering information on overall telemarketing operations would have to be accomplished by reviewing the data at each terminal. With four or five telemarketers, this approach is feasible and is generally less expensive than using one minicomputer with four or five video display terminals.

4. One Minicomputer, Multiple Terminals, Multiple Telemarketers

This system represents the state-of-the-art approach to computer-assisted telemarketing. A minicomputer gives you a powerful, fully integrated database that may be accessed by any telemarketer. If a telemarketer is sick or on vacation, another person may step in easily. This approach is especially attractive because the system's power and speed facilitates its use for both outgoing and incoming telemarketing. The other systems are too slow to be used, on a direct basis, to handle incoming calls. In addition, these systems can access accounts receivable and inventory files readily to determine their status.

The major disadvantage of this approach is comparatively larger financial investment required. The minicomputer and software may require an initial investment of $40,000 to $60,000, but when amortized over five years, the investment more than pays for itself.

HOW TO GET STARTED

A good way to begin is to take advantage of your impending change. Review your objectives and marketing strategy. Analyze your sales track record, including cost per sale. You may elect to use telemarketing to concentrate on your higher priced items. Be sure that your telemarketing approach has profit potential. Don't sell 20-dollar products unless you can sell volume.

At this point, you may want to hire a consultant to help you automate. If you have your own in-house data-processing department, be cautious about getting them involved. Their emphasis on the technical details of data processing may delay your program startup considerably. Ideally, the project manager should have marketing knowledge first, supported by some technical background in data processing.

Before selecting hardware, decide what you want your system to accomplish. List the major functions you want in order of priority; then select software that can help you get the desired results. There is adequate software on the market to prevent the need to reinvent the wheel by creating your own program. There are always exceptions; but, chances are, as unique as your company is, there is software that can accommodate you.

Once you have chosen the appropriate software, then select the hardware to drive it. If you already have data-processing support in your company, by all means utilize your existing hardware if possible. However, once you have made the commitment to automate your telemarketing program, it's important to select software and hardware that will work for you. Don't make the hardware you have fit by forcing it to be used in applications that are not suitable. Remember your telemarketing investment, executed properly, will be a source of additional profits.

Begin training your personnel during the time after choosing your hardware and software and before it is installed. Don't program yourself for failure by trying to teach two new and distinct skills at once: telephone selling and computer operations. By training them in telemarketing skills before the system arrives, you pave the way for smooth transition. You also gradually enlist their support. It's very common for telemarketers, who are primarily verbal rather than systematic, to have a negative first reaction to computers. By involving them early in your program, but not before they have a chance to learn the basics, you ease them into a positive attitude regarding automation.

System installation should not interfere with daily operations. You may even want to run parallel for a while, just to be sure everything is functioning properly. It is a good idea to have a dry run of your system on a weekend or in the evening. This gives your staff time to familiarize themselves with the new system without the press of prime-time calling. Problems that develop at this time are not so serious.

Before your system is due to be installed, be sure your database, including names, addresses, and telephone numbers of your prospects, are on floppy diskettes or tape, depending on the system you utilize. If necessary, use an outside list-processing service or temporary in-house help to be sure this information is ready.

As you gain additional experience with your computere, refine it to maximize its effectiveness. You may decide that you don't need to use certain capabilities. Or, on the contrary, you may decide that you need to enhance even more the capabilities you have. Depending on the caliber of your telemarketing people, you may also elect not to use all of your system's capabilities immediately. You may want to start your telemarketing staff with just one function to ease them into being comfortable with the entire system. You may begin, perhaps, by using the automatic dialing or the screen prompting. This is always a judgment call. It is better to do too little at first than too much. After your people are comfortable with one or two functions, you can then add on one at a time. Using this method, your people gradually become more and more adept at utilizing the system without developing a negative attitude. You, of course, are the best judge of how much your staff can handle.

THE FUTURE

Judging by the history and development of the computer in general, and the applications of telemarketing, we can only expect more and more computer sophistication. In all likelihood your office has become much more automated over the past five years. If you don't have an electronic typewriter, word processor, or micro or minicomputer now, you very likely will in the next year. If not, you are certainly in the minority of companies. We can only expect the progress of labor-saving automation to continue. There is little doubt that you will be automating your telemarketing some time in the future. Why not do it now and profit from an early start?

We can only guess at what some of the new technology will allow us to accomplish. A friend who is a real estate broker suggests better use of computer-assisted telemarketing would be to tape record the telemarketer saying some of the more repetitive portions of the presentation, saving his or her energy for the more demanding and sophisticated parts of the presentation. Rather than say the same key sentences over and over, the telemarketer might merely press a button and the computer would play those statements and questions. Then the telemarketer would take over, using his or her verbal skills and energy to deal with the specific characteristics of the particular call. The technology is already here to allow this. It certainly makes telemarketing more attractive. The direction in which automation leads us is only limited by our imagination.

14

Resources for Telemarketing

In this chapter, I've listed three resources available to you when creating your own telemarketing program. These three software products are so outstanding that I have chosen to highlight them. They are available now—fully tested and debugged—and will certainly help you develop an efficient, effective telemarketing program.

MANAGING PROSPECTS WITH MARKETFAX

In the preface to the MARKETFAX manual, the program is described as follows: "MARKETFAX is a marketing and correspondence management software package that provides the features of data base manager and word processor. The combination of these features provides the first 'Human communications accounting' system for large and small businesses."

If, like most of us, you are not especially computer literate, the above paragraph will have little meaning to you. On the other hand, once you become acquainted with the software, you will appreciate readily what it can do for you and your company in terms of increasing sales.

Two Databases

What MARKETFAX has done is combine the ability to mix and match two separate files. The first group of files is your prospect or customer data base. This is simply a name and address file of all those companies you have targeted as prospects, or perhaps existing customers you wish to develop further. This file allows you to store up to 512 characters of information for each prospect. The information is conveniently organized and coded in an extremely useful and concise manner. This means that you can select on a predetermined basis those prospects that meet specific criteria.

For example, once you have accumulated your database of customers, you may decide you want to send a special mailing to all those prospects in the state of Minnesota who have 50 employees or more, and are in the construction business and have received at least one previous letter from your company. MARKETFAX accomplishes this selection in seconds.

A second major filing characteristic of MARKETFAX is its ability to retain a virtually unlimited file of modifiable form letters. These letters are generally two paragraphs long, although they can be any desired length. MARKETFAX uses the two-paragraph approach because its research has determined that a two-paragraph business letter is the most effective.

MARKETFAX allows the user to match its two files. This means you can send any prospect on your data base any letter in your letter file. It also allows the user to dash off a quick note as needed for unique situations.

Automatic Letters

What is most unique about MARKETFAX is its ability to prepare and print automatically a series of letters on a predetermined ba-

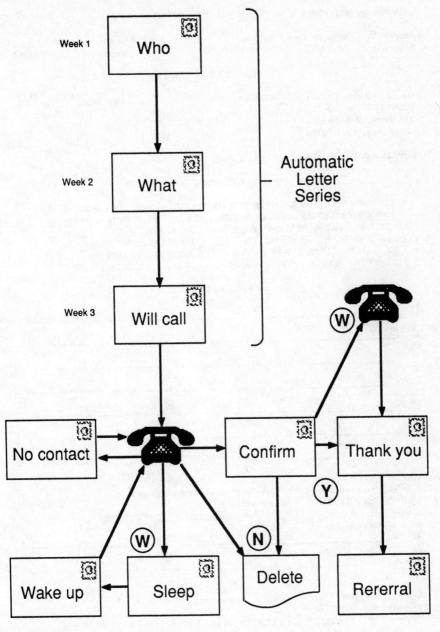

FIGURE 14-1

December 31, 1986   **** ACTION REPORT ****

Report for: Stanley Leo Fidel
Situation: CALL4APPT   Letter No.:   T8
                                                     Response: VARIABLE

** YOUR CONTACT **

Ms. Sue Akins   President   555-3434
COSMETICS 'R' US
345 North Broadway
Santa Ana, CA 92701

COMCL:00001 (Next action: on January 7.)

*** INSTRUCTIONS / NEXT ACTION ***

CALL FOR APPT. HAS RECEIVED PRE OR LEADSLTR, ETC.   December 31
        *** CHECK LETTER HISTORY & CHECK OFF AS APPPROPRIATE ***
FILL IN TIME, DAY & DATE ON ADDIN1   [ ] 19, YES
[ ] 20, SEND INFO;   [ ] 32, CK   [ ] 21, LATER - FUTURE
[ ] 22, LATER - 1 TO 2 WEEKS   [ ] 23, NO CONTACT
[ ] 24, NO - ARCHIVE   [ ] 25, NO - DELETE

** FREE FORM LETTER **

[1.1]_____

[1.2]_____

[1.3]_____

[2.1]_____

[2.2]_____

[2.3]_____

Days till action _____ Date next action _____

OLD INFORMATION:
ADDIN1: Interested in Tele-Marketing to expand business
ADDIN2: does $100,000 in commissions

NEW INFORMATION:
ADDIN1:_____

ADDIN2:_____

Initials: SLF   Qualifiers: PRS DISTR
Transfer to: AGENT
History: 861231:T8   1231:T8 0827:t:L10 0721:40 0721:40 0
M-T-D: 15   Y-T-D: 15

FIGURE 14-2

214

sis. Let us suppose your marketing strategy calls for sending three letters to the prospects on your mailing list. Each letter will contain a business reply card. If a prospect does not respond to a mailing, he or she will receive the next mailing automatically. If the prospect does respond, he or she receives a phone call.

MARKETFAX allows you to send the appropriate letters automatically, or notifies your salespeople of those who are to receive phone calls. This saves an enormous amount of time you would otherwise spend managing your prospects. Once the initial letter is mailed, each additional letter in the sequence will be sent on schedule with no need for human intervention. Suppose you want to send letters to 300 different prospects, but you want to send only 100 letters each week. MARKETFAX allows you to do the following:

Week 1: 100 letters are mailed to the first 100 prospects.

Week 2: 100 letters are sent to the second 100 prospects, and 100 follow-up letters are sent to the first 100 prospects.

Week 3: 100 letters are sent to the third 100 prospects. 100 follow-up letters are sent to the second 100 prospects. 100 final letters are sent to the first 100 prospects, and so on.

Automatic Follow-Up

In the fourth week, your telemarketers receive an action report, containing the first 100 names and numbers for telephone follow-up. If any of your prospects returns the business reply card, an operator simply puts that information into the system, that prospect is removed from the letter series, and the telemarketing representative is notified by the system to make a phone call. This assures you of a systematic approach to marketing where no viable lead falls through the cracks.

What is unique about MARKETFAX is that follow-up letters will be generated automatically with no operator determination. Other marketing software is available, but no other package has this feature of generating a series of letters automatically.

Telemarketer's Assistant

In addition to sending correspondence, MARKETFAX will also scan the data base for the next prospect or customer to call, then it will dial the telephone number if it is being used with a modem. MARKETFAX also gives telemarketers on-screen prompts to guide them through their telephone presentations. It even offers *branching** in the event of questions or objections, which allows your telemarketer to be as effective as possible, while assuring management that no important information is being omitted from the presentation. In addition to sending correspondence and persistently telemarketer, MARKETFAX can also create call reports and print your letter lists and prospect lists. It will also print reports and labels, sort your lists, and help you convert data from other list sources. It is a very flexible marketing program.

Systematic Telemarketing

A key thrust of this marketing software approach is that every phone call will result in either a contact with the decision maker or no contact. If a contact is made, the decision maker will respond in one of three ways, either saying "Yes" to the request for an appointment or a sale, saying "No," saying "Call me later." Since there are only four basic results of the phone call, MARKETFAX keys in to each possible result and prepares the appropriate letter. If there is no contact, MARKETFAX sends out something like the following:

"I am sorry I haven't been able to get through to you, although I have tried calling you several times.

"You most certainly will receive value from spending no more than one minute on the phone with me, and I would greatly appreciate your courtesy."

---

*Branching is a computer function that allows the telemarketer to touch the appropriate button on the keyboard and receive a visual prompt, right on the computer screen, to the next sequential part of the presentation. This can be a feature/benefit, a question, an answer to a question, or a rebuttal to an objection.

If the response to your call has been positive, MARKETFAX can send a letter as follows:

> "Thank you for spending a few minutes on the telephone with me today. I look forward to meeting you next Wednesday at 10:00 A.M. at your office.
>
> "After you see what I have to show you and discuss it with me, I know you'll feel the time was well spent."

If the response has been negative, MARKETFAX will send something like the following:

> "Thank you for spending some time with me on the telephone today. I'm sorry you have no interest in exploring our services any further at this time.
>
> "We will be contacting you from time to time to inform you of new developments that you will find interesting. Thank you for your consideration."

If your prospect says, "Call me later," MARKETFAX will send the following appropriate letter:

> "Thank you for speaking with me on the telephone today. I'm sorry this was not a good time for you, and I'll be calling you again in two weeks as you requested.
>
> "At that time, you will certainly find what I have to say will be of interest to you. Thank you for your consideration."

Regardless of the outcome of your telemarketer's call, MARKETFAX sends an appropriate letter, thus enhancing the relationship between your company and your prospects. If your prospects don't buy now, your company's name and image will be brought to their attention again in a professional manner. The next time, the outcome may be different. If your prospects do buy now, they receive the professional courtesy of a written thank you. This fosters repeat business.

You can use MARKETFAX in one of two ways:

1. Each telemarketer can have a personal computer with the MARKETFAX software installed in it.

2. One personal computer with the MARKETFAX program can support your telemarketing group. In the latter, you will not be as effective as when each individual uses MARKET-FAX, yet it will also not require as great an investment.

You may decide to install one system at first and then add on as your results justify.

The MARKETFAX software is specifically designed for use on a personal computer. It is extremely cost-effective when there are up to five telemarketers in your group. When the number exceeds five, you should consider a multiuser system.

TEL-ATHENA

Tel-ATHENA is a multiuser software package intended to be used with a minicomputer, although it may be used on some PCs. It works with the PICK operating system and is extremely efficient, fast, and powerful. It accommodates as many users as the corresponding computer hardware permits. It may be used for both outbound and inbound telemarketing.

Tel-ATHENA is intended to be used on-line to support the telemarketer. Each telemarketer has a video display terminal, which is connected to a minicomputer that uses Tel-ATHENA software. What is unique about Tel-ATHENA is its ease of use. It is extremely flexible and can be adapted to your needs without using a programmer to configure it.

In addition to generating correspondence, forms and scripts, Tel-ATHENA has many other capabilities, some of which are described here.

Computer Tape Processing

Tel-ATHENA has the ability to read and write information from and to computer tape in virtually any format. This allows data bases such as customer lists to be transferred into the telemarketing system from other computer systems. It also permits information such as customer orders to be transferred from the telemarketing system into other computer systems inexpensively via magnetic tape.

Screen Seating

Screen seating allows the telemarketer to select any information from any customer file on the system and fit it into variable fields showing on the screen. Information pertinent to each call is inserted into the on-screen script electronically before the call is made. For example, the buyer's previous orders can be integrated into the presentation *automatically,* thus personalizing the presentation, which improves the closing rate dramatically.

Work Scheduling

With work scheduling, management can establish schedules for callbacks by telemarketers, even taking into consideration the time zone from which calls are being made and the time zone being called. It also schedules the work by month, day, and hours during each day. This prevents telemarketers from scheduling callbacks on weekends or holidays, or at other times when no one will be available to receive the call.

Security and Work Assignment

This is a function that allows users to access the portions of the system they need and no others. Each user has a unique ID and password, which offers a greater level of security than is otherwise available.

Operational Mode Control

Most useful for training, this feature enables telemarketers to train on the system without affecting any live data, making entries without actually changing the existing data base.

Callback Scheduling

When a telemarketer calls prospects whose lines are busy or who won't take the call just then, the callback can be scheduled for 30 minutes later or any other time. "No" answers can be automatically scheduled for callback in an hour or on the next workday. Any other callbacks can be specified by the telemarketer during the call.

Information Codification

Management uses this feature to categorize free form information into new groups that can be included in data analysis and project reports, thus adding important marketing facts to your data base.

Data Analysis

Tel-ATHENA is equipped to enable management to run statistical analysis on data recorded during prior calls. The results can then be printed in standard formats, processed for management reports, or even be represented graphically for use in other formats.

Correspondence and Forms Generation

Using this portion of the program, project supervisors prepare standard letters and preprinted forms to generate automatically, customized with information recorded from any call. It allows your sales group to send out professional, personalized communications with virtually no effort, and in hardly any time.

Graphic Generation

A feature that enables management to define and produce graphs and charts—line charts, bar charts, and pie charts—these graphics then can be added to letters, reports, and proposals, making your communications even more impressive.

Report Generation

Management can produce reports of any desired data with the following features:

1. The pages will be titled and numbered.
2. Information will be selected and sorted according to whatever criteria are desired.
3. Numbers will be segmented, subtotaled, and totaled as desired, automatically.

Project Reporting

Allowing management to monitor the performance of each telemarketing representative automatically, these reports will show:

1. Start time
2. Stop time
3. Time worked
4. Number of calls attempted
5. Number of calls answered
6. Number of calls not answered
7. Number of calls busy
8. Average length of each call
10. Number of calls in call category

This valuable feature offers to management powerful tools to control and evaluate the production of its telemarketing group.

Communications

Remote terminals and printers that can communicate with the telemarketing computer system allow you to have people working from home who are part of the entire system. You can also print orders at remote shipping locations or generate management reports at the home office even when the telemarketing takes place at a branch office. There are many other applications possible with your own communications system.

Electronic Mail

Users send and receive messages to and from one other with this feature, permitting the quick, efficient dissemination of information in an essentially paperless environment.

Reference File Management

This enables users who have no programming expertise to create, build, and update unlimited numbers of information files, files used typically by your telemarketers when they need information during a call. Such things as product prices, state tax rates, zip codes, and related business locations are typical information files.

Data Base Management

The PICK operating system has its own powerful data base. Since Tel-ATHENA is an integrated part of the PICK operating system, data base management is incorporated in the software automatically.

Tel-ATHENA truly represents the state of the art in computer-assisted telemarketing. It also represents a sizeable investment in computer hardware and software. Investigation of tel-ATHENA is warranted if your company's annual sales are in excess of $4 million.

The Wonder of WATSON

Watson is a brilliantly designed new software package with accompanying hardware that allows you to establish a sophisticated voice mail system, allowing a group of individuals to send and receive voice messages without human intervention. Systems like this have, until now, been available only in conjunction with expensive telephone systems that cost tens of thousands of dollars.

With Watson, it is possible to turn your computer into a state-of-the-art voice mail system for under $800.

Your salespeople, consultants, and customers can use Watson to keep in touch with each other 24 hours a day.

Individual User Codes

Each user of the system is assigned a unique identification code. Callers address messages to a particular user by entering that user's ID code. If you like, your telephone receptionist can transfer callers to Watson and enter the appropriate user's ID code so that the caller can then leave a message for the Watson user.

Message retrieval is accomplished by calling Watson and entering your ID code and even a secret password, if desired. There are a number of exciting new features that Watson makes available. For example, you can instruct Watson to call you at another number and forward messages from important callers. Users can reply to messages as they listen to them; insert comments into a message and redirect it to another user; and check the date, time, and originator of any message.

Voice Mail

For an example of how Watson works, let's suppose you are a sales manager for your company. Your name is Tom Jones and you're on the road working with one of your salespeople. You call your office and the telephone receptionist transfers you to the Watson mail extension. After business hours, the company telephone system would automatically direct outside calls to the same Watson mail extension.

Watson answers, "Hello, this is the Watson system of the ABC company. If you are a user, enter your code number now. Otherwise, please wait for the tone and leave a message."

You enter your ID code by pressing "* 1234 #" on your telephone touchtone pad. (These features work only from a touchtone phone, or equivalent.) Watson then says, "Enter password followed by 'pound' key." You press "456 #."

Watson says "Three messages," and continues, "9 play, 7 record,

6 forwarding, 4 hangup." You press 9 to play your messages. The first is from one of your regional sales managers, Barb Field. Her message is, "Tom, J.M. is ready to buy. Can I agree to $900 per unit?" You press 5 to reply and say, "Barb, try to get $950. But go along with them if you have to." Then you press "#" to stop recording and Watson replays the message.

The second message is from Phyllis Cohen, the vice-president of marketing. She says, "Tom, I need your sales report right away." You press "4" to check the message date. Watson says, "Today at 3:30 PM, Phyllis Cohen, 23." (23 is Phyllis Cohen's extension.) You press 5 to reply, and say "Phyllis, we'll be closing J.M. That gives us a total of 10,000 units for this month. I'll be calling in later if you have any questions."

Watson asks, "Remove all messages? 9 yes, 6 no." You press 9 to delete the messages you just received. Watson repeats the main menu, "9 play, 7 record, 6 forwarding, 4 hangup."

You press 7 to record a message for Charles Todd, vice president of manufacturing. Watson asks, "Destination mailbox?" You dial Charles' extension: 31. After the tone you say, "Charles, we're about to close that J.M. order. Can you order an extra 3000 units beginning next month?"

In case you get another message from Phyllis, you decide to set up Watson for call forwarding. You press "#" to stop recording, then you hear the main menu again and press 6 for forwarding. Watson says, "Enter phone number followed by pound key." You dial the forwarding number "9* 6225211 #." (The 9* tells Watson to dial for an outside line and pause for a dial tone). Watson repeats the forwarding number and asks if it is O.K.. You press 9 for yes and then 4 for hangup.

An hour later, you are at your customer's office and the phone rings. Someone answers the phone and hears, "Tom Jones. Forwarding message from Watson mail. Please enter your password." The phone is handed to you and you hear the same message repeated. You interrupt it by dialing your password. Watson plays the message, "Tom, this is Phyllis again. I would like you to meet with the president and myself tomorrow about the J.M. sale at 10:00 A.M."

Additional Features. As you can see, Watson saves a great deal of time and avoids what commonly is called "telephone tag." There are several other valuable features to the Watson system. It contains an electronic rolodex file of up to 500 names. There is an internal modem, which allows you to press a button and automatically dial the number of anyone on your electronic rolodex. You can program Watson so that specific callers will receive a personalized message from you. No one else can hear their messages. There is an electronic calendar file as well as the ability to dictate notes and letters. Watson can be used to communicate from computer to computer, as well.

A truly innovative addition is the ability to forward your messages to another location by calling Watson. As you change locations, you can have your messages keep up with you.

Outgoing Calls. Another module of Watson now available, VIS, allows you to make outgoing calls automatically. For example, let us suppose you are the sales manager of a company and you want to notify all your individual salespeople about a price change. You can call your message into Watson once and have Watson automatically notify each of your salespeople of the change.

You can also use Watson to make outgoing calls to prospects and customers. It is highly programmable, so you can structure your message to receive and record information as well as transmit it. This allows you to conduct surveys automatically. There is a wealth of other applications that relate to telemarketing. One, which will interest all those who hate to repeat the same message or part of the message all day long, records the repetitive portion of the message in Watson. This way, the telemarketer will pick up the line to participate in the more interesting, nonrepetitive facets of a conversation.

For example, you can record, "Hello, this is Bruce Smith of Books Unlimited. I'd like to speak to the president of the company. What is his or her name, please?" Only after the receptionist answers will Bruce speak. By eliminating a great deal of the boring, repetitive tasks of telemarketing, Watson allows humans to enjoy the more fulfilling aspects of their work. Isn't this what modern technology is all about?

Appendix A

Sample Telemarketing Manual

TABLE OF CONTENTS

PROGRAM OVERVIEW FOR CALLERS

THE COMPANY

For ten years, VIDEX/VIDEOTRAIN, INC., a Los Angeles-based subsidiary of Spring Enterprises, has been the preeminent leader in the field of audiovisual (AV) corporate education. It offers the broadest spectrum of film strips, slides, cartridges, video cassettes (both stop action and full motion), and allied materials available to train business professionals in corporations across the U.S.A. and worldwide.

VIDEOTRAIN, the original product line, is a name synonymous with very good but very elementary training programs, one recognized by most executives from their basic business education. Primary emphasis now is on establishing VIDEX as *the* innovative producer of consistently superior advanced AV products, without losing the positive association of the VIDEOTRAIN reputation. To that end, VIDEX continues its commitment to (1) create a high quality, creatively produced AV product, a "no frills" didactic approach packing a great deal of technical information and complex skills-teaching without sacrificing professionalism, and (2) presenting state-of-the-art information by utilizing the nation's top experts in each field as consultants. Business specialists are on hand as in-house consultants for any technical questions or comments from executives.

THE TARGET MARKET

Of the thousands of companies in the United States, 3500 are already VIDEX customers. The remaining companies represent a vast, largely untapped market; many of them may have heard of VIDEX, or purchased products previously, but some have gone two or three years without follow-up. Some regular customers may buy one to four times a year, while others haven't bought for several years.

Sales are currently engendered through inbound calls; outbound calls are made when time allows, and not according to any fully adhered-to system.

VIDEX wants to expand exposure to its products with an aggressive telemarketing program directed to:

1. President or
2. Director of Training

or other title variation, such as Director of Marketing, or Human Resources—essentially, the decision maker(s) involved in the selection, purchase, and use of AV training materials.

Since corporations vary greatly in size, the number of decision makers may also vary greatly: A small company may have a single decision maker in complete charge of the budget, while a large company may have a substantial budget but many decision makers. We are targeting those companies with 25 to 500 employees. This will allow the greatest number of sales with a minimum amount of delay.

The usual approach to a sale is through a 14-day preview of an AV film or video cassette, usually for a $25 fee, with follow-up in two weeks. For the balance of 1985, this fee is being waived. It is hoped that more previews will be converted to sales, and that the current preview-to-sale rate—now at 25%—will be increased by 10%.

THE PRODUCTS

VIDEX has produced over 1000 AV education and training materials used in basic business education, retraining, upgrading skills, and continuing education. Each year the company brings to market 50 to 70 new programs, introduced by way of catalogues, direct mail announcements, and public relations news releases.

A selection of 7 motion video packages, consisting of from 2 to 12 individual titles, forms the nucleus of this telemarketing effort. For your reference, these product categories are identified and detailed in the product section. The basic cost of each film or video is $395.

The new method of all-action motion video is a more sophisticated technique than the stop-action video transfer, which relies on a "fade in, fade out" method of moving from topic to topic. For teaching purposes, however, the continual motion videocassettes still can be stopped at any time in order for a point to be made (or for learning reinforcement) by the trainer.

In VIDEX'S words, "We haven't abandoned our traditional software formats such as film strips, slides, and cartridges, all of which are still widely used—especially in schools. We do believe that program content . . . can be enhanced by the motion video format, depending on the topic." To underscore this statement, VIDEX offers a trade-in opportunity to companies wishing to upgrade to this medium.

THE OBJECTIVES

The objectives of the telemarketing thrust are sevenfold:

1. To expand VIDEX'S active customer base by 3,500 (doubling the current base).
2. To increase revenue by $2.5 million over the next 12 months.
3. To improve preview-to-purchase rate: films, from 10% to 20%; videos, from 25% to 35%.
4. To develop a consistently sucessful tracking system.
5. To integrate optimally the telemarketing arm with existing departments.
6. To gather research data for future product development and marketing strategy.
7. To build awareness of VIDEX'S highly professional products and services.

CALL FLOWCHART INTRODUCTION

The call flowchart is actually a roadmap that shows how an ideal telemarketing call should progress from initial contact to close. Every stage performs a certain role in taking the caller to a successful conclusion. The key points in each stage are bulleted, and serve only as reference. In essence, the call flowchart contains the skeleton of the presentation guide, and should not be expected to contain specific phrases, buzz words, and dialogue that is more fully developed in the presentation. (See Figure A-7.)

TELEPHONE PRESENTATION INTRODUCTION

The step-by-step structure of the telephone presentation enables almost any type of caller to adapt his or her technique to the established flow of the presentation. The specific language can and should be adjusted to fit a caller's personal comfort level, but the integrity of the steps as outlined should be preserved. They assure a natural progression from start to finish. The sequenced steps protect against loss of control by the caller, and prevent conversations of excessive length that defeat the program's purpose. Most important, the structured approach makes every contact with a lead as compelling as it can possibly be, no matter how the caller happens to feel. It guarantees an effective presentation consistently.

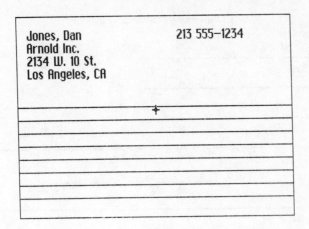

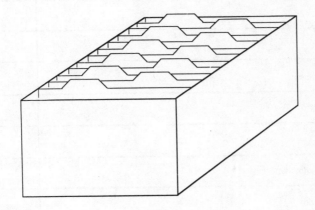

FIGURE A-1

TELEPHONE PRESENTATION: VIDEX

STEP 1: LOCATE CON-
TACT

(Use Full Name of Pros-
pect Whenever given)

To Receptionist:
"Hello, this is (FIRST LAST NAME) of
VIDEX. May I speak with the President
of the company?" (OR: Director of Training, OR: Director of Marketing, OR: Director of Human Resources, or other
appropriate office as indicated on prospect's card.)

Daily Telemarketing Representative Summary

Project: _____

TSR: _____

Date: _____

	In: _____ Out: _____	Totals
Hours:		
Calls:		
Contacts:		
Presentations:		
# of Sales:		
Sales $:		
# of Appointments:		
Lead source:		
Info.:		
NIs:		
CBs:		
NAs:		
Misc.:		

FIGURE A-2

Project: _____ Date: _____ Week: _____ Ending: _____

ID	TSR	Total hours	Total calls	Total # of contacts	Total # of sales	Total sales volume	% hit rate	Total presen-tations	Total appoint-ments	Total # of	Total # of lit. requests	Total # of NI	Total # of CBs	Total # of NAs
	Training													
	Working	Total hours	Total calls	Total # of contacts	Total # of sales	Total sales volume	% hit rate	Total presen-tations	Total appoint-ments	Total # of	Total # of lit. requests	Total # of NI	Total # of CBs	Total # of NAs

FIGURE A-3

233

Telephone Survey Sheet

Salesperson _____   Solicitor _____

Date _____

Company _____

_____

Type of business _____   Phone ( ) _____

Person _____   Title _____

Person _____   Title _____

Printing reg.	Type	2/4 Color	Quantity	When	How often
Direct mail	_____	_____	_____	_____	_____
Catalogs	_____	_____	_____	_____	_____
Brochures	_____	_____	_____	_____	_____

Letters _____ _____ _____ _____ _____

Blister/boxes _____

Other _____

Misc. information

What do you like about your present supplier?

How many do you have?

What could be improved on by your present printing suppliers?

Who is involved in decisions of ordering printing?

When is next printing job coming up?

_____

Hot	Warm	Cold	Agency

Send letter _____

Call back on _____

FIGURE A-4

FIGURE A-5

Prospect Call Sheet

Date _____ Tele-Marketer _____

Name _____ Phone # _____

Title _____

☐ Salesperson to visit

Date _____ Time _____ ☐ AM ☐ PM

Name of business _____

☐ Literature to be sent

Address _____

City _____ State _____ Zip _____

Level of interest: 1 Very interested

2 Fairly interested

Type of business _____

3 Mildly interested

# of employee _____ Credit rating _____

Annual sales rev. _____

Comments _____

Previous suppliers _____

_____

Prospect source _____

_____

Estimated sales potential _____

Call date	N.A.	Call back	Call details	Services/ products sold	Gross sale	Additional sales		
						Upgraded sale	Item	$ Value

235

Date ———   Incoming Call Log   Name ———

Name	Address	Phone #	Called about	Source	Outcome

FIGURE A-6

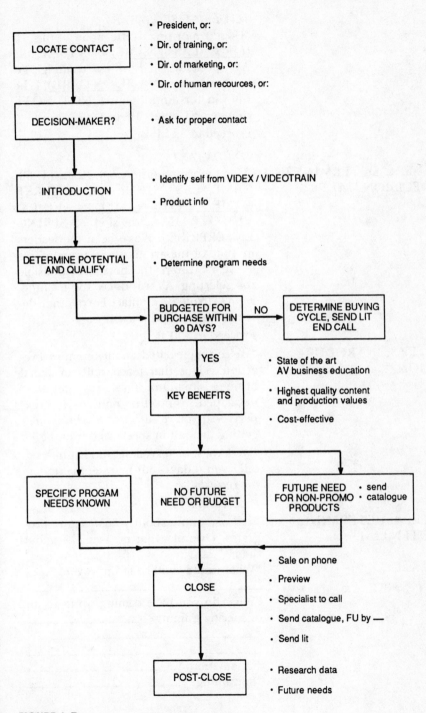

LOCATE CONTACT	• President, or:
	• Dir. of training, or:
	• Dir. of marketing, or:
	• Dir. of human recources, or:

| DECISION-MAKER? | • Ask for proper contact |

| INTRODUCTION | • Identify self from VIDEX / VIDEOTRAIN |
| | • Product info |

| DETERMINE POTENTIAL AND QUALIFY | • Determine program needs |

BUDGETED FOR PURCHASE WITHIN 90 DAYS? — NO → DETERMINE BUYING CYCLE, SEND LIT END CALL

YES

KEY BENEFITS	• State of the art AV business education
	• Highest quality content and production values
	• Cost-effective

SPECIFIC PROGAM NEEDS KNOWN   NO FUTURE NEED OR BUDGET   FUTURE NEED FOR NON-PROMO PRODUCTS   • send • catalogue

CLOSE	• Sale on phone
	• Preview
	• Specialist to call
	• Send catalogue, FU by —
	• Send lit

| POST-CLOSE | • Research data |
| | • Future needs |

FIGURE A-7

TO OFFICE SECRETARY:
"Good morning (afternoon), this is (FIRST LAST NAME) of VIDEX, the AV specialists in business training. I'd like to speak to (NAME ON CARD). Is he (she) in for a minute? (IF NOT, NOTE change on Contact Form.)
Proceed to STEP 2

STEP 2: DETERMINE IF DECISION MAKER

TO CONTACT:
"Good morning (afternoon), ____(FIRST NAME, LAST NAME) this is (FIRST NAME, LAST NAME) of VIDEX/ VIDEOTRAIN, a division of SPRING ENTERPRISES. We've been the leaders in state-of-the-art business training for 10 years. You're the person responsible for selecting AV products for training, right?" (Note on Contact Form other decision makers in this area)
Proceed to STEP 3

STEP 3: INTRODUC-TION

"We're very excited about our new live-action videos that teach skills in actual business situations. These cassettes were developed using the nation's top experts—so you're safe in knowing you're getting the best in specialized training."

"We have some excellent opportunities to offer you today—but first, let me update my records."
Proceed to STEP 4

STEP 4: DETERMINE POTENTIAL

"Tell me a little about your training programs. Overall, what do you like about them?" ____
"What would you like to improve?" ____
_____

"What do you have coming up in terms of specific training?" _____
_____
_____

"Orientation?" _____
"Retraining?" _____

NOTE responses to all of above on Contact Form.

"Do you keep records?"

"What kind of budget do you have?"
NOTE responses to all of above on Contact Form.

"If you got really excited about our videos, and saw that they really suited your needs, would you have the budget available within the next 90 days?" _____

IF NO:"

"When would the money open up?"
NOTE on Contact Form.

"If we could demonstrate that it was more cost-effective to use our videos in your training program, would that free up the budget?"
NOTE on Contact Form.

STEP 5: SUMMARY AND

"Let's see ... (Read back information and qualifications you have recorded on Contact Form; e.g., 'You will be covering nonverbal communication skills next fall, your budget is open,' etc.

"I know something about you. Now let me tell you a little more about us. Here's what makes us the innovative leaders in AV Training programs:

STATE-OF-THE-ART HEALTH CARE INFORMATION USING THE BEST CONSULTANTS IN THE COUNTRY. All our programs are developed with top experts recommended by specialty organizations and professional associations. Is expert training important to you?"

HIGHEST QUALITY CONTENT AND PRODUCTION VALUES. We spend thousands and thousands of dollars to assure the highest calibre result. How does that sound?"

In Fact ... over $2 million per year is spent on new programming

- COST-EFFECTIVE; consider the dramatic savings possible with AV programs: You can play them again and again so they can be used to train your whole staff at very little cost, right?

Your people can view them at their convenience, so it doesn't interfere with their work schedules. That's a plus, too, isn't it?

Your staff can stop and start the tape so they learn at their own individual rate. Isn't that effective?

Also, they can supplement your training staff and increase learning effectiveness. Doesn't that make sense?

Proceed to STEP 6

STEP 6: CLOSE

A. IF SPECIFIC PROGRAM NEEDS HAVE BEEN MENTIONED:

Since you say that you have need for 1 nonverbal communication, I suggest you use our NVC series. It's a package of 3 cassettes. You can choose the whole package, or individual titles such as 'USING BODY LANGUAGE TO SELL.' The package sells for $750, or you can choose individual videos at $275 each. (Note: Refer to comments on each package on page __.)

Or, if you choose 5 videos, we will give you 3 free. Which do you prefer? "VIDEX has a 30-day return policy—the most liberal preview/return policy in the industry. So you can feel safe, right? Which do you use—Beta or VHS or 3/4?" "Fine. I'll ship your cassettes out today."

B. IF NO SPECIFIC PROGRAM IS MENTIONED:

"Let me tell you about our new releases. (NOTE: refer to comments on Package Description sheet, p.__.) "Which one of these would you be most interested in reviewing?"

NOTE on Contact Form.

The package sells for <u>750</u>, or you can select individual titles for $295. Or, if you buy five, we'll give you three free. "What's better for you—the whole program, or individual videos?

"VIDEX has a 30-day return policy—the most liberal preview policy in the industry. Do you use Beta, VHS, or 3/4?"

"Fine. I'll ship your cassettes out today."

C. *IF DON'T PURCHASE OVER THE PHONE:*

"I can understand that; still I'd really like to get the video cassette(s) out today for you to <u>preview</u>. By the way . . . there's no charge for this, and you have 14 days to look at them. Fair enough?"

"If you preview a video and like it, is there any reason you wouldn't decide to keep it? I'll be calling you in a couple of weeks."

D. *IF NEEDS MORE TECHNICAL INFORMATION:*

"I'll be happy to have one of our specialists get back to you by <u>(date)</u> to answer your questions."

E. *WANTS TO SEE CATALOGUE:*

"I'll send the catalogue out today, and see that you're called by <u>(date)</u>."

F. *LAST RESORT*

Thank politely, send literature.

STEP 7: POSTCLOSE: RESEARCH AND FUTURE NEEDS

"Briefly, would you tell me who else is involved in making decisions about AV material?"

(NOTE on Contact Form, ask to be transferred IF FEASIBLE.)

"Who is your supplier of AV materials, if you don't purchase from VIDEX? Is there any particular reason you HAVEN'T chosen VIDEX products?"

(NOTE on Contact Form)

"When you see our catalogue, you're going to find many programs that will be perfect for future needs. We'll be checking back soon to talk about them. I know you'll feel good about VIDEX products."

BACK-UP DATA

OBJECTIONS AND ANSWERS

Objection—   "We don't have the money."

Answer—

- "I can certainly understand that, and still your people could use the training, right? If money were no object, which videos would you want?" (Write Names Down)

"Good. You send your people to seminars don't you? What about finding some money in your seminar and travel budget? You know, we're only talking about $295 for training you can use again and again and again, right?"

"I'll get that out to you and you'll have 30 days to find the money—fair enough?"

Objection—   "Still too expensive."

Answers—   "Here are some other ways we can help you save money."

- "If you trade in your old films with similar titles for the new videos, we'll arrange a $75 discount on each video. Do you have any old films that you don't use very much?"
- "Also, every 5 programs you buy, we'll give you 3 more programs free. That's a savings of $885, isn't it?"

Objection—   "What if it's not what I need?"

Answers—   "Seeing is believing—that's the beauty of the preview program. If what you see doesn't suit your needs, simply send the videos back to us within 14 days, and don't pay for them. What could be fairer than that?"

Objection—   "What about outdated material?"

Rebuttal—

"Our state-of-the-art information is produced using top consultants in every area, with program content geared to today's business environment and the latest technology. VIDEX MATERIAL IS STATE-OF-THE-ART."

"If a video is revised within six months to a year after purchase, we'll give you an equal trade. Does that make you feel better?"

QUESTIONS AND RE-SPONSES

Question—

"What about service? And delivery?"

Response—

"We have 800 number phone lines to serve you, with representatives who'll respond immediately to your needs. We have a 30-day return policy, and a superior shipping record. We ship UPS for delivery within two weeks. If you request it, we can ship UPS BLUE for emergencies (at your expense, of course)."

Appendix B

RESOURCES

The listings in this section are largely derived from the 1987 Tele-Professional Buyer's Guide, reproduced with their permission. Tele-Professional is one of the premier Tele-Marketing periodicals in America. I have made every effort to assure that the listings are accurate, but cannot guarantee that there are no errors. Most of the companies listed are *not* known to me, so please do not assume that their placement here is a recommendation. Those that are known to me and that I recommend are preceded by an *.

ACD's (Automatic Call Distributors)

Audiocom, Inc.
Penthouse 401
8100 Oak Lane
Miami Lakes, FL 33016
Stuart Ginsberg
305-825-4653

Bonner-New Inc.
4418 Calliope Street
New Orleans, LA 70125
Michael Puinno
504-821-0534

Candela Electronics
926 W. Maude Ave.
Sunnyvale, CA 94086
Ken Durey
408-738-3800

Code-A-Phone Corporation
Div of the Conrac Corporation
16261 S.E. 130th Ave.
Clackamas, OR 97015
Gary Bennett
503-655-8940

Combined Telecom Resources
416 Dunailie Drive
Nashville, TN 37217
Eve Fierce
615-361-0469

Dacon
8 Industrial Ave.
Upper Saddle River, NJ 07458
Jane Marlow, Adm. Mgr.
201-825-4640

Data Plus, Inc.
7205 Lockport Place
Suite E
Atlanta, GA 30307
James Marck, CEO
800-368-3747
202-289-6900

Davox
4 Federal
Billerica, MA 01821
Bill Bradley
617-667-4455

Dictronics Inc.
85 Franklin Street
Needham, MA 02192
Jim Brown
617-444-2010

Digital Transmission, Inc.
315 Eisenhower Lane South
Lombard, IL 60148
Joe Baier/Steve Pope
901-683-5677
901-686-0866

Dytel Corporation
50 E. Commerce Drive
Schamburg, IL 60173
Bill Nigh
312-519-9850 x5216

GTE Supply
P.O. Box 30402
Salt Lake City, UT 84130-0402
Ray Bufford
801-537-5222

Innings Telecom Corporation
P.O. Box 134
Georgetown, CT 06829
Richard Mellin
203-938-3172

Intrastate Telecommunications
1550 Deer Park Avenue
Deer Park, NY 11729
Al Kammerer - Pres.
516-252-2255

Jackson Communications
1250 Broadway,
17th Floor
New York, NY 10001
John Wassenbergh, VP Mktg.
212-563-1200

Microlog
4 Professional Drive
Suite 116
Gaithersburg, MD 20879
Mary Peters
800-562-2822

Midwest Telephone Supply Inc.
925 N. Bluemound Drive
Appleton, WI 54915
Jack Reynolds
414-739-6341

Northern Telecom, Inc
P.O. Box 1222
Minneapolis, MN 55440
Joseph A. Scott,
Mkgt. Mgr.
800-328-8800
612-932-8238 MN

Opcom
110 Rose Orchard Way
San Jose, CA 95134
Beth Baltimore
408-943-0878

Plant Equipment Inc
28075 Diaz Road
Temecula, CA 92390
Patty Cummings
714-676-4802

Qualitel Services, Inc.
2871 Metropolitan Place
Pomona, CA 91767
Lou Carlson
714-596-1675

Ric Systems
446 Lancaster Avenue
Frazer, PA 19355
Richard Gavalis
215-647-6677

Rockwell International, Switching Systems
1431 Opus Place
M/S 933-400
Downers Grove, IL 60515
312-454-1752

Solid State Systems
1300 Shiloh Rd. N.W.
Kennesaw, GA 30144
Laura Kamenitsa,
Mgr Mkt Comm.
404-423-2229

South Central Bell Corporation
Div of Bell South Corp.
600 N. 19th Street,
19th Floor
Birmingham, AL 35203
Jackie Cook
800-633-6272

Standard Telecommunications
175 Louis Street
S Hackensack, NJ 07606
Zina Hassel
201-641-9700

Tadiran Electronics Industries
5733 Myer Lake Circle
Clear Water, FL 33520
John Dabnor
813-532-3222

Teknekron Infoswitch
P.O. Box 612487
DFW Airport, TX 75261
Andrew Waite
817-354-0661

Tel Plus International
800 N. Federal Highway
Boca Raton, FL 33431
Denise Behringer, Director
305-997-9999

Telcom Technologies
3072 East G Street
Ontario, CA 91764
Rose Relich
714-980-5000 x216

Telephone Support Systems Inc.
2001 Marcus Ave.
Lake Sucess, NY 11040
Bernard P. Allen
516-352-6800

Telephonic Equipment Corp.
17401 Armstrong Ave.
Irvine, CA 92714
Henry McNulty, Dir Mkt
714-250-9400 x400

Teletech Communications Inc.
174 Classon Avenue
Brooklyn, NY 11205
Jacob Schlesinger, Pres.
718-783-8383

William B. Allen Supply Co.
300 N. Rampart Street
New Orleans, LA 70112
Bill Kanelos
504-525-8222

Zeta Digital Systems Inc.
2233 Northwestern Ave.
Waukegan, IL 60087
Bill Sultan, VP Mktg
312-244-0974

Agencies, Direct Marketing

ADC Alan Drey Company, Inc.
600 Third Avenue
New York, NY 10016
212-661-0440

Bankers Marketing Services Inc.
872 Massachusetts Ave.
Cambridge, MA 02139
Richard Bingaman
800-854-0014

Blitz Media Direct
Communications Tower
102-TP7
Middle Island, L.I., NY
11953-0102
Andrew S. Linick, Ph.D.
516-924-8555

CMP Direct Marketing Services
600 Community Drive
Manhasset, NY 11030
800-645-6278

Cahners Direct Marketing Services
1350 E. Touhy Ave.
Des Plaines, IL
60017-5080
800-323-4958

Chicago Assoc. of Direct Mktg.
600 South Federal,
Suite 400
Chicago, IL 60605
312-922-0439

Chilton Direct Market & List
1 Chilton Way
Radnor, PA 19089
215-964-4365

Consumers Marketing Research Inc.
600 Huyler Street
South Hackensack, NJ
07606
Geoffrey Nelson
800-225-0634
201-440-8900 NJ

DMS Direct Marketing Support
1865 Miner Street
Des Plaines, IL
60016-4791
312-298-9730

Design Three-sixty Direct Marketing
1011 Madison Ave.
South Milwaukee, WI
53172
John Bryzycki
414-768-6900

Direct Marketing Technology
5400 Newport Drive #11
Rolling Meadows, IL
60008
312-577-1020

Direct Mktg. Guaranty Trust
141 Canal Street
Nashua, NJ 03061
603-882-9500

Executive Services Companies
901 North International
Pkwy.
Richardson, TX 75081
214-699-1271

Flair-Direct
214 West Erie Street
Chicago, IL 60610
312-943-5959

Four Star Associates, Inc.
260 Duffy Avenue
Hicksville, NY 11802
Ed Schibler
516-822-4100

I.T.L.
24423 Southfield Road
Ste 100
Southfield MI 48075
Thomas Tharp
313-569-5800

John Tighe & Partners
72 West 85th Street
New York, NY 10024
212-873-2520

Kestnbaum & Company
221 North La Salle
Street
Chicago, IL 60601
312-782-1351

LCS Industries, Inc.
120 Brighton Road
Clifton, NJ 07012
800-524-1388

Mail Management Group, Inc.
2101 West Alice Ave.
Phoenix, AZ 85021
602-997-4447

North American Communications Group, Inc.
2400 Westwood Avenue
Richmond, VA 23230
Paul R. Simmons
804-353-4453

PSA Direct Marketing Group
2711 Toledo Street
Torrance, CA 90503
213-328-9623

Richard Siedlecki Direct Marketing
2674 East Main St.
Suite C-170
Ventura, CA 92630
805-658-7000

SCI Direct Marketing Systems
10101 Bren Road East
Minnetonka, MN 55343
612-933-4200

The Interface Group, Inc.
300 First Avenue
Needham, MA 02194
617-449-6600 x4082

Visions Marketing Services
451 E. Ross Street
Lancaster, PA 17602
Allan Geller
800-222-1577
800-222-1570 PA

Wiland & Associates, Inc.
141 Fifth Ave. 7th Floor
New York, NY 10010
212-475-4400
213-395-3445

W.S. Ponton, Inc.
The Ponton Building
5149 Butler St.
Pittsburgh, PA 15201
Harvey Rabinowitz
800-628-7806

Association

American Telemarketing Association
1800 Pickwick Avenue
Glenview IL
(800) 441-3335

Automatic Dialers

Alphone Intercom Systems
1700 130th Ave N.E.
Bellevue, WA 98007
Jim Morrison
206-455-0510

Arion
17819 S. Lysander Dr.
Carson, CA 90746
Dante Wilson
213-532-3400

Arnus Corporation
1305 Conkling
Utica, NY 13501
Patrick Ciandella
315-793-8500

B.A. Pargh Company Inc.
1283 Murfreesboro
Road
Nashville, TN 37217
Bernard Pargh
800-BAP-1000

Bonner-New Inc.
4418 Calliope Street
New Orleans, LA 70125
Michael Puinno
504-821-0534

Brand-Rex Company
1600 W. Main Street
Williamantic, CT 06226
Bruce Gordner
203-456-1706

Buscom
490 Gianni Street
Santa Clara, CA 92054
Trevor Squirrell
408-988-5200

Candela Electronics
926 W. Maude Ave.
Sunnyvale, CA 94086
Ken Durey
408-738-3800

Computer Research Inc.
3901 Nome Unit 2
Denver, CO 80239
Bill Hamilton
303-373-2331

Comtel Broadcasting Corp.
13 Harbour Town Center
Noblesville, IN 46060
Bob Haverstick
317-877-6050

Corliss Data Systems
77 Hartland St.
East Hartford, CT 06108
Mo Kenneally
203-282-0131

DRW Corporation
7744 West 78th Street
Minneapolis, MN 55435
Dennis Pelletier
612-829-0938

Davox
4 Federal
Billerica, MA 01821
Bill Bradley
617-667-4455

Dukane Corporation
2900 Dukane Drive
St. Charles, IL 60174
Jim Shane
312-584-2300

Entrac Inc.
416 C. Avenue N.E.
Cedar Rapids, IA 52401
Spencer Cardwell Jr.
319-565-2602

Fannon Courier Corporation
15300 San Fernando Mission Blvd.
Mission Hills, CA 91345
Murry Trotiner
818-898-2237

Gordon Kapes Inc.
7250 N Cicero Avenue
Lincolnwood, IL 60646
Carolyn Cashel
312-676-1750

KTI Corporation
1666 N., Firman, Ste. 400
Richardson, TX 75081
Steve Wagner
214-669-9590

L.P. & Associates
(Former Tel Enterprises)
622 No. 22nd Drive
Phoenix, AZ 85015
Lou Polett
602-265-5016

Microlog
4 Professional Drive
Suite 116
Gaithersburg, MD 20879
Mary Peters
800-562-2822

Micro Peripheral Corporation
2565 152nd N.E.
Redmond, WA 98052
Mark Perrin
206-881-7544

Mid Atlantic Marketing Inc.
17017 Flatwood Drive
Rockville, MD 20855
Matt Wolk
301-258-5066

Millicom Inc.
733 Third Avenue
New York, NY 10017
Phil Callahan
212-687-0055

Nova Communications
68 Royal Range Road
Sandown, NH 03873
William Berg
603-887-2657

Omni Communications
319 Lynnway
Lynn, MA 01903
Laurie TM Manager
617-596-2000

Profidex Corp
90 West Street
New York, NY 10006
Steven Haber
212-732-6795

Profit Growth Inc.
2699 Walter Avenue
Northbrook, IL 60062
Fritz Kreiss
312-498-9043

Racom
5504 State Road
Cleveland, OH 44134
S. Silverstine
216-351-1755

Selkirk Associates, Inc.
Kenmore Box 216
Boston, MA 02115
Tony Merlo
617-536-7200

Skutch Electronics
209 Kenroy Lane #7
Roseville, CA 95678
Judy McCulloch
916-786-6186

South Central Bell Corporation
Div of Bell South Corp
600 N. 19th Street,
19th Floor
Birmingham, AL 35203
Jackie Cook
800-633-6272

Southern Bell Telephone
Div of Bell South Corp
500 N. Orange Ave.
Orlando, FL 32801
Yvonne Vickey
305-237-3701

TBS International
959 E. Collins
Richardson, TX 75081
214-690-9436
Jack Zimmerman

Telecorp Systems, Inc.
5825-A Peachtree
Corners, E.
Norcross, GA 30092
Dana Webster, VP
800-334-9907

Telephone Concepts Inc.
Div of Esgeco Ltd.
2971 Flowers Road S.
Ste. 165
Atlanta, GA 30341
Kathy Anderson
404-992-1932

Tri-Ed Inc.
11372 Trask #109
Garden Grove, CA 92643
Bill Winn
800-228-7433

Valcom Inc.
1111 Industry Avenue S.E.
Roanoke, VA 24013
Donald Buck
703-982-3900

Voad Systems
3304 Pico Blvd.
Santa Monica, CA 90405
Patrick Ryan
213-450-2929

Burn-Out Consultants (Stress Management)

Linda Blakeley, Ph. D.
435 N. Bedford Dr.
Suite #310
Beverly Hills, CA 90210
213 273-9042

Elaine Fidel, MSW
201 S. Alvarado Street
Suite #707
Los Angeles, CA 90057
213 483-5511

Call Accounting Equipment/ Services

Affinitech Corporation
2252 Welsch Industrial Court
St. Louis, MO 63146
Bryan Baehr
314-569-3450

Aim Telephone Inc.
14 Gloria Lane
Fairfield, NJ 07006
William Juliano
203-227-8600

Autotel Information Systems
4944 N. County Road 18
Minneapolis, MN 55428
Christopher Santill
612-533-7888

CVTC
4205 Grove Avenue
Gurnee, IL 60031
Laura Hinze, Mktg Dir
312-249-5560

Commonwealth Communications Inc.
416 Elm Ave.
Kingston, PA 18704
Daniel Schall
717-283-4888

Control Key Corporation
100 Summit St.
Peabody, MA 01960
Wayne Barnett,
Ntl Sales Mgr
617-532-6990

DMW Group Inc.
2020 Hogback Road
Ann Arbor, MI 48104
Bruce Wilson, Mkt Mgr.
313-971-5234

Enhanced System, Inc.
6961 Peachtree
Industrial Blvd.
Norcross, GA 30092
Michael Mittel
404-662-1503

Graybar Electric Company
34 N. Meramec
St. Louis, MO 63105
Don Folkmer
314-727-3900

Homisco, Inc.
190 Lee Burbank Highway
Revere, MA 02151
Ronald Contrado
617-286-1220

Infortext Systems Inc.
1067 E State Parkway
Schaumburg, IL 60173
Tim Kelly, Exec VP
312-490-1155

Instor Corporation
199 Jefferson Dr.
Menlo Park, CA 94025
Nancy Engles, Ad Mgr
415-326-9830

KTI Corporation
1666 N. Firman Ste. 400
Richardson, TX 75081
Steve Wagner
214-669-9590

Lang Systems Inc.
1010 O'Brien Drive
Menlo Park, CA 94025
Seth Neumann
415-328-5555

Midwest Telephone Supply Inc.
925 N. Bluemound Drive
Appleton, WI 54915
Jack Reynolds
414-739-6341

Moscom
300 Main Street
East Rochester, NY 14445
Ron Tucker
716-385-6440

NEC Telephones, Inc.
8 Old Sod Farm Road
Melville, NY 11747
Don Hoffman/
Ivan Launer, Ad Mgr.
516-753-7000

National Systems Corp.
221 N. Lasalle Street
Chicago, IL 60601
Jim Kargman
312-726-3211

Newcastle Communications
270 Lafayette Street
9th Floor
New York, NY 10012
Ed Nicholas
212-431-7220

Nova Communications
68 Royal Range Road
Sandown, NH 03873
William Berg
603-887-2657

Opus Telecom Inc.
96 Eames Street
Farmingham, MA 01701
Jay or Barbara Gainsboro, Owners
617-875-4444

Prophecy Development Corp.
2 Park Plaza
Boston, MA 02116
Frank Foster/
Sean Cavanaugh
617-451-3430
617-451-1885

Skutch Electronics
209 Kenroy Lane #7
Roseville, CA 95678
Judy McCulloch
916-786-6186

Soft-Com Inc.
22 W. 21st Street
New York, NY 10010
Karen Miller
212-242-9595

Summa Four Inc.
2456 Brown Avenue
Manchester, NH 03103
Greg Falan
603-625-4050

Sykes Datatronics Inc.
375 Orchard Street
Rochester, NY 14606
Chip Chapman
716-458-8000

Techtran Inc.
200 Commerce Drive
Rochester, NY 14623
Mike Masiello
716-334-3246

Telamon Corporation
8134 Zionsville Road
Indianapolis, IN 46268
Albert Chen, Managing Dir
317-875-0045

Tel Electronics Inc.
705 East Main
American Fork, UT 84003-2138
801-756-9606

Tie Communications Inc.
8 Progressive Drive
Shelton, CT 06484
Joseph Monachino, Adv Mgr
203-926-2000

Xiox Corporation
577 Airport Blvd.
Ste. 700
Burlingame, CA 94010
Barbara Brown, Dir of Adv.
415-375-8188
408-727-1943

Cathode Ray Tubes

Alfa Telesystems Inc.
111 New York Ave.
Lake Hopatcong, NJ 07849
Bill Osborne
201-663-2318

Citifax Corporation
3667 Woodhead Dr.
Northbrook, IL 60062
Ruth Conners
312-291-9645

Communication Services
Div of Honeywell Inc.
Honeywell Plaza

Minneapolis, MN 55408
Michael Fox
612-870-5999

CRC Information Systems
435 Hudson Street
New York, NY 10014
212-620-5678

Electro Rent Corporation
4131 Vanowen Place
Burbank, CA 91505
Patrick Johanson
818-843-3131

GTE Communications
Div GTE Corporation
1907 U.S. Highway 301 North
Tampa, FL 33619
Lois Elwood
813-623-4000

ITT Communications Services
100 Plaza Dr.
Secaucus, NJ 07096
Christopher Hoppin, VP/Dir Adv
201-330-5111

Mar-tel Communications, Inc.
375 S. Washington Avenue
Bergenfield, NJ 07621
Lawrence Steinberg, Pres.
201-385-7171

McDonnell Douglas Applied Communications Systems
20705 Valley Green Drive
Cupertino, CA 95014
Bill Sernoff
408-446-8177

Megaphone
Div of Voad Systems
3304 Pico Blvd.
Santa Monica, CA 90405
Patrick Ryan
213-450-5979

Peirce-Phelps Inc.
2000 N. 59th Street
Philadelphia, PA 19131
Henry Grove
215-879-7180

South Central Bell Advanced Systems
505 N. 20th Street
Ste. 850
Birmingham, AL 35203
Cynthia Wingo
205-879-2121

Standard Telecommunications
175 Louis Street
S. Hackensack, NJ 07606
Zina Hassel
201-641-9700

Tel Plus International
8000 N. Federal Highway
Boca Raton, FL 33431
Denise Behringer, Director
305-997-9999

Telecom Resources
123 N Centennial Way
Ste. 206
Mesa, AZ 85201
Nita Bishop
602-834-1233

WMD Micro Distributors Inc.
109 Galther Drive
Mt. Laurel, NJ 08054
Brenda Sharkey
609-778-4600

Consultants

ACT Communications, Inc.
109 N. Main
Ector, TX 75439
L.B. Burrow
816-471-4945

Audiocom, Inc.
14445 N.W. 77th Avenue #203
Miami Lakes, FL 33014
Ron Deblinger, President
305-825-4653

Adelie Corporation
125 Cambridge Park Drive
Cambridge, MA 02140
Charles Khuen/
Harriette Chandler
617-354-0400

Advent Management Associates
110 W. Union St.
P.O. Box 3203
West Chester, PA 19381-3203
215-431-2196

Advertir
495 Old York Rd.
#431
Jenkintown, PA 19046
215-969-2891

American Media Inc.
1454 30TH Street
West Des Moines, IA 50265
(515) 224-0919

Ameritel Corporation
124 S. Wisconsin Ave.
Neenah, WI 54956
Craig Leipold
414-727-3900

Amrigon
25 W. Long Lake Rd.
Bloomfield Hills, MI
48013
Richard Smith
313-258-2300

**Andcor Companies,
Inc.**
600 S. County Road 18
Ste. 575
Minneapolis, MN 53426
Alison White
612-546-0966

**Andrew S. Linick,
Ph.D.**
Tall Trees 960 Dept. TP7
Middle Island, NY
11953-0102
Andrew S. Linick, Ph.D.
516-924-3888

Angel A.F. Associates
404 Walker Lake Ontario
Rd.
Hilton, NY 14468
Angel Agel-Frederich
716-964-8375

**Ann K. Bradley
Associates, Inc.**
3990 Old Town Ave.
Ste. 105C
San Diego, CA 92110
Jacqui Roche
619-295-2942

Arlen Communications
7315 Wisconsin Ave.
600E
Bethesda, MD 20814
301-656-7940

Scott Ashby
2520 Grand Ave. #310
Kansas City, MO 64108
816-474-9038

**Ashworth Associates,
Inc.**
P.O. Box 4707
Laguna Beach, CA
92652
Leonard J. Trosino
714-671-2236

**Assoc. for Human
Achievement**
1728 Morgan Lane
Redondo Beach, CA
90278
Linda Seard,
Operations VP
213-379-2510

Atkins and Associates
2455 N.E. Loop 410
Ste. 300
San Antonio, TX 78217
512-657-5775

**Atlanta Direct
Marketing**
6951-J Roswell Road
Atlanta, GA 30328
William H. Dyke,
President
404-393-0427

**BM&T Consultants
LTD, Inc.**
P.O. Box 98 G
Morris Plains, NJ
07950-9098
John Bienkowski
201-539-2265

**Bell Canada Phone
Power**
483 Bay Street
8th Floor South Tower
Toronto, ON M5G2E1
Jerry Brown
416-581-5130

**Richard L.
Bencin**
7922 Seth Paine Street
Brecksville, OH 44141
216-526-6726

**Bill Bishop &
Associates**
834 Gran Paseo Drive
Orlando, FL 32825
Bill Bishop, Owner
305-257-7355

Business By Design
125 S. Avenue 53
Los Angeles, CA
90042-4533
Ken Mann
213-256-1000

CBC
2399 North Fruitland Dr.
North Ogden, UT 84404
804-744-3866

Carcione & Associates
1698 N.E. 28th St.
Pompano Beach, FL
33064
Samuel Carcione
305-429-0534

Charles A. Winchester
850 Seventh Ave. #702
New York, NY 10019
212-582-0895

**Coffman
Systems, Inc.**
13140 Midway Place
Cerritos, CA 90701
Bill Bryce, Sales Mgr.
213-926-6653

COM Direct
2102 Business Center
Dr.
Irvine, CA 92715
714-851-5015
213-385-1771

ComTel Marketing, Inc.
288 Lancaster Avenue
Malvern, PA 19355
Jeff Wooden
215-647-8781

Commonplan Assoc.
30B Sugar Creek Villas
Greer, SC 29651
Melissa Hagye
803-292-0503

**Communication and
Management**
522 S. Guadalupe Ave.
Ste A
Redondo Beach, CA
90277
Martin Andrews
213-316-2886

**Communications
Consultants**
Box 55 Main St.
Asbury, NJ 08802
Daralyn Runge
201-689-7600

**Concepts Marketing
Consultants**
2755 American Way Dr.
Ste. 8
Memphis, TN 38118
Skip Padgett
901-366-7576

**Connors
Telemarketing**
54 Winstead Ave.
Dedham, MA 02026
Joseph T. Connors
617-329-1121

**Considine &
Associates**
110 S. Euclid St.
Ste. 103
Pasadena, CA 91101
Ray Considine,
President
818-449-4210

Consoil and Associates
5 Riverside Dr.
New York, NY 10023
212-874-7362

Consultel
70 Boston Post Rd.
Wayland, MA 01778
Douglas Mitchell
617-358-5555

**Contract Marketing
Consultants**
2755 American Way
Drive
Memphis, TN 38118
H.E. (Skip) Padget
901-366-7567

**Corp Development
Consultants**
P.O. Box 8944
Newport Beach, CA
92660
Ed Doyle
714-759-6919

**Creative Computer
Consulting**
9748 Los Coches
Suite 10
Lakeside, CA 92040
Gary Olsson/Chris Wille
619-561-9922

**Creative Marketing
Systems**
1350 Grand Ave.
San Marcos, CA 92069
619-744-8833

**Creative Response
Marketing**
3423 E. Chapman Ave.
Ste. C
P.O. Box 2100
Orange, CA 92669
714-639-6918

Cross Information Co.
1881 9th Street
Boulder, CO 80302
T. Cross
303-444-7799

Customtel
P.O. Box 26695
Minneapolis, MN 55426
Robert Hood
615-542-0800

**Dair Computer
Systems**
3440 Kenneth Dr.
Palo Alto, CA 94303
415-494-7081

**Data Base
Management**
345 Park Ave. S.
8th Floor
New York, NY 10010
212-685-4600

Direct Marketing
75 S. Union St.
P.O. Box 309
Lambertville, NJ 08530
609-397-3500

Direct Marketing/R&D
95 Shoshone
Buffalo, NY 14214-1019
716-835-4933

Direct Marketing Systems, Inc.
P.O. Box 238
Wynnewood, PA 19096
Paul R. Mohr
215-649-5688

Diversified Consultants
590 Salem Ave.
York, PA 17404
717-845-8991

Don Nagel Enterprises
P.O. Box 938
Shingle Springs, CA 95682
916-677-1801

Dove Assoc.
31 Milk St.
Boston, MA 02109
617-542-5520

Drucker & Halloran
3308 Library Lane
Minneapolis, MN 55426
612-922-1396

Duluth Area Chamber Of Commerce
325 Harbor Dr.
Duluth, MN 55802
218-722-5501

Data Station Systems Inc.
2769 E Atlantic Blvd.
Pompano Beach, FL 33062
Joe Cordney
305-942-0990

David Alan Yoho
10803 W Main St.
Fairfax, VA 22030
David Yoho
703-591-2490

Double Five, Inc.
P.O. Box 267
DeBary, FL 32713
Stan Billue
305-668-4058

Drothier & Smith Associates
26021 Southerfield Rd.
Lathrup Village, MI 48076
Mary Doris Smith
313-569-5430

EBW Direct Marketing
136 Madison Ave.
New York, NY 10016
212-684-5220

ELRA Group
725 Greenwich Street
Suite 300
San Francisco, CA 94133
Dr. Gerhard J. Hanneman
415-781-1191

Earl I. Wilson & Associates
6355 Topanga Canyon Blvd., Suite 507
Woodland Hills, CA 91367
818-340-6201

Ed Yeaker Assoc.
990 Post Road
Scarsdale, NY 10583
914-472-8936

El-Most Productions
P.O. Box 41291
Dallas, TX 75241
214-224-8080

English and Associates
6404 Bresslyn Rd.
Nashville, TN 37205
615-356-6846

Earl Palmer Brown Co./Phila.
1845 Walnut St.
Philadelphia, PA 19103
215-299-2800

Ernst Associates, Inc.
59 E. 54th Street
Suite 64
New York, NY 10022
Michael Dougherty
212-688-4898

FGI & Affiliated Publishing Companies
80 Scenic Drive, Ste. 7
Freehold, NJ 07728
201-780-7020

Factor Learning Design, Inc.
P.O. Box 1420
Leesburg, VA 22075
Steve Sunberg
703-777-6988

Fahigren & Swink
120 E. 4th Street
Cincinnati, OH 45202
513-241-9200

*Fidel Communications Company
One Wilshire Building
Suite 1210
Los Angeles, CA 90017
(213) 622-5211

Foremost Telemarketing Group
15222 Keswick St.
Van Nuys, CA 91405
David Essex
800-225-5343
818-988-6900

Fund Raising Services
366 Adelaide St. East,
Ste. 321
Toronto, ON M5A3X9
Ken Wyman, Director
416-362-2926

GDA Associates
P.O. Box 5295
Pittsburgh, PA 15206-5295
412-661-2692

GSW Consultants
4550 Kearny Villa Rd.,
#112
San Diego, CA 92123
Joel Winitz
619-571-5551

GWL Associates
169 South Buchanan Avenue
Louisville, CO 80027
Glenn Lippman
303-665-9630

General Telephonics Corp.
7002 Blvd. East,
Ste. 414M
Guttenberg, NJ 07903
Frank Rinaldi
201-868-1116

Glenn Bammann Communications
818 S. Second St.
Dekalb, IL 60115
815-756-6132

Gregory John Sheffield
Rt. 1
Box 37
Lockwood, NY 14859
607-598-2586

HSB Direct Marketing
240 Eglinton Ave. E
Toronto, ON M4P1K8
John Spilsburg
416-486-8096

Hardy Business Service
P.O. Box 13
Zelienople, PA 16063
Joe Hardy, President
412-483-4219

Haskal and Associates
200 N. Robertson,
Ste. 202
Beverly Hills, CA 90211
Aaron Haskel
213-274-5981

Helix Communications
400 Camelot Building
P.O. Box 13400
Pittsburgh, PA 15243
412-344-0344

Holtje Associates
2560 Glengyle Drive
Vienna, VA 22180
703-281-9528

Industrial Consulting Center
P.O. Box 34
Long Beach, CA 90801
Dr. Les Lee
213-431-7677

International Resource Development
6 Prowitt St.
Norwalk, CT 06855
203-866-7800

Information Bureau
402 W. Interstate 30
Garland, TX 75043
214-226-8000

Information Bureau
402 W. Interstate 30
Garland, TX 75043
214-226-8000

Ingalls Associates, Ltd.
1908 Mt. Vernon Avenue
P.O. Box 2514
Alexandria, VA 22301
703-548-1271

Inquiry Handling Services
200 Parkside Dr.
San Fernando, CA 91340
Bernie Otis,
818-365-8131

Integrated Systems Planning
724 Dulaney Valley Rd.
Towson, MD 21204
Jacquie Spear
301-825-1670

Jerrold P. Applebaum
40-07 201 St.
Bayside, NY 11361
718-423-5052

Joe Camba-Consultant
P.O. Box 517
Mt. Juliet, TN 37122
Joe Combs
615-754-4000

John M. Hess
Chautauqua Park
Boulder, CO 80302
303-449-9541

John P. Lodsin &
Associates
1600 Willoughby Rd.
Ste. A100
P.O. Box 5533
Knoxville, TN 37928
615-573-3000

K. Stoeger Associates
1704 Linden St.
Des Plaines, IL 60018
312-299-6008

Ken Wyman &
Associates
366 Adelaide Street, E.
#231
Toronto, ON M5A3X9
416-362-2926

Klafter Marketing
45 North Station Plaza
Suite 205
Great Neck, NY 11021
516-466-8665

Krantz Associates,
Inc.
445 Watching Avenue
Watchung, NJ 07060
Boris Krantz
201-757-3300

LC&S Direct
100 Cedar Street,
Ste. A-32
Dobbs Ferry, NY 10522
Carol Krajewski,
President
914-693-2834

Lawson Research
Institute
2504 Hazelwood Ave.
Dayton, OH 45419
513-299-5341

Linkin
Communications
10710 National Place
Los Angeles, CA 90034
213-837-8400

List America
1202 Potomac St. N.W.
Washington, D.C. 20007
202-298-9206

Lawrence Butner
Advertising
228 E. 45th St.
New York, NY 10017
212-682-3200

Lee Richardson,
Consulting
P.O. Box 1106
Columbia, MD 21044
Lee Richardson,
Consultant
301-596-4899

MTEL Marketing
23850 Commerce Park
Road
Beechwood, OH 44122
Don Oliver
216-292-7420

MacDantz Direct
120 W. Fayette
Baltimore, MD 21202
301-837-2120

Marathon
Telemarketing
Systems
P.O. Box 725051
Atlanta, GA 30339
Steve Warshawer
404-422-3913

Marketing
Connections
One Annabel Lane,
Ste. 212
San Ramone, CA 94583
415-866-1818

McKinney Marketing
Group
345 E. 86th St.
New York, NY 10028
212-289-9125

Mira Research Center
1 Mira Station
P.O. Box 23037
Lansing, MI 48909
517-337-1525

Mitterling Method, Inc.
36 Admiralty Cross
Coronado Cays, CA
92118
Bob Anderson
619-721-1540

Modular Marketing
1841 Broadway
New York, NY 10023
212-581-4690

Mr. Mailer/Leads Plus
2471 John Young Prkwy.
Orlando, FL 32804
Gordon
305-295-6767

NCRI List
Management
45 Legion Dr.
Cresskill, NJ 07626
Irv Silverman
201-894-8300

NEFCO
840 Montgomery Ave.
Narberth, PA 19072
Marvin Cohen
215-664-5505

NTI
60 Whitlock Place,
Suite F
Marietta, GA 30064
Becky H. Cox
404-426-8985

NYNEX
100 Church Street,
Rm. 810
New York, NY 10007
Bernard Cohen
212-513-9602

Name-Finder Lists
2121 Bryant
Suite 304
San Francisco, CA
94110
Larry Shobs
414-641-5208

National Telemarketing
56 Shogum Road
Randolph, NJ 07869
Eugene Kordahl
201-361-3500

Nelson Panullo
Jutkins Dir. Marktg.
2121 Cloverfield Blvd.
Santa Monica, CA
90404
213-829-3444

New Business
Development
660 La Casa Via
Walnut Creek, CA
94598
Diane Sanchez
415-943-6736

Nik Vitullo Advertising
Agency
427 Chestnut Street
Union, NJ 07083
201-688-8383

Omega
444 Market Street,
Fifth Floor
San Francisco, CA
94111
Sharane L. Springer,
TM Mgr.
415-543-1836

Original Designs By
Anna
4139 Mountwood Rd.
P.O. Box 2999
Baltimore, MD 21229
301-947-1015

PSI Telemarketing
2945 W. Peterson
Avenue
Chicago, IL 60659
Barbara Borowsky
312-878-0800

Paramount Lists
3126 Peach St.
P.O. Box 3552
Erie, PA 16508
814-459-8787

Paul D. Ricker,
Marketing Cons.
1000 Coconut Creek
Parkway
Pompano Beach, FL
33066
305-973-2223

Peg Fisher &
Associates
1201 S. Wisconsin
Racine, WI 53404
414-633-1675

Perception Plus
100 East St. Vrain,
Ste. 105
Colorado Springs, CO
80903
Evelyn Eman, President
303-471-0111

Perceptive Marketers
Agency
1920 Chestnut St.
Philadelphia, PA 19103
Randy Orlow
215-665-8736

Philip Office
Associates
750 Talbott Tower
Dayton, OH 45402
513-461-1300

Phone Bank Systems,
Inc.
220 Mac
E. Lansing, MI 48823
Tom Page, President
517-332-1500

Principal Associates
4112 Majestic Lane
Fairfax, VA 22033
703-968-7779

Protector
2699 Walters Avenue
Northbrook, IL 60062
312-498-9043

Pyramid
Communications
P.O. Box 15288
Sacramento, CA 95851
Bob Frank, Consultant
916-447-1900

RFM Associates
35 Atkins Avenue
Trenton, NJ 08610
609-586-5214

RMH Telemarketing
300 E. Lancaster
Avenue, Suite 204-D
Wynnewood, PA 19096
MarySue Lucci,
Executive VP
215-642-2438

RSVP Marketing
450 Plain St. Ste. 5
Marshfield, MA 02050
Edward C. Hicks
617-837-2804

**Ramdad Marketing
Consultant, Ltd.**
19 W. 44th Street, Ste.
1000
New York, NY 10036
Alan M. Feinberg
212-840-2719

**Ransom and
Associates**
106 East Pacemont Rd.
Columbus, OH
43202-7100
614-267-7100

**Raymond L. Jackson
Consulting**
108 N. Church St.
Snow Hill, MD 21863
301-632-0300

**Redwood Training
Associates**
1115 Foothill Street
Redwood City, CA
94061
Michael A. Brown
415-364-2527

**Remington
Associates**
535 East Moreland
Ste. 135
Phoenix, AZ 85004
Stephanie J. Remington
602-955-7770

**Richard N. Kaufman &
Associates, Ltd.**
495 Connecticut Avenue
Norwalk, CT 06854
Richard Kaufman
203-838-2000

Richter Distributing
801 Orapax St.
P.O. Box 1109
Norfolk, VA 23501
804-622-7339

**Robert Day
Communications**
8826 Dorrington Ave.
Los Angeles, CA 90048
213-858-0520

**Rockingham,
Jutkins
Marketing**
3422 Schooner, Suite 11
Marina del Rey, CA
90292
Ray Jutkins
213-306-7901

**Ron Weber &
Associates**
727 Campbell Avenue
West Haven, CT 06516
203-776-3484

**S. Michael
Associates, Ltd.**
P.O. Box 184
Bellwood, IL 60104
S. Michael Zibrun, Pres.
312-547-5530

SM Marketing
14288 Central Avenue
Chino, CA 91710
714-591-4883

**SNET Telemarketing
Consulting Services**
2 Science Park
New Haven, CT 06511
Luke Brennan
203-497-4866

SRI International
333 Ravenswood
Avenue
Menlo Park, CA 94025
415-859-6322

**SST Telemarketing
Services**
3930 Walnut Street
Fairfax, VA 22030
Jerry Werhel
703-352-5235

**Salesleaders/Creative
Marketing**
4615 Delashmitt 1436
P.O. Box 15336
Chattanooga, TN 37343
615-870-3393

**Samuel Krasney
Assoc.**
2204 Morris Ave.
Ste. 302
Union, NJ 07083
212-883-0835

**Saron
Telecommunication
Network**
301 W. 53rd St.
New York, NY 10019
212-315-2077

**Selkirk
Associates**
333 Newberry Street
Boston, MA 02115
Elizabeth Mead
617-536-7220

**Smith, Dorian and
Burman**
1100 New Britain
Avenue
West Hartford, CT 06110
203-522-3101

Softel
1974 Las Encinas
Los Gatos, CA 95030
Judy Lanier
408-866-2284

**Software Intelligence
Corp.**
1941 N.E. 54th St.
Ft. Lauderdale, FL
33308
Amhad Morandi
305-564-5220

Sonecor Network
No. 2 Science Park,
1st Floor
New Haven, CT 06511
Luke Brennan, Manager
800-922-0829

**Stephen Dunn &
Associates**
1422 Washington Blvd.
#1
Venice, CA 90291
Sarah Wrightson
213-392-8591

**Strategic Serv. for
Management**
233 Kneeland Avenue
Yonkers, NY 10705
Samuel S. Frumkies,
Director
914-965-7552

**Systematic
Telemarketing Inc.**
6603 Queen Ave. South
Suite H
Richfield, MN 55423
Dan Krueger
612-861-6157

TARP Inc.
706 7th Street, S.E.
Washington, DC 20003
John Goodman
202-544-6313

**TM (Telemarketing/
Telecommunications
Mgmt.)**
468 Armour Dr., N.E.
Atlanta, GA 30324
404-876-7260

TOP Associates, Inc.
1900 The Exchange
Atlanta, GA 30339
Debbie Dodds
800-233-3585

**Technology Transfer
Institute**
741 10th Street
Santa Monica, CA
90402
Randy Burns
213-394-8305

**Tel-Design
Management Inc.**
150 River Rd. Ste. J-1
Montville, NJ 07045
David Tirpak, President
201-299-9600

Tel/Mar & Associates
16376 Santa Bianca
Hacienda Heights, CA
91745
David Murray
818-369-8056

Tele-Analysis
42 Colleen Circle
Trenton, NJ 08638
Gene Blicharz,
Consultant
609-771-6952

Tele-Profit Group
Thames Point Marina
1900 Thames St.,
Suite 310
Baltimore, MD 21231
Patricia McCabe
301-276-2716

Tele-Vision
18511 Hawthorne Blvd.
Suite 260
Torrance, CA 90504
Steve Noble
213-372-3686

**Telecom Consultants
Group, Inc.**
120 South Riverside
Plaza, Suite 2260
Chicago, IL 60606
William Mashek
312-454-9396

**Telecommunication
Networks Consulting**
1511 Farsta Court
Reston, VA 22090
Walt Roehr
703-435-1787

Telecon, Inc.
269 B Willow Street
Teaneck, NJ 07666
201-836-5694

**Telemarketing
Consultants**
100 Cedar St.
Dobbs Ferry, NY 10522
Carol Krajewski
914-693-2834

**Telemarketing
Professionals**
57 Tunnel Road
Berkeley, CA 94705
Carolyn Mills
415-986-8981

**Telemarketing
Recruiters**
114 E 32nd St.,
Ste. 1202
New York, NY 10016
212-213-1700

**Telemarketing
Sciences**
15840 Ventura Blvd.
#450
Encino, CA 91436
Alex Goodman, Advisor
818-789-2888

**Telemarketing
Specifics**
1433 Candelero Drive
Walnut Creek, CA
94598
Sally S. Saunders
415-930-8944

**Telemarketing
Systems Consulting
& Brokerage**
221 Camaritas Avenue,
Ste. E
So. San Francisco, CA
94080
Paul Braschi, Pres.
415-583-1640

**Telemarketing
Technologies, Inc.**
245 Unquowa Road,
Ste. 136
Fairfield, CT 06430
Jonathan Hylan
203-254-3982

**Telephone Look-Up
Service**
337 New Rodgers Road
Levittown, PA 19056
215-752-8206

**Telephone Marketing
Resources**
33 West 60th St.,
9th Floor
New York, NY 10023
Jeri Gantman, VP
212-307-0175

Teleplan Inc.
Field Point Circle
Greenwich, CT 06830
Barbara C. Manley
203-661-4312

**Telesolutions—Nelson
Communications**
2001 Beacon Street
Brookline, MA 02146
Kevin R. Currie
617-891-3800

Telestrategies
347 5th Ave.
New York, NY 10016
Glenn Lebawitz
212-725-5040

Tele Systems
10550 Westoffice Dr.,
Ste. 104
Houston, TX 77042
713-784-3439

The Ergotec Group
Four Burnham Parkway
Morristown, NJ 07960-5301
Daniel T. Stusser
201-984-9000

The PLS Group
11325 Seven Locks
Road, Suite 226
Potomac, MD 20854
Julie Van Zetta
301-983-8508

The Stenrich Group
160 Fifth Avenue
New York, NY 10010
Steven Isaac, President
212-255-7273

**The Telephone
Marketing Group**
501 Washington Lane
Jenkintown, PA 19046
Steven Lynn, President
215-576-7000

The Telexcel Co.
3004 Pacific Avenue
Marina del Rey, CA
90291
George Walther
213-821-4100

Thomas Fobbri
1138 Audre Ave.
Mountain View, CA
94040
415-964-1965

**Tim David Marketing
Services**
113 W. 78th St.
Suite One
New York, NY 10024
212-580-9111

**Tom McCarthey
Associates**
P.O. Box 3302
San Diego, CA 92103
619-260-3753

Tomorrow Today
3279 20th Street
San Francisco, CA
94110
415-641-4103

Total Marketing
20122 Imperial Cove
Lane
Huntington Beach, CA
92646
Cheri Boone
714-968-3681

**Triad Marketing
Resources (TMR)**
1350 Ashley Square
Winston-Salem, NC
27103
Bobbi Gemma
919-760-4782

**U.S. Telemarketing
Inc.**
5300 Oakbrook
Parkway Bldg. 300
Norcross, GA 30093
Jean Villanti
404-381-0100

**Urban Decision
Systems**
2040 Armacost Ave.
P.O. Box 25953
Los Angeles, CA 90025
213-820-8931

**Vidocom
L.D. Bevan Company,
Inc.**
5740 Corsa Avenue,
Ste. 106
Westlake Village, CA
91362
Roger T. Ellis
818-889-3653

Voicepro
352 University Ave.
Westwood, MA 02030
Helen C. Jensen
617-326-8386

**WRD & Inc. (William
R. Duffy & Associates)**
201 E. 36th Street
New York, NY 10016
212-682-6755

W.S. Ponton, Inc.
The Ponton Buiding
5149 Butler St.
Pittsburgh, PA 15201
Harvey Rabinowitz
800-628-7806

**Walters
Communications**
195 Lake Avenue
Worcester, MA 01604
Dennis Ravenelle
617-754-5375

**Walton
Communications**
14677 Midway Road,
#219
Dallas, TX 75244
214-392-9222

**Washington Crossing
Associates**
315 River Road
Washington Crossing,
NJ 08560
David Thompson
609-737-0052

**Wm.R. Biggs/Gilmore
Advertising**
P.O. Box 6069
Hilton Head, SC 22938
803-785-3989

WREN Marketing
5437 S. Cimarron
Littleton, CO 80123
212-682-6755

Data Base Management Services/ Processing

Brad Bern Corporation
8250 Winton Rd.
Cincinnati, OH 45231
Mike Bunning
513-931-5111

CCX Network, Inc.
301 Industrial Blvd.
Conway, AR 72032
Jim Bradshaw,
Comm. Mgr.
501-329-6836

**Consumers Marketing
Research, Inc.**
600 Huyler St.
S. Hackensack, NJ
07606
Geoffrey Nelson
201-440-8900
800-225-0639

**DataBase Solutions,
Inc.**
744 Office Parkway
Suite 225
St. Louis, MO 63141
Dallas Gravatt
314-991-0647

**New England
Information System**
P.O. Box 646
Hanover, MA 02339
Douglas T. Prescott,
President
617-826-9550

**Rexnord Data
Systems**
4701 W. Greenfield Ave.
Milwaukee, WI 53214
Geoff Watters
414-648-3203

Data Communications Products

ABI Communications

Group Services
P.O. Box 3627
Wenatchee, WA
98801-0058
Michele Leyden
509-663-1535

ATE Data, Inc.
Div. of ATE Enterprises,
Ste. 800
Cincinnati, OH 42502
Beth Beach
513-381-7424

AT&T
Communications
International
1 Pierce Place
Itasca, IL 60143
201-221-6658

American Laser
Systems Inc.
106 Fowler Road
Goleta, CA 93117
Lorriane Shallenberger
805-967-0423

American Satellite
Company
Subsidary of Comtel
1801 Research Blvd.
Rockville, MD 20850
James Sobczak
301-251-8333

Brand-Rex Company
1600 W. Main Street
Willimantic, CT 06226
Bruce Gardner
203-456-1706

Canoga Data Systems
21218 Vanowen Street
Canoga Park, CA 91303
Larry Totter
213-481-8506

Compuscan, Inc.
81 Two Bridges Road
Fairfield, NJ 07006
Gerald Labie
201-575-0500

Computer Transceiver
Systems
E. 66 Midland Ave.
Paramus, NJ 07652
Joe Tribucher
201-261-6800

Contel Information
Systems Inc.
Div. Continental
Telecomm, Inc.
130 Steamboat Road
Great Neck, NY 11024
Gene Sochsenmaier
516-829-5900

Cylix Communications
Corp.
800 Ridge Lake Blvd.
Memphis, TN 38119
Kim Ring
901-761-1177

DLS Video Inc.
6020 Poling
Elida, OH 45807
Ben Young
419-227-2424

Digital
Communications
Assoc.
100 Alderman Drive
Alpharetta, GA 30201
James Lee
404-442-4224

Digital Transmission,
Inc.
315 Eisenhower Lane
South
Lombard, IL 60148
Joe Baier/Steve Pope
901-683-5677
901-686-0866

Economy Data
Products Inc.
2134 N.W. 108th Street
Des Moines, IA 50322
Gary McClain
515-270-6000

Electro Rent
Corporation
4131 Vanowen Place
Burbank, CA 91505
Patrick Johanson
818-843-3131

Electro Standard Lab.
Inc.
P.O. Box 9144
Providence, RI 02940
Raymond Sepe,
President
401-943-1164

Energy Sciences
Electronics Group
13456 S.E. 27th Place
Bellevue, WA 98005
Joseph Corsi
206-881-2661

F-Tec
15 Seeley Avenue
Piscataway, NY 08854
Fred Day
201-562-1100

Grass Valley Group
Div Tektronics Inc.
P.O. Box 1114
Grass Valley, CA 94945
Randy Wood
916-478-3167

Innovative Electronics
4714 NW 165 St.
Miami, FL 33014
Shelly Dolan,
Mktg Com Mgr
305-624-1644

Integrated Scientific
Systems
1181 Aquidneck Ave.
Middletown, RI 02840
Jerry Bernard,
Mkg Mgr.
800-847-ISYS
800-847-4388

Interand Corporation
3200 W. Peterson Ave.
Chicago, IL 60659
Linda Phillips
312-478-1700

International
Electronic Mail
21686 Stevens Creek
Blvd.
Cupertino, CA 95014
408-446-4367

Keystone Distributing
Company
Div Medcomp
Technologies Inc.
120 Kisco Avenue
Mount Kisco, NY 10549
Mike Warman
914-241-7121

Microdyne
Corporation
491 Oak Road
P.O. Box 7213
Ocala, FL 32672
904-687-4633

Modulation Associates
897 Independence
Avenue
Mountain View, CA
94043
J. Walter Johnson
415-962-8000

Multipoint
Communications Corp
Div TIW Systems Inc.
1284 Geneva Drive
Sunnyvale, CA 94089
Rob Wellins
408-734-9300

Network Solutions
8229 Boone Blvd.
7th Floor
Vienna, VA 22180
Gary Desler
703-442-0400

RCA Global
Communication
60 Broad Street
New York, NY 10004
Dan Dwyer
201-885-2261

RMS Group Inc.
43-59 10th Street
Long Island City, NY
11101
B. Surj
718-784-1616

Racal-Milgo
Div of Racal Electronics
P.O. Box 407044
Ft. Lauderdale, FL
33340-7044
James Norman
305-476-4004

SKC Communication
Products
13804 W. 78th Terrace
Lenoxa, KA 66216
Paul Ameen, Pres.
913-268-0177

Selscore Technologies
Div of Switchcraft Inc.
P.O. Box 470580
Tulsa, OK 74147-0580
Kermit Ross
918-252-1578

Siecor Corporation
489 Siecor Park
Hickory, NC
28603-0489
Joseph Hicks
704-327-5821

Sykes Datatronics Inc.
375 Orchard Street
Rochester, NY 14606
Chip Chapman
716-458-8000

Teltone Corp
10801 120th Ave. NE
Kirkland, WA 98033
John Welliver,
Cust Support Mgr
206-827-9626

U.S. Telecom—
Corporate Network
Services
1815 Century Blvd.
Atlanta, GA 30345
Kim A. Jacobs
404-982-1723

Voice Computer
Technologies
5730 Oakbrook Parkway
Ste. 175
Norcross, GA 33093
Colleen Moonen
404-441-2303

256

Votan
4487 Technology Drive
Fremont, CA 94538
Bruce Ryan
415-490-7600

WORDSERV
38-30 209th St.
Bayside, NY 11361
Philip Klein
718-225-8218

Electronic Mail Systems

CommSel
MCI Mail Agent
1014 Santiago Drive
Newport Beach, CA
92660
Jerry Klein
714-646-2440

Computer Task Group
800 Delaware Ave.
Buffalo, NY 14209
Mary Kileen
716-882-8000

Computer Transceiver Systems
E. 66 Midland Ave.
Paramus, NJ 07652
Joe Tribucher
201-261-6800

Comtel Broadcasting Corp
13 Harbour Town Center
Noblesville, IN 46060
Bob Haverstick
317-877-6050

Electronic Mail Corporation of America
143 Sound Beach
Avenue
Greenwich, CT 06870
Philip F. Pagano
203-637-8800

ITT Dialcom
1109 Spring St.
Silver Spring, MD 20910
Trey Taylor,
Marketing Mgr.
301-587-0680

International Electronic Mail
21686 Stevens Creek
Blvd.
Cupertino, CA 95014
408-446-4367

MCI Communications Corp.
1133 19th St. NW
Washington, DC 20036
Karen Selko
202-887-2238 Karen

Radionics
920 Holt Road
Rochester, NY 14580
Scott Ladin
716-872-2100

Via Titus Inc.
475 E. Main Street
Patchogue, NY 11772
Donald MacLay
212-553-3542

Votan
4487 Technology Drive
Fremont, CA 94538
Bruce Ryon
415-490-7600

Western Union
1 Lake Street 4-10
Upper Saddle River, NJ
07458
Joanne Rinkus
201-825-2635

Facsimile Equipment

Alden Electronics Inc.
40 Washington Street
Westborough, MA 01581
Lawrence Farrington
617-366-8851

Allen Business Machines Inc.
1816 S. Calhoun St.
Fort Wayne, IN 46804
Melody Luchi
219-744-4259

Fujitsu
3190 Miraloma Ave.
Anaheim, CA 92084
Sue Shelby, Adv. Mgr.
714-630-7721

Gammalink Synchronous Communication
2452 Embarcadero Way
Palo Alto, CA 94303
Michael Lutz
415-856-7421

Harris/3M
2300 Parklake Drive, NE
Atlanta, GA 30092
Betty Crowe
404-621-1139

Murata Business Systems
4801 Spring Valley
Suite 108B
Dallas, TX 75244
Jane Arak
214-392-1622

Panafax Corp
10 Melville Park Rd
Melville, NY 11747
John Plet
516-420-0055

South Central Bell Advanced Systems
505 N. 20th Street,
Ste. 850
Birmingham, AL 35203
Cynthia Wingo
205-879-2121

Teleautograph/ Omnifax
8700 Bellanca Ave.
Los Angeles, CA 90045
Frank May
213-641-3690

Financing and Leasing

Cheshire
404 Washington Blvd.
Mundelein, IL 60060
312-949-2500

Coastal Leasing Company
2820 E. 10th Street
Greenville, NC 27835
Don Blanchard
919-752-3850

Directions, Peppler & Assoc.
133 East County Line
Road
Barrington, IL 60010
Patrick Peppler
312-790-1544

East West Leasing
1472 St. Francis Drive,
Suite 2
Santa Fe NM 87501
Kirpal Singh Khalsa,
Partner
505-984-2178

Goldome
1 Fountain Plaza
Buffalo, NY 14203
L.G. Brind Armour
716-847-5871

Intech Leasing Corporation
10 Signal Road
Stamford, CT 06902
Joseph P. Fullop
203-324-1300

International Dev. Marketing
750 13 Street SE
Washington, DC 20003
Peter Nelson
202-546-1900

Krueger
1330 Bellevue
P.O. Box 8100
Green Bay, WI 54308
414-468-8100

Leasecomp Inc.
1336 Citizens Parkway
Ste. G
Morrow, GA 30260
Phil Harris
404-961-9350

Prudential Systems Inc.
7330 Adams Street
Paramount, CA 90721
John Robbins, Pres.
213-531-1223

Pacom Leasing Corporation
1221 S.W. Yanhill,
Ste. 210
Portland, OR 97205
800-532-7374

Samuel F. Carcione & Associates
Tax accounting &
financial pln.
1698 N.E. 28th Court
Pompano Beach, FL
33064
Samuel F. Carcione
305-718-0234

Fulfillment Services

AT&T American Transtech
8000 Baymeadows Way,
Rm 53143
Jacksonville, FL 32216
304-636-1941
800-241-3354 x2524

Automatic Fulfillment Services
8 South Morris Street
P.O. Box 305
Dover, NJ 07801
201-366-8722

BSA, Inc.
39 Cindy Lane
Ocean, NJ 07712
201-493-8062

Business Services, Inc.
902 Freehanville Drive
Mt. Prospect, IL 60056
312-296-9300

Cybernetics Systems International Corporation
99 Ponce de Leon Blvd., 9th Floor
Coral Gables, FL 33134
305-443-1651

Directel
229 Huber Village Blvd.
Westerville, OH 43081
614-890-1705

Dyment Distribution, Services
20026 Progress Dr.
Strongsville, OH 44136
216-572-0725

Essex Enterprises
909 Orchard Street
Mundelein, IL 60060
312-949-6008

Fulfillment Corp. of America
205 W. Center Street
Marion, OH 43302
614-383-5231

Fulfillment Plus, Inc.
1626 Locust Ave.
Bohemia, NY 11716
516-563-2250

Fulfillment Unlimited
2727 Scioto Parkway
Columbus, OH 43220
614-771-1875

Hallmark Data Systems
5500 W. Touhy Ave.
Skokie, IL 60077
312-674-6900

Hayden Business Support Services
1 Chris Court
Dayton, NJ 08810
A. Scott Marsilio
201-329-9150

Inquiry Handling Services
200 Porkside Dr.
San Fernando, CA 91340
Bernie Otis, Mktg. Cons.
818-365-8131

MCRB
11633 Victory Blvd.
North Hollywood, CA 91609
213-877-5384

Marke Techs
115 Brand Rd.
Salem, VA 24156
703-389-8121

Markline Info Systems, Inc.
411 Waverly Oaks Rd.
Waltham, MA 02154
800-343-8572

Nationwide Fulfillment Systems
Sunset Blvd.
Ridgely, MD 21660
800-638-5189

Nice Corp.
4357 S. Airport Park Plaza
Ogden, UT 84405
801-621-6423

Package Fulfillment Center
2105 Lakeland Ave.
Ronkonkoma, NY 11779
516-588-7520

Progressive Distributing Serv.
1370 Belfield Street
Grand Rapids, MI 49509
616-243-2107

Sisk Fulfillment Service
P.O. Box 463
Federalsburg, MD 21632
800-638-2567

Synergy Marketing Group
79 Sagmaw Drive
Rochester, NY 14623
Raymond Del Monte
716-232-1177

Tomare Enterprises, Inc.
3141 Lehigh Street
Allentown, PA 18103
215-791-1414

Towne Advertisers Mailing Services Inc.
511 E. Goetz Ave.
Santa Ana, CA 92707
Mary Anne Witsoe
714-540-3095

U.S. Fulfillment Services
125 Rowell Court
Falls Church, VA 22046
Timothy F. Cotton
703-241-0600

Furniture/Office Products for Phone Rooms

Aspects Inc.
11615 Pendleton Street
Sun Valley, CA 91352
(213)768-9000

Center Core Systems
250 Corporate Court
South Plainfield, NJ 07080
Scott Sander, VP Mkt.
201-561-7755

Cygnet Technologies Inc.
1296 Lawrence Station Road
Synnyvale, CA 94089
Bob Sumbs, Dir of Mkt
415-498-1111

DLS Video Inc.
6020 Poling
Elida, OH 45807
Ben Young
419-227-2424

Esgeco Ltd.
2971 Flowers Road South
Atlanta, GA 30341
G. Meidlien
404-949-6008

Fujitsu Imaging Systems of Amer.
Corporate Dr.
Commerce Park
Danbury, CT 06810
Tom Shimko
203-796-5780

Interand Corporation
3200 W. Peterson Ave.
Chicago, IL 60659
Linda Phillips
312-478-1700

Magnetic Systems Inc.
P.O. Box 11
Wellesley, MA 02181
Steve Drowne
617-237-0420

National Partitions
340 W. 78th Road
Hialeah, FL 33014
305-822-3721

SSBS/Cannon
Division of Alco Standard
2580 Alta Arden Way
Sacramento, CA 95825
Carl Beckly
916-486-9988

Steelcase
Grand Rapids, MI 49501

Telematrix Ind Inc.
5 Harris Court
Great Neck, NY 11021
Dean Garfinkel
516-482-8280

The Brewster Corporation
50 River Street
Old Saybrook, CT 06475
Thomas O'Connor
203-388-4441

Hardware for Telemarketing Automation

American Telemark, Inc.
4333 Maywood Avenue
P.O. Box 58108
Los Angeles, CA 90058
George McCall
213-583-8678

Audiocom, Ltd.
8100 Oak Lane
Penthousc 401
Miami Lakes, FL 33016
Stuart Ginsberg
305-825-4653

Automated Phone Exchange Corp
4931 S. 900 E.
Salt Lake City, UT 84117
Brent Rasmussen
801-265-2000

Automated Telemarketing Inc.
222 S. 9th Street
Ste. 3060, Piper Tower
Minneapolis, MN 55402
Michael A. Boylan
612-349-6609

Behaviorial Management
6 Pine Tree Drive
St. Paul, MN 55112
Mary Imgrund
612-483-5750

Bill Rosenberg & Associates
3 Versallies Street
Cranston, RI 02920
Ryan Loveless
401-728-4929

Brooks Power Systems
3569 Bristol Pike
Bensalem, PA 19020
Joe Brooks
215-244-0264

CRC Information Systems
435 Hudson Street
New York, NY 10014
212-620-5678

Cado Systems
700 Century Park South
Suite 128
Birmingham, AL 35226
Steve Van Gilder
205-979-3407

Coffman Systems, Inc.
13140 Midway Place
Cerritos, CA 90701
Bill Bryce, Sales Mgr.
213-926-6653

Commercial Data Systems Corp
100 S. Pioneer Dr.
Smyrna, GA 30080
Jennifer Davis
404-799-1000

Communication Consultants Inc.
Box 55 Main Street
Ashbury, NJ 08802
Daralyn Durar
201-537-4046

Computer Consoles Inc.
97 Humbolt Street
Rochester, NY 14609
Robert Lofaso
716-482-5000

Computertalker
Div of Computervoice Inc.
1730 21st Street
Santa Monica, CA 90404
Ron Anderson
213-828-6546

Computime, Inc.
401 N. 117th Street
Omaha, NE 68154
Jim Rose/
Martin Hensley
402-330-1311

Cygnet Technologies Inc.
1296 Lawrence Station Rd.
Sunnyvale, CA 94089
Bob Sumbs, Dir of Mkt.
415-498-1111

DataCorp Business Systems
28300 Euclid Avenue
Cleveland, OH 44092
John Fisher,
VP Sales and Mkt.
216-731-8000

Datamap
6874 Washington Ave. So.
Eden Prairie, MN 55344
Grant Warfield
612-941-0900

Dialogic Communications Corp
1106 Harpeth Industrial Court
P.O. Box 8
Franklin, TN 37064
Gary Fitzhughes,
VP Mktg.
615-790-2882

Digital Equipment Corporation
129 Parker St.
MA 01754
Henry Heisler
617-264-1577

IBM Corporation
301 Merritt Seven
Norwalk, CT 06856
Darby T. Coker, Dir Adv.
203-849-6000

Independent Telecommunications Systems Inc.
9 Heritage Oak Lane, Ste. 7
Battle Creek, MI 49015
Jennifer Brazzel
616-979-2600

Intellisys Technologies
1933-#102
O'Toole Avenue
San Jose, CA 95131
Hayes Kolb
408-435-0666

Interactive Telemarketing Inc.
8585 Stemmons Fwy., Ste. 1107-N
Dallas, TX 75247
Jeff Symon
214-631-2277

International Computerized TM
2260 Cabot Blvd. West
Langhorne, PA 19047
Steve Sedmark
215-757-0200

International Software Sales
12 Wade Road
Latham, NY 12110
Sandra Rudin, VP
518-783-1982

Jayness Associates
Div Audiocost Inc.
110 Powers Building 16 W Main
Rochester, NY 14614
J. Schirano
719-262-6400

Liason Data Corporation
2680 Bishop Drive Ste. 214
San Ramon, CA 94583
Tony Parkhill
415-830-4700

MTI Systems Corporation
38 Harbor Park Drive
Port Washington, NY 11050
Cliff Leventhal
800-645-6530

Marathon Telemarketing Systems
P.O. Box 725051
Atlanta, GA 30339
Steve Warshawer
404-422-3913

Marketing Information Systems
411 North Rockwell
Chicago, IL 60618
312-491-3885

Market Network
17905 Sky Park Circle Unit P
Irvine, CA 92714
John Sherwood, President
714-261-2412

Melita Electronic Labs
P.O. Box 5120
Scottsdale, AZ 85261
Michael Domer
602-998-3600

Message Processing Systems, Inc.
8848 Red Oak Boulevard
Charlotte, NC 28210
Sam LoBue
704-527-8888

Metro Telemarketing Systems
1600 E Little Creek Rd
Norfolk, VA 23518
Carl Freed
804-583-8383

Micro Peripheral Corporation
2565 152nd N.E.
Redmond, WA 98052
Mark Perrin
206-881-7544

Nec Information Systems
1414 Mass Ave.
Boxborough, MA 01719
Peter Furgison
617-264-8000

Northern Telecom, Inc.
P.O. Box 1222
Minneapolis, MN 55440
800-328-8800
612-932-8238 MN
Joseph A. Scott,
Mkgt. Mgr.

OSCAR, Inc.
375 South Washington
Bergenfield, NJ 07621
Ron Leeds
201-385-8300

Omega International
550 Pharr Rd. Ste. 750
Atlanta, GA 30305
404-237-8977

Peerless Technologies Corp
11843 Starcrest
San Antonio, TX 78247
Janis Maxymof
512-494-3647

Peridata International
Division of Lantor
13650 Gramercy Place
Pasadena, CA 91325
Dave Callahan
213-217-9155

Prime Computer Corp
Prime Park
Natuck, MA 01760
Arlene A. DiRocco
800-322-2450 Mass
800-342-2540 U.S.

Profit Growth Inc.
2699 Walters Avenue
Northbrook, IL 60062
Fritz Kreiss
312-498-9043

Qualitel Services, Inc.
2871 Metropolitan Place
Pomona, CA 91767
Lou Calson
714-596-1675

Ric Systems
446 Lancaster Avenue
Frazer, PA 19355
Richard Gavalis
215-647-6677

**Rockwell
International,
Switching
Systems**
1431 Opus Place
M/S 933-400
Downers Grove, IL 60515
312-454-1752

**SKC Communication
Products**
13804 W. 78th Terrace
Lenexa, KA 66216
Paul Ameen, Pres.
913-268-0177

Softech Inc.
15 W Tenth Street
Ste. 900
Kansas City, MO 64105
William Zimmerman
816-472-5605

Spectracom
90 W. Easy Street
Simi, CA 92065
Dan Hillard
805-527-2326

**TBS
International,
Inc**
959 E Collins
Richardson, TX 75081
Jack Zimmerman
214-690-9436

Target Systems Corp
33 Boston Post Rd. W.
Marlboro, MA 01752
Jerry Croteau,
Vice Pres.
617-460-9026
617-263-5331

**Teknekron
Infoswitch**
1784 Firman Drive
Richardson, TX 75081
Lou Temple
214-644-0570

**Telebroad-
Casting
Systems**
P.O. Box "D,"
Sunny Lane
Beach Lake, PA 18405
717-729-8206

**Teleconnect
Company**
500 2nd Ave. SE
Cedar Rapids, IA 52403
800-REACHUS
319-366-6600

Telecorp Systems, Inc.
5825-A Peachtree
Corners, E.
Norcross, GA 30092
Dana Webster, VP
800-334-9907

**Teledirect
International Inc.**
402 W. 35th Street
Davenport, IA 52806
Kenneth Ryan
319-391-5562

**Telemarketing Corp. of
America**
350 Park Ave.
Suite 7220
New York, NY 10118
Steven Bryan, VP Mkt
212-736-2530

Telemarketing Inc.
5919 Jonquil Lane
Minneapolis, MN 55442
John Meegan
612-559-1119

**Telephone Support
Systems**
2001 Marcus Ave.
Lake Success, NY
11040
Glenn Friedman
516-352-6800

**Televation
Telecommunications**
2723 Curtis Street
Downers Grove, IL
60515
Robert Groetzenbach
312-852-9695

Televector, Inc.
505 Eighth Avenue
New York, NY 10018
Morton Aaronson
212-947-7573
212-662-7000

Time Electronics
50 Frankford Street
Fitchburg, MA 01420
Lori Ballancourt
617-342-4210

**Trans World
Telephone**
2550 Medina Road
Medina, OH 45256
Leo Hooper
216-722-5500

**Tri-County
Telecommunications
Inc.**
7059 Reseda Blvd.
Reseda, CA 91335
Tim Thelen
818-705-8199

UNISYS
Township Line &
Jolly Road
Blue Bell, PA 19424
Jeff Houdret
215-542-4011

Zaisan Inc
1290 Page Mill Road
Palo Alto, CA 94304
Jerry Kennedy, VP Mkt
415-493-7841

**Zeta Digital Systems
Inc.**
2233 Northwestern Ave.
Waukegan, IL 60087
Bill Sultan, VP Mktg
312-244-0974

Headsets
and
Accessories

ACS Communications
250 Technology Dr.
Scotts Valley, CA 95066
Terry Foster
408-438-3883

Aim Telephone Inc.
14 Gloria Lane
Fairfield, NJ 07006
William Juliano
203-227-8600

**Allied
Telecommunications**
60 Oxford Road
Newton Centers, MA
02159
Gerald Sheffield
617-969-3550

Audiocom Inc.
8100 Oak Lane
Penthouse 401
Miami Lakes, FL 33016
Stuart Ginsberg
305-825-4653

**Automation
Electronics Corp.**
344 40th Street
Oakland, CA 94609
Randy Wilson
415-828-2880

**B.A. Pargh Company
Inc.**
1283 Mufreesboro Road
Nashville, TN 37217
Bernard Pargh
800-BAP-1000

**Communications
Sources Inc.**
123 N. Centennial Way
#206
Mesa, AZ 85201
George Boyce
602-273-1800

Communitech, Inc.
449 N. York Road
Elmhurst, IL 60126
Neal Shact
312-941-9060

Danavox, Inc.
6400 Flying Cloud Drive
Eden Prairie, MN 55344
Polly Carver
800-826-4656
612-941-0690

Decabe Industries
P.O. Box 52068
Atlanta, GA 30333
Mr. Whitiker
404-264-4466

**Executive Systems,
Inc.**
2112 Spencer Road
Richmond, VA 23230
Art Putnam
804-288-0041

GBH Distributing
1312 E Harvard Suite D
Glendale, CA 91205
Von Bedikian,
Reg. Sls. Mgr.
213-664-3235
818-246-9900

**Innovation
Specialities**
1900 Powell Street,
Ste. 1135
Emeryville, CA 94608
Royce Kirlanovich
800-624-1784
415-652-2411

Megaphone
Div of Voad Systems
3304 Pico Blvd.
Santa Monica, CA
90405
Patrick Ryan
213-450-5979

Plantronics
345 Encinal Street
Santa Cruz, CA 95060
David Hodges
408-426-5858
415-986-3415

**Power & Telephone
Supply Co.**
2668 Yale Avenue
Memphis, TN 38182
Laburn Dye
901-324-6116

**S&M Associates
Communications**
5721-J Bayside Road
Virginia Beach, VA
23455
Steve McClellen
804-460-5333

**Stromberg-Carlson
Com. Systems**
Div of Plessey
400 Rinehart Road
Lake Mary, FL 32746
Randall Pugh
305-849-4808

**Tele-Communications
Inc.**
2909 Hilcroft Ste. 650
Houston, TX 77057
Avis Rupert
800-641-6416

Telephone Connection
600 W. Broad Street
Richmond, VA 23230
Bill Stelmack
804-288-7000

**Tri-County
Telecommunications**
7059 Reseda Blvd.
Reseda, CA 91335
Tim Thelen
818-705-8199

Tri-Ed Inc.
11372 Trask #109
Garden Grove, CA
92643
Bill Winn
800-228-7433

UNEX
A Dynatech Company
Ventel Headsets
3 Lyberty Way
Westford, MA 01886
Robert Birch,
National Sls Mgr
617-692-9505

**Unique
Communications**
1951 John's Drive
Glenview, IL 60025
Kay Jackson, President
312-222-0867

Valcom Inc.
1111 Industry Avenue
S.E.
Roanoke, VA 24013
Donald Buck
703-982-3900

Voad Systems
3304 Pico Blvd.
Santa Monica, CA
90405
Patrick Ryan
213-450-2929

**Wicom/Weiser
Industries**
6027 Etiwanda
Tarzana, CA 91356
Isaac Weiser
818-708-1881

Ziehl Associates Inc.
306 Jericho Tnpk
Floral Park, NY 11001
Joan E. Ziehl,
Sales Manager
516-437-1300

Incentives and Awards

**Bottomline
Promotions**
115-01 Lefferts Blvd.,
Ste. 6
South Ozone Park, NY
11420-2488
Alan Reiter
718-843-5440

Buck Knives
1900 Weld Blvd.
El Cajon, CA 92020
Marge Staples
800-854-2257
619-449-1100

Chase Bag Company
2900 Vance St.
Reidsville, NC
27323-1677
William F. Ludington
919-342-1313
213-582-8211 LA

**Cookie Of The Month
Club**
Box 155, Kaolin Road
RD-1
Avondale, PA 19311
Helen Doordan
215-268-8030

D. Klein
60 Industrial Road
Lodi, NJ 07644
Anthony Shaw
201-778-4200

**Dark Star Screen
Products**
1703 Kingston Drive
Muncie, IN 47304
Cathy Spangler
317-282-4764

**General Electric
Premium Incen.**
P.O. Box 24459
Louisville, KY 40224
Bob Rolland
502-452-3495

Hoover Company
North Canton, OH
44720
Bob Rowan
216-499-9200

K-Products Inc.
Industrial Air Park
Orange City, IA 51041
Ryan Ashteroff
712-737-4925

**Leisuretime
Photo**
5400 No. Dixie Hwy.,
Ste. 9
Boca Raton, FL 33431
305-997-6173

**Longines-Whittnauer
Watch Co.**
145 Huguent
New Rochelle, NY
10802
Robert Mazzone,
Dir. Spec. Mkt
914-576-1000

**Omaha Steaks
International**
Dept. 4990
P.O. Box 3300
Omaha, NE 68103
Bill Cartee
402-391-3660

**Original Incentives
Inc.**
8070 Beechmont Ave.
Cincinnati, OH 45230
Frank Kroger
405-474-2882

Panasonic Company
Mail Stop 1F1 MTEC
One Panasonic Way
Seacaucus, NJ 07094
Ren Franse
201-392-4466

Presto Industries Inc.
Eau Claire, WI 54703
Bob Brewer
715-839-2121

**Sears Roebuck &
Company**
Sears Tower
D/727G, BSC 12-43
Chicago, IL 60684
312-875-7152
800-626-9304

**Sterling Novelty
Company**
3445 Amonia Circle
Colorado Springs, CO
80918
Gary Smith
303-590-9080

Texas Instruments
P.O. Box 655303
M/S 3658
Dallas, TX 75265
Keith Lewis
214-997-2488

USA Marketing
2182 Camp Ave.
Merrick, NY 11566
Norm Eisenberg
516-868-6893

**Weston-Reed
Industries, Inc.**
5425 Grosvenor Blvd.
Los Angeles, Ca 90066
213-450-9000

Key Systems

**Bell Atlanticom
Systems Inc.**
1400 Spring St.
Silver Springs, MD
20901
Sara Thompson
800-252-BELL

**CMX Communications
Inc.**
1300 N Florida Mango
Road
West Palm Beach, FL
33409
Bill Bailey
305-684-4700

APPENDIX B 261

Code-A-Phone Corporation
Div of The Conrac Corporation
16261 S.E. 130th Ave.
Clackamas, OR 97015
Gary Bennett
503-655-8940

Comm Services Inc.
1240 E. Joppa Road
Towson, MD 21204
Richarad Pujia
301-337-5544

Crest Industries Inc.
6922 N. Meridian
Puyallup, WA 98371
Earl Mason
206-927-6922

Eagle Telephonics Inc.
375 Oser Avenue
Hauppauge, NY 11788
Jim Perrone
516-273-6700

Era Telecommunications
168 5th Avenue
New York, NY 10010
R. Abada
212-807-6771

Executone Inc.
550 Triangle Parkway
Norcross, GA 30092
Jim Hollander
516-681-4000

F-Tec
15 Seeley Avenue
Piscataway, NY 08854
Fred Day
201-562-1100

Fujitsu
3190 Miraloma Ave.
Anaheim, CA 92084
Sue Shelby, Adv. Mgr.
714-630-7721

GTE Communications
Div GTE Corporation
2500 W. Utopia Road
Phoenix, AZ 85027
Rick Adams
602-581-4272

IPC Communications Inc.
600 Steamboat Road
Greenwich, CT 06830
Joseph Wilson
203-661-7500

IWATSU America, Inc.
430 Commerce Blvd.
Carlstadt, NJ 07072
Patty Schachter,
Mkt. Mgr.
201-935-8580

Intervoice Inc.
1850 N. Greenville #184
Richardson, TX 75081
Don Crosbie
214-669-3988

Intrastate Telecommunications
1550 Deer Park Avenue
Deer Park, NY 11729
Al Kammerer, Pres.
516-242-2255

Mid Atlantic Marketing Inc.
17017 Flatwood Drive
Rockville, MD 20855
Matt Wolk
301-258-5066

NEC Telephones, Inc.
8 Old Sod Farm Road
Melville, NY 11747
Don Hoffman/
Ivan Launer, Ad. Mg.
516-753-7000

North Supply
600 Industrial Parkway
Industrial Airport, KS 66031
Tom Housh,
Mkt. Com. Mgr.
913-791-7000 x1833

Northcom Group Inc.
600 Industrial Parkway
Industrial Airport, KS 66031
Dan Moody
913-791-7000

Phone Ware, Inc.
7534 La Jolla Blvd.
La Jolla, CA 92037
William J. Nassir
619-459-3000

RCA Telephone Systems
Route 38
Bldg. 204-1
Cherry Hill, NJ 08358
John Travares
609-486-5539

San/Bar Business Telephone Systems
9999 Muirlands Blvd.
Irvine, CA 92714
Dick Walther
800-527-4837

Scientific Telecom
508 Lamar Street
Greenwood, MS 38930
Alan
601-354-0400

Telamon Corporation
8134 Zionsville Road
Indianapolis, IN 46268
Albert Chen,
Managing Dir.
317-875-0045

Tie Communications Inc.
8 Progressive Drive
Shelton, CT 06484
Joseph Monachino,
Adv. Mgr.
203-926-2000

Tone Commander Systems Inc.
P.O. Box 1039
Redmond, WA 98052-1039
Dennis Nixion
206-883-3600

Toshiba America Telcom Div.
2441 Michell Drive
Tustin, CA 92680
Vivian Averton,
Mkt. Comm. Super.
714-730-5000

Trilluim Telephone Systems
Div. of Mitel Inc.
1567 Sunland Lane
Costa Mesa, CA 92626
Greg Hawkins
714-557-3300

U.S. West
6200 S. Quebec
Ste. 450
Ingelwood, CO 80111
Mickie Clark, Adv. Mgr.
303-889-6246

Walker Telecommunications Corp.
200 Oser Avenue
Hauppauge, NY 11788
Marty Chase
516-435-1100

Westech Communications Inc.
3700 Pacific Highway
Suite D
Olympia, WA 98503
Vernon Goldsby
206-459-9436

Lists & Directories

Contacts Influential
4220 Long Beach Blvd.
Long Beach, CA 90807
(213) 422-6522

Data Base Management, Inc.
345 Park Avenue South
New York, NY 10010
(212) 685-4600

Local Area Network Systems

American Laser Systems Inc.
106 Fowler Road
Goleta, CA 93117
Lorriane Shallenberger
905-967-0433

Applied Telemarketing Associates
2696 Chamblee-Tucker Road
Atlanta, GA 30341
Michael J. Burke
404-451-4334

Arnus Corporation
1305 Conkling
Utica, NY 13501
Patrick Ciandella
315-793-8500

Chesapeake and Potomac Telephone Company
11710 Beltsville Drive
Beltsville, MD 20705
Cathy Ochs
301-595-2314

Combined Telecom Resources
416 Dunailie Drive
Nashville, TN 37217
Eve Fierce
615-361-0469

Contel Information Systems Inc.
Div Continental Telecomm. Inc.
130 Steamboat Road
Great Neck, NY 11024
Gene Sochsenmaier
516-829-5900

GNU Communications Inc.
438 S. Main
Milpitas, CA 95035
Skip Brown
408-262-5038

Gandalf Data Inc.
Div Gandalf Technologies Inc.
1020 S. Noel Avenue
Wheeling, Il 60090
Michael Salustri
312-541-6060

Hedges Communications Company
1949 E. Sunshine
Corporate Center 2-100
Springfield, MO 65804
Steve Thompson
417-881-3425

ITT Communications Services
100 Plaza Dr.
Seacaucus, NJ 07096
Christopher Hoppin,
VP. Dir. Adv.
201-330-5111

Innovative Electronics
4714 NW 165 St.
Miami, FL 33014
Shelly Dolan,
Mktg. Com. Mgr.
305-624-1644

Jayness Associates
Div Audiocost Inc.
110 Powers Building 16
W Main
Rochester, NY 14614
J. Schirano
719-262-6400

Network Solutions
8229 Boone Blvd.
7th Floor
Vienna, VA 22180
Gary Desler
703-442-0400

OKI Telecom
Div OKI America Inc.
4405 International Blvd.
Norcross, GA 30093
Dave Rowan
404-925-9200

Peirce-Phelps Inc.
200 N. 59th Street
Philadelphia, PA 19131
Henry Grove
215-879-7180

Siecor Corporation
489 Siecor Park
Hickory, NC
28603-0489
Joseph Hicks
704-327-5821

Support Systems International
150 S. Second Street
Richmond, CA 94804
Greg Richey
415-234-9090

Telenova Inc.
102-B Cooper Court
Los Gatos, Ca 95030
George Gunkel
408-395-2260

U.S. Telecom— Corporate Network Services
1815 Century Blvd.
Atlanta, GA 30345
Kim A. Jacobs
404-982-1723

WMD Micro Distributors Inc.
109 Galther Drive
Mt. Laurel, NJ 08054
Brenda Sharkey
609-778-4600

Long Distance Services

AT&T Communications
23461 South Pointe Dr.
Ste. 200
Laguna Hills, CA 92653
800-222-0400

GTE Sprint
P.O. Box 974
Burlingame, CA 94010
415-692-5600
800-521-4949

Global Unlimited Service
1472 St. Francis Drive
Ste. 2
Santa Fe, NM 87501
Kirpal Khalsa
505-984-2178

MCI Communications Corp.
1133 19th St. NW
Washington, DC 20036
Karen Selko
202-887-2238

Tele Connect
500 2nd Ave. S.E.
Cedar Rapids, IA 52403
319-366-6600
800-REACHUS

Worldwide 800
777 Summer St.
Stamford, CT 06901
Stanly Scheinman
203-323-7773

Look-Up Phone Number Service

Consumer Marketing Research Inc.
600 Huyler Street
S. Hackensack, NJ 07606
Geoffrey Nelson
201-440-8900 NJ
800-225-0634

Data Base Management
345 Park Ave. S.
8th Floor
New York, NY 10010
Richard Blume
212-685-4600

Donnelley Marketing
P.O. Box 10250
1515 Summer Street
Stamford, CT 06904
Robin Rosic
203-357-8697
203-357-8746 Robin

Executive Marketing Services
568 S. Washington St.
Naperville, IL 60540
800-EMS-7311
312-355-3003

Nynex Information Resources
100 Church Street
New York, NY 10007
Debora Swee
215-513-9799

Pacific Bell
2600 Camino Ramon,
Room 4S250
San Ramon, CA 94583
Barry Evans,
Sales & Mkt. Mgr.
415-823-3571
415-823-3559

Paramount Lists Inc.
3126 Peach St.
Erie, PA 16508
Ralph Genovese
814-459-8787

Sheer Communications, Inc.
9 Albertson Avenue
Albertson, NY 11507
Arnold Sheer
516-484-3381

Telematch
6501 Loisdale Court
Ste. 1101
Springfield, VA 22150
Holly Brunk,
Dir. Client Svcs.
703-971-2547
703-644-9300

Telephone Look-Up Service
937 New Rodgers Rd.
Levittown, PA 19056
Mort Rifkin
215-752-8206

Market Research

Account-A-Call Corp
4450 Lakeside Dr.
Burbank, CA 91505
Jim Snyder, Pres.
818-846-3340

Bank-Aide, Inc.
734 W. Port Plaza
Ste. 225
St. Louis, MO 63146
Larry Hempel
314-434-8899

CRC Information Systems
435 Hudson Street
New York, NY 10014
212-620-5678

Datapro Research
1805 Underwood Blvd.
Delran, NJ 08075
Nancy Myers
800-DATAPRO

Digital Dispatch, Inc.
1580 Rice Creek Road
Minneapolis, MN 55432
612-571-7400

Gordon S. Black Corporation
1661 Penfield Road
Rochester, NY 14625
David H. Clemm
716-248-2805

Interviewing Service of America
16005 Sherman Way
Van Nuys, CA
91406-4024
Michael Halberstam
Lynne Denne
818-989-1044

Kapuler Telemarketing
3436 No. Kennicott
Arlington Heights, IL
60004
Sandra Greenfield
312-870-6700

Larry Tucker, Inc.
607 Palisade Ave.
Englewood Cliffs, NJ
07632
201-569-8888

Market Reach, Inc.
2672 Bayshore Frontage
Rd., Suite 506
Mountain View, CA
94043
Stuart P. Silverman,
President
415-969-4441

National Phone Center
151 W. 25th Street
6th Floor
New York, NY 10001
Peter Bakolia, VP
212-929-0500

Opinion Research
North Harrison Street
P.O. Box 183
Princeton, NJ 08542
609-924-5900

Professional Surveys, Inc.
786 Mountain Blvd.
Watchung, NJ 07060
201-755-5260

Response Innovations, Inc.
P.O. Box 166
Hershey, PA 17033
717-566-3849

SMG Research
260 East Avenue
Rochester, NY 14604
Brad Ross,
Market Research Mgr.
716-263-2614

Strategic Int'l Telemarketing
1150 S. Bascom Ave.
San Jose, CA 95128
408-971-9733

Telemarket Place, Inc.
3000 Dundee Road
Northbrook, IL 60062
800-344-5200

Telemarketing Management Assoc.
415 W. Golf Rd., Ste. 14
Arlington Heights, IL
60005
Ms. Jean VondeHaar,
Pres.
312-228-9250

Telemarketing Systems Consulting & Brokerage
221 Camaritas Avenue,
Ste. E
So. San Francisco, CA
94080
Paul Braschi, Pres.
415-583-1640

The Marketing Research Workshop, Inc.
1350 15th Street
Fort Lee, NJ 07024
Glenn Weissman
201-461-5365

Trinet Inc.
9 Campus Drive
Parsippany, NJ 07054
Ed Keon
201-267-3600

Visions Marketing Services
451 E. Ross Street
Lancaster, PA 17602
Allan E. Geller
800-222-1577
800-222-1570 PA

Marketing Services

800 Inc.
277 Coon Rapids Blvd.
Minneapolis, MN 54433
612-584-5570

Account-A-Call Corp
4450 Lakeside Dr.
Burbank, CA 91505
Jim Snyder, Pres.
818-846-3340

American Information Network
8201 Corporate Dr.
Ste. 100
Landover, MD 20785
800-424-INFO

American Passage College Marketing
6211 W. Howard Street
Chicago, IL 60648
Stuart Hochwert
312-647-6860

Associated Marketing
402 Maple Ave. West,
Suite C
Vienna, VA 22180
George H. L'Heureux
703-280-4040
703-281-4040

B.J. Knuth Associates
957 North Liberty Street
Elgin, IL 60120
Betty Knuth, President
312-888-4531

Brandywine Marketing Services
1300 First State Blvd.
Ste. A
First State Ind'l Park
Wilmington, DE 19804
302-999-6996

C. Itoh Digital Products, Inc.
19750 South Vermont
Avenue
Suite 220
Torrance, CA 90502
Pat O'Neil,
Sales Manager
800-423-0300

Civic Data
523 Superior Avenue
Newport Beach, CA
92663
Daniel Joynt
714-646-1623

Coe Marketing Inc.
230 E. Ohio, Ste. 303
Chicago, IL 60611
Camille Wietek,
Acct. Mgr.
312-951-5580

Decker Communications
150 Fourth Street
San Francisco, CA
94103
Jeannine Marschner
415-546-6100

Duns Marketing Services
49 Old Bloomfield Ave.
Mountain Lake, NJ
07046
Ms. Pat Brown
201-455-0900

Evergreen Advertising & Marketing
20-½ Main Street
Middlebury, VT 05753
802-388-4088

Executive Marketing Services
568 S. Washington
Street
Naperville, IL 60540
800-EMS-7311
312-355-3003

Focus Marketing Services, Inc.
Box 33
Commack, NY 11725
516-361-7373

Hanson Simonsen, Inc.
2015 21st. Street,
Suite 200
Sacramento, CA 95818
Deanna Hanson
916-451-0333

Institute for Mktg. Specialist
121 Middlesex Turnpike
Burlington, MA 01803
617-272-1438

JAMI Marketing Services
2 Executive Drive
Fort Lee, NJ 07024
201-461-8868

Jesse Marketing
22 Walter Street
Pearl River, NY 10965
J. Colodner, Pres.
914-735-7774

K.C. Blair Associates, Inc.
Box 516
Route 202
Lahaska, PA 18931
K.C. Blair
215-794-0794

Marketing Affiliates, Inc.
20 Phillips Road
P.O. Box 2304
Jackson, TN 38302
901-664-1920

Marketing Assoc. of America
2345 Millpark Drive
Maryland Heights, MO
63043
314-429-6900

Marketing Technology, Inc.
9223 Bedford
Omaha, NE 68134
800-228-2668

Marketing-by-Phone
2611 Pleasant Hill Road
Pleasant Hil, CA 94523
415-935-8585

Mass Marketing, Inc.
260 Northland Blvd.
Cincinnati, OH 45246
513-772-6277

NPJ Direct Marketing, Inc.
2121 Cloverfield Blvd.
Santa Monica, CA 90404
Ray W. Jutkins
213-829-3444

SRDS/NRPC Marketing Services
3004 Glenview Rd.
Wilmette, IL 60091
800-323-4601

Stephan Aaron Enterprises
32 Union Hill Rd.
P.O. Box 428
Morganville, NJ 07751
201-536-3869

Team Associates
4823 Willocroft Drive
Willoughby, OH 44094
Frank Spiro, President
216-946-2528

Telephone Concepts Inc.
192 North Street
P.O. Box 1363
Canton, GA 30114
Bernie Anderson
404-977-6080

The Emporium
15 Harris St.
Rochester, NY 14621
Patricia Dunbar
716-263-3589

The Marketing Resources Group, Inc.
116 New Montgomery,
Suite 500
San Francisco, CA 94105
Michael D. Jonas
415-495-4411

The Marz Group
15445 Ventura Blvd.,
Ste. 10
Sherman Oaks, CA 91403
Keith Marz,
Associate Director
818-907-1111

The Thompson Group
201 E. Ogden Ave.
Suite 15
Hinsdale, IL 60521
Charles W. Thompson,
Owner
313-323-1090

United Laboratories Inc.
1400 Jeffrey
Adison, IL 60101
R. Sorrentino,
Mktg. Serv. Mgr.
312-932-45095

Visions Marketing Services
451 E. Ross Street
Lancaster, PA 17602
Alan Geller
800-222-1577
800-222-1570

Voicepro
352 University Ave.
Wentwood, MA 02030
Helen C. Jensen
617-326-8386

W.S. Ponton, Inc
The Ponton Building
5149 Butler St.
Pittsburgh, PA 15201
Harvey Rabinowitz
800-628-7806

Modems

Alfa Telesystems Inc.
111 New York Ave.
Lake Hopatcong, NJ 07849
Bill Osborne
201-663-2318

Jackson Communications
1250 Broadway,
17th Floor
New York, NY 10001
John Wassenbergh,
VP Mktg.
212-563-1200

Nokia-Kinex Corporation
Div of Nokia
6950 Bryan Road
Largo, FL 33543
Steve Ridge
813-536-5553

Monitoring Systems

Augat/Melco
P.O. Box 1100
Seattle, WA 98111
Kathy Herbert - Sales
206-223-1110

GNU Communications Inc.
438 S. Main
Milpitas, CA 95035
Skip Brown
408-262-5030

Gordon Kapes Inc.
7250 N. Cicero Avenue
Lincolnwood, IL 60646
Carolyn Cashel
312-676-1750

Horchak & Associates
2241 1st Street
P.O. Box 7576
Laverne, CA 91750
Drake Jasso
714-569-4398

Lang Systems Inc.
1010 O'Brien Drive
Menlo Park, CA 94025
Seth Neumann
415-328-5555

Magnetic Systems Inc.
P.O. Box 11
Wellesley, MA 02181
Steve Drowne
617-237-0420

Opto-Tech Industries Inc.
2779 Clairmont Road N.E.
Atlanta, GA 30329
Doug Dyer
404-633-6949

Racom
5504 State Road
Cleveland, OH 44134
S. Silverstine
216-351-1755

Scansoft
3847 La Selva Drive
Palo Alto, CA 94306
Virginia Easterday
415-494-3880

Telecommunications Service Specialists Inc.
802 Sixth Ave. North
Fargo, ND 58102
Lori Edlund
701-235-5445

Telematrix Ind. Inc.
5 Harris Court
Great Neck, NY 11021
Dean Garfinkel
516-482-8280

Telephone Connection
600 W. Broad Street
Richmond, VA 23230Bill Stelmack
804-288-7000

PABX's

Comm Services Inc.
1240 E. Joppa Road
Towson, MD 21204
Richard Pujia
301-337-5544

Mitel Inc.
5400 Broken Sound
Blvd. N.W.
Boca Raton, FL 33431
Lyn Riddle,
Ast. Vice Pres.
305-994-3500

OKI Telecom
Div OKI America Inc.
4405 International Blvd.
Norcross, GA 30093
Dave Rowan
404-925-9200

Scientific Telecom
508 Lamar Street
Greenwood, MS 38930
Alan
601-354-0440

Siemens Communication Systems
550 Broken Sound Blvd.
Boca Raton, FL 33431
Bob Hanson
305-994-7510

Solid State Systems
1300 Shiloh Rd. N.W.
Kennesaw, GA 30144
Laura Kamenitsa,
Mgr. Mkt. Comm.
404-423-2229

Southwestern Bell
1010 Pine Street
Ste. 100
St. Louis, MO 63101
Dana Campbell
314-235-7575

Tadiran Electronics Industries
5733 Myer Lake Circle
Clearwater, FL 33520
John Dabnor
813-532-3222

Tele-Resources
Northway 10,
Executive Park
Ushers Road
Ballston Lake, NY 12019
Diana Ennis
518-877-8571

**Walker
Telecommunications
Corp**
200 Oser Avenue
Hauppauge, NY 11788
Marty Chase
516-435-1100

PBX's

Applied Intelysis
4340 Compus Dr.
#3204
Newport Beach, CA
92660
714-852-1175

**Commonwealth
Communications Inc.**
416 Elm Ave.
Kingston, PA 18704
Daniel Schall
717-283-4888

**Communications
Sources Inc.**
123 N. Centennial Way
#206
Mesa, AZ 85201
George Boyce
602-273-1800

**Era
Telecommunications**
168 5th Avenue
New York, NY 10010
R. Abada
212-807-6771

Executone Inc.
550 Triangle Parkway
Norcross, GA 30092
Jim Hollander
516-681-4000

Harris Corporation
Digital Telephone
Systems Div.
1 Digital Drive
Novato, CA 94947
Fred Page
404-256-4000

**IPC Communications
Inc.**
600 Steamboat Road
Greenwich, CT 06830
Joeseph Wilson
203-661-7500

Mitel Inc.
5400 Broken Sound
Blvd. N.W.
Boca Raton, FL 33431
Lyn Riddle,
Asst. Vice Pres.
305-994-8500

**RCA Telephone
Systems**
Route 38
Bldg. 204-1
Cherry Hill, NJ 08358
John Travares
609-486-5539

Telenova Inc.
102-B Cooper Court
Los Gatos, CA 95030
George Gunkel
408-395-2260

**The Telephone
Connection, Inc.**
1220 North Boulevard
Richmond, VA 23230
Bill Stelmack
804-359-1100

**Tone Commander
Systems Inc.**
P.O. Box 1039
Redmond, WA
98052-1039
Dennis Nixion
206-883-3600

**Toshiba America
Telcom Div.**
2441 Michell Drive
Tustin, CA 92680
Vivian Averton,
Mkt. Comm. Super.
714-730-5000

U.S. West
6200 S. Quebec
Ste. 450
Inglewood, CO 80111
Mickie Clark, Adv. Mgr.
303-889-6246

Z-Tel Inc.
181 Ballardvale Street
Wilmington, MA 01887
Kevin Moersch
617-657-8730

Paging
Devices

Bogen
A Lear Siegler Company
50 Spring Street
Ramsey, NJ 07446
Mr. Dean
201-934-8500

Printers

Epson America Inc.
2780 Lomita Blvd.
Torrence, CA 90505
Scott Edwards
213-539-9140

IBM Corporation
301 Merritt Seven
Norwalk, CT 06856
Darby T. Coker, Dir. Adv.
203-849-6000

Market Network
17905 Sky Park Circle
Unit P
Irvine, CA 92714
John Sherwood,
President
714-261-2412

**Nec Information
Systems**
1414 Mass Ave.
Boxborough, MA 01719
Peter Furgison
617-264-8000

UNISYS
Township Line &
Jolly Road
Bluebell, PA 19424
215-542-4011

Prospect
Lists

**ADCO List
Management Services**
600 Third Avenue
New York, NY 10016
212-661-0440

**AZ Marketing
Services, Inc.**
31 River Road
Cos Cob, CT 06807
203-629-8088

**Aaron's Mailing Lists
& Services**
754 N. Maday
San Fernando, CA
91340
818-365-6964

**Action List Services,
Inc.**
15 Warren Street
Hackensack, NJ 07601
201-343-0616

**Allnet Communication
Services**
1180 Ave. of the
Americas, 6F1
New York, NY 10036
212-704-0960

Alvin B. Zeller Inc.
475 Park Avenue South
New York, NY 10016
Alvin Zeller
800-223-0824

Americalist
Division Haines &
Company
8050 Freedom Ave.
N.W.
North Canon, OH 44720
Mike Carver
216-494-9111

**American Business
Lists**
P.O. Box 27347
Omaha, NE 68127
Debbie Smith, Ad. Mgr.
402-331-7169

**American List
Counsel, Inc.**
88 Orchard Road
CN5219
Princeton, NJ 08543
800-526-3973

BFC Mailing Lists, Inc.
1900 Quail Street
Newport Beach, CA
92660
714-476-1154

Business Directories
101 First St. #426
Los Altos, CA 94022
Joel Rosenburg
415-949-1471

CCX Network, Inc.
301 Industrial Blvd.
Conway, AR 72032
Jim Bradshaw,
501-329-6836

Caldwell Co.
2025 Peachtree Rd.
N.E.
Suite E & F
Atlanta, GA 30309
404-351-7372

**Channing L. Bete Co.,
Inc.**
200 State Rd., Suite 202
South Deerfield, MA
01373
413-665-7611

Compilers Plus, Inc.
2 Penn Place,
Pelham Manor
New York, NY 10803
800-431-2914
914-738-1520

Compudata List Marketing Inc.
P.O. Box 64
Pomona, NY 10970
Elaine Sims,
Acct. Executive
800-431-7185
914-638-2811

Consumers Marketing Research Inc.
600 Huylor St.
S. Hackensack, NJ 07606
Jeff Neilson
201-440-8900 NJ
800-225-0634

Coolidge List Marketing
25 West 43rd Street
New York, NY 10036
212-642-0310

Customs Mailing Services
145 Grove Street
Peterbourough, NH 03458
Joel Weissman,
President
603-924-9442

Data Base Management
345 Park Ave. S.,
8th Floor
New York, NY 10010
Richard Blume
212-685-4600

Datamap
6874 Washington Ave. So.
Eden Prairie, MN 55344
Grant Warfield
612-941-0900

Demographic Research Co., Inc.
233 Wilshire Blvd.
Santa Monica, CA 90401
213-451-8583

Demographic Systems, Inc.
325 Hudson Street
New York, NY 10073
212-255-8707

Direct Media List Management
70 Riverdale Ave.
P.O. Box 4565
Greenwich, CT 06830
203-531-1091

Direction "M" Inc.
1385 York Ave. 31A
New York, NY 10021
212-988-5110

Donnelley Marketing
P.O. Box 10250
1515 Summer Street
Stamford,CT 06904
Robin Rosic
203-357-8697
203-357-8746 Robin

Dunnhill International List Company Inc.
1100 Park Central Blvd. South
Pompano Beach, FL 33064
Robert Dunhill, Pres.
212-686-3700 NY
800-223-1882

Executive Marketing Services
568 S. Washington Street
Naperville, IL 60540
800-EMS-7311
312-355-3003

Generation Marketing
1 Lincoln Plaza
New York, NY 10023
Bart Loring, Pres.
212-496-9280

Gordon List Rentals
Division Gordon
Publications
13 Emery Ave.
Randolph, NJ 97869
Val De Geiso
201-361-9060

Green Pages Publishing and Computers
1212 S. University
Ann Arbor, MI 48104
Archie Allan
313-761-9635

Harris Publishing Information, SVCS
2057-2 Aurora Rd.
Twinsberg, OH 44087
Sue DeRemer
216-425-9000

Hautlists by JD
14334 Main Station
St. Louis, MO 63178
Jack Dudak, Owner
314-664-0859

Hitchcock Business List
25 W550 Geneva Road
Wheaton, IL 60188
800-323-2596

J.V. Assoc.
827 Broad St.
P.O. Box 92
Grinnell, IA 50112
Jerry Vitera
515-236-6209

Lead Marketing International
P.O. Box 932
1506 I-35 West
Denton, TX 76205
Linda Lummus
800-433-5575
800-442-3238 TX

Leads Unlimited, Inc.
8400 Bustleton Ave. Ste. 3
Philadelphia, PA 19152
Don Hellinger
215-745-4374

Leroy Harris Agency
P.O. Box 15816
Cincinnati, OH 45215-0816
Leroy Harris
513-554-4158

Lewis Advertising Company
325 E. Oliver Street
Baltimore, MD 21202
James G. Dickman
301-539-5100

List Services Corporation
890 Ethan Allan
P.O. Box 2014
Ridgefield, CT 06877
203-438-0327

List-King, Inc.
12 East Walnut Street
Kingston, PA 18704
717-283-2265

McGraw-Hill Mailing Lists
1221 Avenue of the Americas
New York, NY 10020
212-512-2000

Metro Mail Corp.
901 W. Bond Street
Lincoln, NE 68521
402-475-4591

N.R.D. Marketing
77 Brookside Place
Hillsdale, NJ 07642
Ben Bendit, President
201-666-2212

Name-Finders Lists, Inc.
2121 Bryant Street, Suite 304
San Francisco, CA 94110
Larry Shoobs
415-641-5208 CA
800-221-5009

Nynex Information Resources
100 Church Street
New York, NY 10007
Debora Swee
212-513-9799

PCS Mailing List Co.
85 Constitution Lane
Danvers, MA 01923
Susan O'Brien
800-532-LIST USA
800-622-LIST MA

Pacific Bell
2600 Camino Ramon, Room 49250
San Ramon, CA 94583
Barry Evans,
Sales & Mkt. Mgr.
415-823-3571
415-823-3559

Pacific Business Lists
17261 Simonds Street
Granada Hills, CA 91344
Marcia Higgins
818-368-7178

Paramount Lists, Inc.
3126 Peach St.
Erie, PA 16508
Ralph Genovese
814-459-8787

Penton Lists
111 Chester Avenue
Cleveland, OH 44114
216-696-7000 x2530

Prescott List Management
17 East 26th Street
New York, NY 10010
212-684-7000

R.L. Polk & Company
6065 Atlantic Blvd., Ste. E
Norcross, GA 30071
Paul Reardon
404-447-1280

R.D.M. Sales
3135 No. Ellington Drive
Los Angeles, CA 90068
Robert D. Mantell
213-851-2786

Research Projects Corp.
Pomperaug Ave.
Woodbury, CT 06798
800-243-4360

Ring Group of North America
230 Community Drive
Great Neck, NY 11021
Paul Ruggieri, VP
516-487-0250

Scott Ross Ltd.
P.O. Box 1931
Evanston, IL 60204-1931
312-674-9744

Software Lists, Inc.
8 Windsor Street
Andover, MA 01810
Dawn-Marie Nelson
617-470-3880

Springhouse List Management
1111 Bethlehem Pike
Springhouse, PA 19477
215-646-8700

The Federal Mailing
2701 E. Sunrise Blvd.
Ste. 500
Ft. Lauderdale, FL 33304
Mark Horowitz
800-327-6970

The Kleid Company, Inc.
200 Park Avenue
New York, NY 10166
212-599-4140

W.S. Ponton, Inc.
The Ponton Building
5149 Butler St.
Pittsburgh, PA 15201
Harvey Rabinowitz
800-628-7806

Wordserv
38-30 209th St.
Bayside, NY 11361
Phillip Klein
718-225-8218

Publications

Bill Scott & Associates, Inc.
7370 Beverly Blvd.
Los Angeles, CA 90036
Gaye Williams
213-938-6151

Business Directories
101 First St. #426
Los Altos, CA 94022
Joel Rosenburg
415-949-1471

Clement Communications
P.O. Box 500
Ceneordville, PA 19331
215-459-4200

Custom Publishing Co.
P.O. Box 20205
Castro Valley, CA 94547
Bob Luskey
415-886-1853

Eye on Telemarketing
13650 Gramercy Place
Gardena, CA 90249
(213) 217-1770

Gahona Graphics
37 W. Cherry
Rahway, NJ 07065
201-382-6161

International Dev. Marketing
750 13 Street SE
Washington, DC 20003
Peter Nelson
202-546-1900

Lead Marketing International
P.O. Box 932
1506 I-35 West
Denton, TX 76205
Linda Lummas
800-433-5575 USA
800-443-3228 TX

Market Place Publications
55 Holly Hill Lane
P.O. Box 4515
Greenwich, CT 06830-0515
203-661-0600

Personal Selling Power
P.O. Box 5467
Fredericksburg, VA 22403
703-752-7000

Prentice-Hall
Englewood Cliffs, NJ 07632
201-592-2000

SRDS/NRPC Marketing Services
3304 Glenview Rd.
Wilmette, IL 60091
800-323-4601

Self-Paced Instruction
80 Scenic Dr., Stes. 7&8
Freehold, NJ 07728
Charlene Thompson, Editor
201-780-7020

Telemarketing
Technology Marketing Building
17 Park Street
Norwalk, CT 06851
(800) 243-6002,
(203) 846-2029

Telemarketing Design
15427 Summerwood Drive
Omaha, NE 68137
Art Sobczak
402-895-9399

Telemarketing Insider's Report
P.O. Box 572
Englishtown, NJ 07726
Mary Ann Falzone
201-264-6127

Telephone Concepts Inc.
192 North Street
P.O. Box 1363
Canton, GA 30114
Bernie Anderson
404-977-6080

Telephone Selling Report
5600 Birch
Shawnee Mission, KS 66205
(913) 262-2626

Teleprofessional
Box 123
Del Mar, CA 92014
(619) 755-6500

The Van Vechten Report
80 Scenic Dr., Ste. 8
Freehold, NJ 07728
800-682-5432

Zip Target Marketing Magazine
1825 N Lincoln Plaza
Chicago, IL 60614
312-943-6645

Recruitment & Manpower Planning

Crandall Associates Inc.
Hal Crandall
212-213-1700
312-726-2977

Eric Ericson & Associates, Inc.
1130 Eighth Avenue South
Nashville, TN 37203
615-242-1050

Fenvessy & Schwab, Inc.
645 Madison Ave.
New York, NY 10022
212-758-6800

Karen Gillick & Associates
980 N. Michigan Ave.
Suite 1060
Chicago, IL 60611
312-337-0345

Killion McCabe, Inc.
11884 Greenville Avenue
Dallas, TX 75243
214-239-6000

Lawrence Marketing Search
32 Reni Rd.
Manhassett, NY 11030
Lawrence Kamisher, President
516-627-5361

National Information Services
11300 Rupp Drive
Burnsville, MN 55357
Ron Howe
612-894-9494

Ridenour & Associates
230 North Michigan Ave.
Chicago, IL 60601
312-444-1160

Sally Reich Associates
232 East 50th Street
New York, NY 10022
212-308-3276

Selection Sciences Inc.
256 Presidio Ave.
San Francisco, CA 94115
415-346-7015

Telemarketing Personnel Consultants
33 Jessics Place
Roslyn Heights, NY 11577
George Fredrics, President
516-621-0110

Telemarketing
Recruiters, Inc.
114 East 32nd Street
New York, NY 10016
Connie Caroli
212-213-1818
312-527-1166

U.S. Profiles
Corporation
6825 Manhattan Blvd.
Suite 500
Forth Worth, TX 76112
Sharon Haberer, VP
817-496-6881

Security
Devices

Opto-Tech Industries
Inc.
2779 Clairmont Road
N.E.
Atlanta, GA 30329
Doug Dyer
404-633-6949

Racal-Milgo
Div of Racal Electronics
P.O. Box 407044
Ft. Lauderdale, FL
33340-7044
James Norman
305-476-4004

Selection
Services/
Equipment

Communication
Services
Div of Honeywell Inc.
Honeywell Plaza
Minneapolis, MN 55408
Michael Fox
612-870-5999

E.C. Hunter Associates
Inc.
132 Atkinson Ave.
Syracuse, CA 13207
Fran Hunter
315-476-3811

GTE Communications
Div GTE Corporation
2500 W. Utopia Road
Phoenix, AZ 85027
Rick Adams
602-581-4727

Gandalf Data Inc.
Div Gandalf
Technologies Inc.
1020 S. Noel Avenue
Wheeling, IL 60090
Michael Salustri
312-541-6060

Precision Sales Inc.
1434 Dumont
Richardson, TX 75080
David Floyd
800-543-3000

Plant Equipment Inc.
28075 Diaz Road
Temecula, CA 92390
Patty Cummings
714-676-4802

Stromberg-Carlson
Com. Systems
Div of Plessey
400 Rinehart Road
Lake Mary, FL 32746
Randall Pugh
305-849-4808

Summa Four Inc.
2456 Brown Avenue
Manchester, NJ 03103
Greg Falan
603-625-4050

Support Systems
International
150 S. Second Street
Richmond, CA 94804
Greg Richey
415-234-9090

TCC Ltd.
60 Bloor Street W
Suite 209
Toronto, Canada,
M4W 3B8
416-961-1155

Telecommunications
Service Specialists
Inc.
802 Sixth Ave. North
Fargo, ND 58102
Lori Edlund
701-235-5445

Telephone Concepts
Inc.
Div of Esgeco Ltd.
2971 Flowers Road S.
Ste. 165
Atlanta, GA 30341
Kathy Anderson
404-992-1932

SMDR
Equipment

Affinitech Corporation

2252 Welsch Industrial
Court
St. Louis, MO 63146
Bryan Baehr
314-569-3450

GTE Communications
Div GTE Corporation
1907 U.S. Highway 301
North
Tampa, FL 33619
Lois Elwood
813-623-4000

Infortext Systems Inc.
1067 E State Parkway
Schaumburg, IL 60173
Tim Kelly, Exec. VP
312-490-1155

Instor Corporation
199 Jefferson Dr.
Menlo Park, CA 94025
Nancy Engles, Ad. Mgr.
415-326-9830

KTI Corporation
1666 N. Firman Ste. 400
Richardson, TX 75081
Steve Wagner
214-669-9590

Mountain Enterprises
586 Bonanza
Big Bear Lake, CA
92315
Ed Clarey
714-866-5826

Opus Telecom Inc.
95 Eames Street
Farmington, MA 01701
Jay or Barbara
Gainsboro, Owners
617-875-4444

Tel Electronics
Inc.
705 East Main
American Fork, UT
84003-2138
801-756-9606

Xiox Corporation
577 Airport Blvd.
Ste. 700
Burlingame, CA 94010
Barbara Brown,
Dir. of Adv.
415-375-8188
408-727-1943

Software for
Tele-
marketing
Automation

Adelie
Corporation
125 Cambridge Park Dr.
Cambridge, MA 02140
Jenine Blum
617-354-0400

Aims Plus
1001 South Sherman
Richardson, TX 75081
Debbie Vieau
214-669-8904

Apogee Systems, Inc.
60 Brigham Street
Marlboro, MA 01752
Rodger Pierce
617-481-9339

Arlington Software &
Systems
400 Massachusettes
Avenue
Arlington, MA 02174
Peter Brajer
617-641-0290

Auto-Com
3833 Lansdale Court
Laurel, NJ 20707
Michael Weiner
301-890-8833

Autocomm
2307 Broadway
Santa Monica, CA
90404
Will Gordon
213-207-7216

Automated Phone
Exchange Corp
4931 S. 900 E.
Salt Lake City, UT 84117
Brent Rasmussen
801-265-2000

Automated
Telemarketing Inc.
222 S. 9th Street
Ste. 3060, Piper Tower
Minneapolis, MN 55402
Michael A. Boylan
612-349-6609

Automation
Electronics Corp.
344 40th Street
Oakland, CA 94609
Randy Wilson
415-828-2880

Breakthrough
Systems, Inc.
19 Cleveland Lane
R.D.4
Princeton, NJ 08540
Robert Gibson
609-452-0130

**Brock Control
Systems**
1600 Parkwood Circle,
Ste. 100
Atlanta, GA 30339
800-221-0775

**CRC Information
Systems
(Tel-ATHENA)**
435 Hudson Street
New York, NY 10014
Sherry Greenhaus
212-620-5678

**Camber Business
Systems Inc.**
4975 Lacross Road
Charleston, SC 29418
Roger Davis
803-747-4539

**Commercial
Data Systems
Corp**
100 S. Pioneer Dr.
Smyrna, GA 30080
Jennifer Davis
404-799-1000

**Communicator
Asystance Systems**
112 Sohier Rd Ste. 105
Beverly, MA 01915
V. Lawrence Haug
617-927-8144

**Complementary
Solutions**
4470 Chamblee-
Dunwoody Rd.
Atlanta, GA 30338
Melanie Noble
404-454-8033

**Compucraft Systems
LTD**
2740 Queensview Drive
Ottawa, On Canada
Carmen McLean
613-726-0004

**Computer Consoles
Inc.**
97 Humbolt Street
Rochester, NY 14609
Robert Lofaso
716-482-5000

Computer Task Group
800 Delaware Ave.
Buffalo, NY 14209
Mary Killeen
716-882-8000

Computime, Inc.
401 N. 117th Street
Omaha, NE 68154
Jim Rose/
Martin Hensley
402-330-1311

D&E Software Inc.
8020 C Old Alexander
Ferny Road
Clinton, MD 20735
Don Wood
301-868-6866

**Dart Technologies
Group**
9800 N.W. Freeway,
#202
Houston, TX 77092
N.W. Thomas
713-528-7208

**DataCorp Business
Systems**
28300 Euclid Avenue
Cleveland, OH 44092
John Fisher,
VP Sales and Mkt.
216-731-8000

Data Station Systems, Inc.
2769 E. Atlantic Blvd.
Pompano Beach, FL 33062-
4915
(305) 942-0990

**Digital Equipment
Corporation**
129 Parker St.
Maynard, MA 01754
Henry Heisler
617-264-1577

**Donald G. Luger and
Associates**
3030 Harbor Lane
North
Minneapolis, MN 55441
Donald Luger
612-553-1122

**Drothier & Smith
Associates**
26021 Southfield Road
Lathrup Village, MI
48076
Mary Doris Smith
313-569-5430

Dynair Electronics Inc.
5275 Martin Luther King
Way
San Diego, CA 92114
Robert Jacobs
619-263-7711

**E.C. Hunter Associates
Inc.**
132 Atkinson Ave.
Syracuse, CA 13207
Fran Hunter
315-476-3811

**Excalibur
Sources**
P.O. Box 467220
Atlanta, GA 30346
404-956-8373

**FAX International
[Client Management Sys-
tem]**
4724 S. W. Macadam Ave-
nue
Portland, OR 97201
503-228-6523

Finalsoft Inc
305 S Main St.
N Syracuse, NY 13212
Steven Bergere
315-458-8627

GSI Transcom
1380 Old Freeport Road
Pittsburgh, PA 15238
Sales Department
412-963-6770

**Grynberg Publishing
Corp.**
5000 So. Quebec
Suite 500
Denver, CO 80237
J. Gary Brooks
303-850-7497

**Information
Management Assoc.**
19 Lunar Dr.
Woodbridge, CT 06525
Andrei Poludnewycz
203-397-1100

**Information Services
Division Resort &
Telemarketing
Systems**
P.O. Box 3549
Santa Monica, CA
90403-0549
Ashton International
Corp.
213-392-4080 in CA
800-327-4866

**Interactive
Telemarketing
Inc.**
8585 Stemmons Frwy.
Ste. 1107-N
Dallas, TX 75247
Jeff Syman,
Dir. of Mktg.
214-631-2277

Inter-systems Corp.
259 East Michigan
Avenue
Kalamazoo, MI 49007
Trish Sanchez
616-344-0220

**International
Computer Systems**
8300 Greensboro Drive
McLean, VA 22102
Arun Batavia
703-442-9430

**International Software
Sales**
12 Wade Road
Latham, NY 12110
Sandra Rudin, VP
518-783-1982

James Atherton Inc.
149 Palo de Oro Drive
Islamorada, FL 33036
James Atherton
305-664-8100

Jeb Systems Inc.
34 Daniel Webster Hwy.
Ste. 24
Merrimack, NH 03054
Donna Brock
800-821-1006
603-883-4662

**KBL Marketing
Systems**
8399 Topango Canyon
Ste. 200
Canoga Park, CA 91304
Dan Sarto, Proj. Mgr.
818-348-7554

Ken Launikonis
4068 Mt. Royal Blvd.
Allison Park, PA 15101
Rosemary Launikonis
412-486-9064

Key Systems Inc.
Prospecting Software
512 Executive Park
Louisville, KY 40207
Carlyle Crutcher
502-897-3332
800-223-5637

**Keystone Distributing
Company**
Div Medcomp
Technologies Inc.
120 Kisco Avenue
Mount Kisco, NY 10549
Mike Warman
914-241-7121

LPC, Inc.
1200 Roosevelt Road
Glen Ellyn, IL
60137-6098
312-932-7000

Lantor, Inc.
13650 Gramercy Place
Gardena, CA 92049
Dave Calahan
213-324-7070

**Launikonis
Development Group**
4068 Mount Royal Blvd.
Gamma Building,
Suite 225
Allison Park, PA 15101
Ken Launikonis
412-486-9064

Lowell Corporation
97 Temple St.
P.O. Box 158
Worcester, MA 01613
Rick Mahan,
Sales & Marketing
617-756-5103
617-799-6410

M.W. Ruth Company
510 Rhode Island Ave.
Cherry Hill, NJ 08002
Jay Foreman
609-667-2526

Mar-tel Communications, Inc.
375 S. Washington Avenue
Bergenfield, NJ 07621
Lawrence Steinberg,
President
201-385-7171

Marathon Telemarketing Systems
P.O. Box 725051
Atlanta, GA 30339
Steve Warshawer
404-422-3913

Market Power Inc.
101 Providence Mine
Road, Ste. 106 A
Nevada City, CA 95959
Harriet Maltin
916-432-1200

Marketing & Sales Software, Inc.
213 West Institute Place
Suite 507
Chicago, IL 60610
Thomas Thai, Pres.
312-787-1689

Marketing Information Systems
906 University Place
Evanston, IL 60201
John Kennedy
312-491-3885

Marketing Management Systems
1730-B Corcoran Street
N.W.
Washington, DC 20009
Harry Galliam
202-483-7738

Minitab Inc.
3081 Enterprise Drive
State College, PA 16801
Cheryl Ferrin
814-238-3280

National Political Resourses
602 Cameron Street
Alexandria, VA 22314
Ronald Charnock
800-526-1984
703-683-9090

National Systems Corp
221 N. Lasalle Street
Chicago, IL 60601
Jim Kargman
312-726-3211

*Natural Microsystems Corporation [Watson]
6 Mercer Road
Natick, MA 01760

Neomathics Inc.
486 Concord St.
Carlisle, MA 01741
Mindy Clark
617-369-0419

NICE Corp.
4357 S. Airport Park
Plaza
Ogden, UT 84405
801-621-6423

Northern Telecom, Inc.
P.O. Box 1222
Minneapolis, MN 55440
Joseph A. Scott,
Mkgt. Mgr.
800-328-8800
612-932-8238 MN

Profidex Corp
90 West Street
New York, NY 10006
Steven Haber
212-732-6795

Prophecy Development Corp
2 Park Plaza
Boston, MA 02116
Frank Foster/
Sean Cavanaugh
617-451-3430
617-451-1885

Reality Software
1770 East Galbraith Rd.
Cincinnati, OH 45215
Doug Kinman
513-821-3003

Reserve Six Corporation
501 Avis Drive
Ann Arbor, MI 48108
Del Sandberg
313-761-3869
800-346-6643

Rockwell International, Switching Systems
1431 Opus Place
M/S 933-400
Downers Grove, IL
60515
312-454-1752

Sales & Marketing Systems Inc.
1730-B Corcoran Street
N.W.
Washington, DC 20009
Harry Gilliam
800-832-0030

*Scientific Marketing Inc. [MARKETFAX]
3303 Harbor Boulevard
Suite G-9
Costa Mesa, CA 92626
(714) 957-0225

Scroth Systems Consulting Inc.
P.O. Box 250
Cobalt, CT 06414
Dick Scroth
203-267-0136

Softa Associates
Callmaker Software
1110 N 175th, Ste. 203
Seattle, WA 98133
Gordon Schaeffer
206-542-7481

Softech Inc
15 W Tenth Street
Ste. 900
Kansas City, MO 64105
William Zimmerman
816-472-5605

Software Marketing Associates, Inc.
P.O. Box 1358
Kearney, NE 68848
David T. Waldron
308-236-8989

Software of the Future
Box 531650
Grand Prairie, TX 75053
Norm Bowman,
Dir. Adv.
800-433-5355
214-264-2626

Softworks, Inc.
7700 Old Branch
Avenue
Clinton, MD 20735-9900
Greg Stergar
301-868-4221

Sysmark Information Sys Inc.
49 Aspen Way
Rolling Hills, CA 90274
H. David Taylor Jr.
213-544-1974 Dirct

System Vision Corp.
P.O. Box 281166
San Francisco, CA
94128
415-355-7308

Target Systems Corp.
33 Boston Post Rd. W.
Marlboro, MA 01752
Jerry Croteau,
Vice Pres.
617-460-9026
617-263-5331

Teknekron Infoswitch
1784 Firman Drive
Richardson, TX 75081
Lou Temple
214-644-0570

Teleconnect Company
500 2nd Ave. SE
Cedar Rapids, IA 52403
319-366-6600

Telemagic
P.O. Box 2861
1320 Ocean Avenue,
Ste. E
Del Mar, CA 92014
Michael McCafferty
619-481-8571
800-992-5228

Telemarketing Inc.
5919 Jonquil Lane
Minneapolis, MN 55442
John Meegan
612-559-1119

Telephone Marketing Services
25354 Cypress Avenue
Hayward, CA 94544
Joan Mollen,
VP Client Serv.
415-887-8555

Telesys Associates
19214 North 31st Lane
Phoenix, AZ 85027
Henry Schwarzberg
602-242-2727
602-582-9184

Televector, Inc.
505 Eighth Avenue
New York, NY 10018
Morton Aaronson
212-947-7573
212-662-7000

The Opus Corporation
20251 Century Blvd.
Germantown, MD 20874
James LaVardera
800-225-OPUS
301-428-3222

Transkirt Corporation
Division of MacLean
Hunter Corp.
Transkirt Lane,
Mt. Ebo Park
Brewster, NY 10509
Joe McFann
914-278-7000

Trans World Telephone
2550 Medina Road
Medina, OH 45256
Leo Hooper
216-722-5500

Travis Datartak Inc.
381 Elliot St.
Newton, MA 02164
Andrew Sunberg
617-964-8960
617-244-8368

Valor Telecom Ltd.
378 Schyuler Ave.
Kearny, NJ 07032
Joseph Pannullo,
President
201-997-2000

Westech Communications Inc.
3700 Pacific Highway
Suite D
Olympia, WA 98503
Vernon Goldsby
206-459-9436

Working Stations
11600 Bolling Brook
Rockville, MD 20852
Mike Cohen
301-231-8001

Switching Systems

Gai-Tronics Corporation
P.O. Box 31
Reading, PA 19603
Pete Lang
215-777-1374

Rockwell International Switching Systems
1431 Opus Place
M/S 933-400
Downers Grove, IL 60515
312-454-1752

Tele-conferencing Products/Services

AT&T Communications International
1 Pierce Place
Itasca, IL 60143
201-221-6658

Colorado Video Inc.
Box 928
Boulder, CO 80306
Jim Dole
303-444-3972

Confretech International
240 Applied Technical Center
2801 Younfield
Golden, CO 80401
Bill Drykus
205-281-9375

Connex International
12 West Street
Danbury, CT 06810
Patty Bisbano
203-797-9060

Image Data Corporation
2986 Mainland Drive
San Antonio, TX 78250
Larry Buerk
512-680-2727

International Microwave Corp.
65 Commerce Road
Stamford, CT 06902
Ben Rabinovici
203-323-5599

JOCOM International, Inc.
250 W. 57th Street,
Suite 701
New York, NY 10019
Patricia Crane
212-586-5544

Keiper Associates
4017-D Majestic Lane
Fairfax, VA 22033
Robert Keiper, Pres.
703-378-5999

L.D. Bevan Company Inc.
Div of Vidicom
742-D Hampshire Road
Westlake Village, CA 91361
Roger Ellis
818-889-3653

Private Satellite Company Inc.
215 Lexington Avenue
New York, NY 10016
Joe Rizzo
212-696-9476

Shure Teleconferencing Systems
Div Shure Brothers Inc.
222 Hartrey Ave.
Evanston, IL 60202-3696
Dick Williams

V-Channel
713 Camina Escuela
San Jose, CA 95129
Alan S. Yatagai
408-996-1740

Tele-marketing (Associated Organizations)

Air Quality Engineering
3340 Winpark Dr.
Minneapolis, MN 55427
Lori Jacobson,
Mkt. Assist.
612-544-4426

American Telemarketing Assoc.
1800 Pickwick Avenue
Glenview, IL 60025
Laurie Buehler
312-675-6814
312-724-7700

Conference Management Corporation
P.O. Box 4990
Norwalk, CT
800-243-3238

Hastings Development Council
Landmark Center
Hastings, NE 68901
Cal Johnson
402-461-4100

Imperial Tape Company
1014 Broadway
Santa Monica, CA 90401
Saul Ganz
213-393-7131

Industrial Telemarketing Assoc.
221 Chestnut St.,
Ste. 302
Roselle, NJ 07203
Ken Eisenberg,
President
201-245-3822

Iowa Department of Economic Development
600 E. Court Avenue
Des Moines, IA 50309
515-281-8328

North American Telecom Assoc.
200 "M" Street N.W.,
Ste. 550
Washington, DC 20036
Joan Smith
800-538-6282

Rasmussen and Associates
2548 North Carleton
Grand Island, NE 68803
Steve Rasmussen
308-381-0311

Southwestern Ohio Telemarketing Association
1313 E. Kemper Road,
Ste. 304
Cincinnati, OH 45246
Sandy Ambrose,
President
213-671-1600

Tele-marketing Equipment

Automated Telecommunications
8520 Edenton Court
Fulton, MD 20759
Earl Gill
301-498-7820

Coffman
Systems, Inc.
13140 Midway Place
Cerritos, CA 90701
Bill Bryce, Sales Mgr.
213-926-6653

ConsulTech
58 Kirshon Avenue
Staten Island, NY
10314-2706
Paul Gammarano
718-983-7040

Dascom Communications
17941 Ventura Boulevard
Encino, CA 91436
(818) 881-0410

Executive Systems,
Inc.
2112 Spencer Road
Richmond, VA 23230
Art Putnam
804-288-0041

Microphone
3239 Sweet Drive
Lafayett, CA 94549
Joann Stertridge
415-283-0711

MITEL, Inc.
5400 Broken Sound Blvd.,
N.W.
Boca Raton, FL 33431
(800) MITEL SX

North Supply
600 Industrial Parkway
Industrial Airport, KS
66031
Tom Housh,
Mkt. Comm. Mgr.
913-791-7000 x 1833

Perception Technology
Shawmut Park
Canton, MA 02021-1409
Douglas Keelan
617-821-0320

Seiscor Technologies
Inc.
Div of Switchcraft Inc.
P.O. Box 470580
Tulsa, OK 74147-0580
Kermit Ross
918-252-1578

Southwestern Bell
1010 Pine Street,
Ste. 1000
St. Louis, MO 63101
Dana Campbell
314-235-7575

Teletech
Communications Inc.
174 Classon Avenue
Brooklyn, NY 11205
Jacob Schlesinger, Pres.
718-783-8383

Unique
Communications
1951 John's Drive
Glenview, IL 60025
Kay Jackson, President
312-222-0867

Walker
Telecommunications
Corporation
200 Oser Avenue
Hauppauge, NY 11788
(516) 435-1100

Tele-
marketing
Service
Organiza-
tions—
Inbound

800 Speed Order
Systems (Co)
P.O. Box 32070
Phoenix, AZ 85064
Mr. Lippman, President
602-957-4923

AllBrand
Telemarketing
323 S. Franklin
Suite E138
Chicago, IL 60606-7094
312-922-1790

American Reservation
Systems
1280 W. Peachtree St.
N.W. Ste. 325
Atlanta, GA 30367
800-USA-8787

Astro Marketing
5445 N 103rd Street
Omaha, NE 68134
Mary Rhone, VP
800-247-9999

CVTC
4205 Grove Avenue
Gurnee, IL 60031
Laura Hinze, Mktg. Dir.
312-249-5560

Carlson Mktg.
Lettershop Svcs.
401 13th Ave.
P.O. Box 239
Howard Lake, MN
55349
612-543-3737

E.S. Advertising
Services
1890 E. 40th Street
Cleveland, OH 44103
216-881-8909

Execucall 800 Plus
8250 Winton Road
Cincinnati, OH 45231
Tom Cummingham/
Margie Dupps
800-543-3005

General Sound
Telephone
1216 Washington Street
Allentown, PA 18102
Dona Banys
215-435-1515

Interstate
Telemarketing
626 N. 109th Plaza
Omaha, NE 68154
402-493-2300

John Ross Enterprises
Inc.
23611 Chagrin Blvd.
Suite 101
Cleveland, OH 44122
John Ross
800-223-5580 USA
800-442-4545 Ohio

Kearney Telecomm
Center, Inc.
P.O. Box 1358
Kearney, NE 68848
David Waldron
308-236-8989

L.R. Yielding Assoc.
Greathill Road Industrial
Park
Nawgatuck, CT 06770
203-723-1485

Lark Associates
P.O. Box 56
North Brunswick, NJ
08902-0056
201-828-1067

Media Service Center
1515 E. Burnside
Portland, OR 97214
503-288-5849

Mediaplus
15 W. 44th St.
New York, NY 10036
212-840-2866

Market Track Inc.
2110 Powers Ferry Rd.
Ste. 301
Atlanta, GA 30339
Jamie Baskin
404-951-0681

New England 800
604 Main St.
P.O. Box 800
Rockland, ME 04841
800-CALL-NOW

Operator 800
P.O. Box 2489
Syracuse, NY 13220
Paul Yonge
800-962-1480 NY
800-448-4511 USA
800-255-1133 CANADA

Primenet
925 Delaware Street
S.E.
Minneapolis, MN 55414
Mary Strom
612-379-6900
612-332-8820 Krist

Spitech Corporation
One Greentree Center
Suite 201
Marlton, NJ 08053
Craig Spicer
609-596-7370

TMR
(Telecommunications
Marketing Resource,
Ltd.)
25 Greenwich Avenue
Warwick, RI 02886
Bill Rosenberg
800-345-6733

Telemarketing
Promotions
1038 Beacon Street
Newton Centre, MA
02159
617-527-6033

Telephone Concepts
Unltd.
3730 Lehigh Street
Suite 201
Whitehall, PA 18052
Joanne Kuchera
215-437-4000
800-527-6400

The Endowment
Company
P.O. Box 499
Fairfield, IA 52556
Mark Scheckman
515-472-5662

UNISYS
130 Jamesburg Rd.
Dayton, NJ 08810
800-222-0966

US Sales & Marketing Inc.
P.O. Box 920054
Norcross, GA 30092
William Davis
404-446-1611

Valentine-Radford
1100 Commerce Tower
Kansas City, MO 64105
Susan Spaulding
816-842-5021

Tele-marketing Service Organiza-tions— Outbound

800 Speed Order Systems (Co)
P.O. Box 32070
Phoenix, AZ 85064
Mr. Lippman, President

Alba International
51 S.W. Le Juene Rd.
P.O. Box 14099
Miami, FL 33134
305-445-5331

Albertella Associates
777 14 St. N.W.
Washington, DC 20005
202-347-2936

Americall Telemarketing
3010-A Woodcreek Drive
Downers Grove, IL 60515
George Kestler
312-810-0525
312-810-1707

American Airlines Direct Marketing Corporation
P.O. Box 619160, 5H80
Dallas/Ft. Worth Airport, TX 75261-9160
Sales and Marketing
Greg Ogden
800-325-2580

American Direct Marketing Svcs.
1261 Record Crossing
Dallas, TX 75235
Kim Carlson
214-634-2361

American Direct Response
16005 Sherman Way
Suite 216
Van Nuys, CA 91406-4024
Michael Halberstam/ Lynne Denne
818-989-5349

American Preferred Readers Svc
P.O. Box 1123
Fort Lauderdale, FL 33302
305-536-9336

American Telephone Marketing
2070 Chain Bridge Road, #380
Vienna, VA 22180
Fred Vasofsky
703-790-3636

APAC Corporation
9950 W. Lawrence
Schiller Park, IL 60176
Steve Glaser
800-822-2722
312-671-6100

B.P. Enterprises, Inc.
P.O. Box 509
West Barnstable, MA 02668
Paul Caron, President
617-428-0289

Britcom Telemarketing
2200 South Main Street
Lombard, IL 60148
J. Bishop, VP
312-932-7300

CSI Precision Target Marketing
100 Denton Ave.
New Hyde Park, NY 11040
516-747-1800

Card Share
3250 N. 93rd Street
Omaha, NE 68134-4720
Gregg Christoph
800-348-1000

Clark Equipment Credit Corp.
Teleprocessing Services Group
Circle Drive
Buchanon, MI 49107
John Blair
616-697-8175

Classic Image
510 Rhode Island Ave.
Cherry Hill, NJ 08002
609-667-2526

Community Benefits
1109 N. Thompson St.
Richmond, VA 23230
804-358-4991

Computer Assisted TM Corp.
200 Carleton Avenue
East Islep, NY 11730-1222
Stuart Gittelman
516-277-7000

Copy Van
2211 Dickens Rd.
P.O. Box 6819
Richmond, VA 23230
804-285-7841

Customer Development Inc.
4701 N. War Memorial Drive
Peoria, IL 61614
Kathey Beers
309-686-1900

Datacomp
31 Airpark Road
Princeton, NJ 08540
Steve Sproviero
609-924-8000

Direct Marketing/QMC
4124 Fields Dr.
Lafayette Hill, PA 19444
215-233-2890

Doyle's Discount Center
5547 S. Peck Ave.
P.O. Box 2132
La Grange, IL 60525
312-352-0429

Data Comp Telemarketing
31 Airpark Road
Princeton, NJ 08540
Stephen Sproviero
609-924-8000

Direct Connections
11211 Katy Freeway, Ste. 440
Houston, TX 77079
Laura Miller
713-464-7233

Direct Telemarketing Services
1780 Stoney Hill Dr., Ste. C
Hudson, OH 44236
William J. Braden
216-650-4700

EBSCO Telephone Services
P.O. Box 3157
Kent, OH 44240
Bob Prosise
216-673-2826

E. Phelps Nichols & Associates
800 Roosevelt Rd.
E-306
Glen Ellyn, IL 60137
312-790-9677

Entertel, Subs. Entrtnmnt Public
619 Mass
Lawrence, KS 66044
913-841-1200

Electronic Marketing Associate
12 Voice Road
Carle Place, NY 11514
Steven Granat
516-741-9000

Eugene A. Griffin
269-1-0 Grand Central Parkway
Floral Park, NY 11005
718-224-1643

Farmer Data Bank
1999 Shepard Road
St. Paul, MN 55116
Judy Jacaks
800-322-9322 x438
800-322-9322 x422

Fifth Medium Marketing
2701 W. Howard Street
Chicago, IL 60645
Barbara Bebee/ Melody Johnson
312-761-1660

Fingerhut Corporation
4400 Baker Rd.
Minnetonka, MN 55343
Charles Smith, Manager
612-932-3684

George N. Pegula Agency
400 Lackawanna Ave.
Scranton, PA 18503
717-343-4745

Grass-Tech
P.O. Box 114
Berkeley Heights, NJ 07922
201-665-0241

Greentree Film Distributors
1200 N. Mill Road, Suite B
Northfield, NJ 08226
609-272-0016

Grolier Telemarketing, Inc.
Old Sherman Turnpike
Danbury, CT 06816
Dante Cirilli
800-842-0014 USA
800-952-9044 Conn

H&G Direct
Division of Hicks
& Greist
220 E. 42nd Street
New York, NY 10017
212-907-9300

HJV Telemarketing
3600 W. Broad Street
Ste 675
Richmond, VA 23230
Barb Curtis
800-552-6995 in VA
800-531-3343 USA

Harris Associates
433 Walnut Street
Reading, PA 19601
215-374-9359

**Heritage
Telemarketing**
Div Heritage Publishing
4100 Heritage Drive
North Little Rock, AR
72117
Phil Sheldon
501-945-5000

**Image Makers,
Communication
Specialists**
422 Market Street
P.O. Box 286
Parkersburg, WV 26102
304-424-6466

Impact Telemarketing
788 Hadden Avenue
Collingswood, NJ 08108
Edward Ducoin
609-858-5394

**Idelman
Telemarketing
Inc**
7415 Dodge St.
Omaha, NE 68114
Dale Broekemeier,
President
Steve Idelman, CEO
402-393-8000
800-642-0700

Insight Inc.
P.O. Box 55
Stillwater, MN 55082
Roy Wahlberg,
Project Admin.
612-439-7048

**International
Telemarketing
Services, Inc.**
501 Forbes Boulevard-M
Lanham, MD 20706
Glenda Singer
800-826-0793

**Interviewing
Service of
America**
16005 Sherman Way
Van Nuys, CA
91406-4024
Michael Halberstam/
Lynne Denne
818-989-1044

**JC Communications
Services, Inc.**
55 E. Washington
Chicago, IL 60602
Joseph Culotta
312-372-4747

**Lead Marketing
International**
P.O. Box 932
1506 I-35 West
Denton, TX 76205
Linda Lummus
800-433-5575
800-443-3238 TX

**Lester
Telemarketing**
19 Business Park Drive
Branford, CT 06405
Bob Lester
203-488-5265

**Lewis & Associates
Telemarketing**
1611 Ingersoll Avenue
Des Moines, IA 50312
James Lewis
515-244-4708

Louis Lines, Inc.
4900 Fredrick Pike #60
Dayton, OH 45414
Eleanor C. Lewis
513-277-7707

MPACT Telemarketing
300 W. 5th Street,
Suite 840
P.O. Box 2266
Austin, TX 78701
Len Bussey
512-479-1554

**MSI Marketing
Specialties, Inc**
560 Greenbrier, Ste. 202
Oceanside, CA 92054
Roger Rosdahl
800-222-7279

**Mark Geller &
Associates**
941 Oakwood Avenue
Fullerton, CA 92635
714-529-4628

**Marketing
Connections**
One Annabel Lane,
Ste. 212
San Ramone, CA 94583
415-866-1818

**Marketing Motivators,
Inc.**
3725A No. 126th Street
Brookfield, WI 53005
Lawrence A. Pentler
414-783-6800

**Marketing Square
Communications**
1100 Centerpoint Drive
Box 508
Stevens Point, WI 54481
David Garber
715-344-4609

Market Trak Inc.
2110 Powers Ferry Rd.
Ste. 301
Atlanta, GA 30339
Jamie Baskin
404-951-0681

Marketron
33 Winrock Center
Suite 548
Albuquerque, NM 87110
505-831-4173

**Megadial
Communications, Inc.**
551 Fifth Ave., Ste. 1020
New York, NY 10017
Owen Amerling
212-557-9130

Meyer Associates, Inc.
14 N. 7th Ave.
St. Cloud, MN 56301
Sally Jo Baumgartner
612-259-4000

**Modern
Communications**
Fund Raising Specialties
1936 M.V.A. #135
Gaithersburg, MD
20879
Marvin Cherna
301-977-0283

N.J. Associates
6 Columbia Place
Princeton Junction, NJ
08550
609-799-0563

NTI
60 Whitlock Place,
Suite F
Marietta, GA 30064
Becky H. Cox
404-426-8985

National Credit Audit
4701 N. War Memorial
Drive
Peoria, IL 61615
309-686-1900

**National Phone
Center, NPC**
151 W. 25th Street
6th Floor
New York, NY 10001
Peter Bakolia, Exec. VP
212-929-0500

**Nevus
Communications
Group**
905 Bonifant St.
Silver Spring, MD 20910
301-495-0276

**New Resi Data
Marketing**
77 Brookside Place
Hillsdale, NJ 07642
201-666-2212

**New Resources
Telemarketing**
109 E. Third Street
New Richmond, WI
54017
Michael J. Pedro
715-246-5060

North Coast Direct
3645 Warrensville
Center Rd.
Cleveland, OH 44122
Jan
216-991-2161

**Odell, Roper and
Associates**
7316 Wisconsin Ave.
Ste. 507
Bethesda, MD 20814
Peter S. Embrey
301-657-9821

On-Line Telemarketing
555 West 57th Street
Ste. 1515
New York, NY 10019
Richard Roll
212-974-1125

**Paul A. Lewis
& Associates**
3250 W. Market St.
Akron, OH 44313
216-864-7646

**Phone Power
Unlimited**
91 Palmer Dr.
P.O. Box 3034
Wayne, NJ 07470
201-956-1085

Public Interest Communications
7700 Leesburg Pike
Suite 301
Falls Church, VA 22043
703-237-5200

Precision Target Marketing Inc
100 Benton Ave.
New Hyde Park, NY 11040
Richard Feary
516-747-1800

Profit By Phone
171 Main Street
Ste. B104
Ashland, MA 01721
Michael Love
617-881-7411

Progressive Marketing Services
3649 W. 183rd Street
Hazel Crest, IL 60429
Kevin Lane
312-957-5200

Publisher's Clearing House Telemarketing
382 Channel Drive
Pt. Washington, NY 11050
Karen Schloss
516-883-5432

RCA Global Communications
60 Broad Street
New York, NY 10004
Dan Dwyer
201-885-2261

RMH Telemarketing
300 E. Lancaster Avenue, Suite 204-D
Wynnewood, PA 19096
MarySue Lucci,
Executive VP
215-642-2438

RSVP Marketing
450 Plain St. Ste. 5
Marshfield, MA 02050
Edward Hicks
617-837-2804

Response Communications Inc.
1040 Kings Highway N.
Ste. 630
Cherry Hill, NJ 08003
Bob Pensky, Pres.
404-256-1500
609-482-2600

SST Telemarketing Services
3930 Walnut Street
Fairfax, VA 22030
Jerry Werhel
703-352-5235

Sales Leads
242 Sunset
Vernon Hills, IL 60061
312-364-3124

Stackpole Books/Cameron-Keller
P.O. Box 1831
Harrisburg, PA 17105-1831
717-234-5041

Strategic Int'l Telemarketing
1150 S. Bascom Ave.
San Jose, CA 95128
408-971-9733

Sturner & Klein
11900 Parklawn Drive
Rockville, MO 20852
301-881-2720

Syntex Medical Diagnostics
900 Arastradero Road
Palo Alto, CA 94304
Gordon C. Fiala
415-494-1086 x 1228

T And A Marketing
1155 15th St. N.W.
Washington, DC 20005
202-857-0990

TMI Telecommunications Marketing, Inc.
12165 W. Center Road, Ste. 60
Omaha, NE 68144
Fred Stevens
800-445-8800

Tech-Vest Resources
1946 Greenpoint Dr.
St. Louis, MO 63122-5248
612-965-0184

Total-Tel USA
140 Little Street
Belleville, NJ 07109
201-751-5510

Techni-Call
20775 Western Avenue
Torrance, CA 90501
Steve Noble
213-618-9994
415-595-3341

Tel Sel
527 Tunxis Hill Rd.
Fairfield, CT 06430
Denis Garvey, President
203-366-4252

Tele-Mark Services, Inc.
223 Jericho Turnpike
Mineola, NY 11501
516-746-4055

Tele-Vision
18511 Hawthorne Blvd.
Suite 260
Torrance, CA 90504
Steve Noble
213-372-3686

Telecommunications Marketing
12165 W. Center Road, Ste. 60
Omaha, NE 68144
Fred Stevens,
VP of Mktg.
800-445-8800

Telecross Corp
842 W. 4th Ste. A-101
Waterloo, IA 50701
Diana Mason
800-835-2767
319-235-4469

Teleforce
901 Campisi Way,
Ste. 205
Campbell, CA 95008
David Marin
408-377-3800

Telemarketing Management Assoc.
415 W. Golf Rd., Ste. 14
Arlington Heights, IL 60005
Ms. Jean VondeHaar,
President
312-228-9250

Telemarketing Results, Inc.
2070 Chain Bridge Rd.
Suite 400
Vienna, VA 22180
Glen Snyder, Pres.
703-442-5795

Telemarketing Services Inc
25 Van Zant St.
Norwalk, CT 06855
Nancy Galli,
VP Operations
203-854-1000

Telemarketing Temps
1313 E. Kemper Road
Suite 304
Cincinnati, OH 45246
Dan Hellmuth
513-671-1600

Telemarketing USA
1001 Connecticut Avenue NW
Suite 828
Washington, DC 20036
Deborah Beck
202-452-0050

Telephone Concepts Unltd.
3730 Lehigh Street
Suite 201
Whitehall, PA 18052
Joanne Kuchera
215-437-4000
800-527-6400

Telephonics
16913 Enterprise Dr.
P.O. Box 4516
Scottsdale, AZ 85261
(Fountain Hills)
800-528-4700

The Adman
1044 Bellefontaine Ave.
P.O. Box 1869
Lima, OH 45802
419-227-6407

The Apac Corporation
9950 W. Lawrence Ave.
Schiller Park, IL 60176
Steve Glaser
312-671-6100

The Cable Agency
301 Eastwood Circle
Virginia Beach, VA 23454
804-463-3845

The Marketing Resources Group, Inc.
116 New Montgomery,
Suite 500
San Francisco, CA 94105
Michael D. Jonas
415-495-4411

The Stenrich Group
160 Fifth Avenue
New York, NY 10010
Steven Isaac, President
212-255-7273

The Telemarketing Company
5300 W. Lawrence
Ste. 8
Chicago, IL 60641
Mary Shanley
312-545-0407

The Telephone Marketing Group
501 Washington Lane
Jenkintown, PA 19046
Steven Lynn, President
215-576-7000

Times Journal
Telemarketing
Co.
6320 Augusta Drive
Springfield, VA 22150
703-644-9300

Trans America
Telemarketing
605 14th St. N.W.
Ste. 700
Washington, DC 20005
Charles Cadigan
202-383-8300

Traxell
Marketing Inc.
9031 N Dearwood Drive
Milwaukee, WI 53223
Tom Zabjek
414-357-8700

UNISYS
130 Jamesburg Rd.
Dayton, NJ 08810
800-222-0966

U.S. Fulfillment
Services
125 Rowell Court
Falls Church, VA 22046
Timothy F. Cotton
703-241-0600

US Sales & Marketing
Inc.
P.O. Box 920054
Norcross, GA 30092
William Davis
404-446-1611

Vector
Communications, Inc
2231-D Commerce
Avenue
Concord, CA 92520
J. Michael
415-676-5329

Vigure Company
7777 Leesburg Pike
Ste. 500
Falls Church, VA 22043
J.R. Thompson
703-356-0441

Visions
Marketing
Services
451 E. Ross Street
Lancaster, PA 17602
Allan Geller
800-222-1577
800-222-1570 PA

Voice Computer
Technologies
5730 Oakbrook Parkway
Ste. 175
Norcross, GA 33093
Colleen Moonen
404-441-2303

William B. Allen
Supply Co.
300 N. Rampart Street
New Orleans, LA 70112
Bill Kanelos
504-525-8222

Working Stations
11600 Bolling Brook
Rockville, MD 20852
Mike Cohen
301-231-8001

World Book
Telemarketing
799 Roosevelt Road,
Bldg. 3
Glen Ellyn, Il 60137
Peggy Hunter
312-858-4703

Xtend
Communications
171 Madison Avenue
New York, NY 10016
212-725-2010

Tele-
marketing
Service
Organiza-
tions—
Inbound
and
Outbound

800 Speed Order
Systems
P.O. Box 32070
Phoenix, AZ 85064
Marlene Wilde
602-957-4923

A&B Practical
Supplies
105 Fir Street
Suite 333
La Grande, OR 97850
503-963-9811

A.J. Wood
One Winding Drive
Philadelphia, PA 19131
215-473-7100

ACTS
10999 Reed Hartman
Highway, Ste. 113
Cincinnati, OH 45242
James Eavey
513-891-8855

ADDS
Telemarketing
155 Pasadena Avenue
South Pasadena, CA
91030
Norm Pensky
800-233-7487

AMPAD Corp
104 Lower Westfied
Road
Holyoke, MA 01040
John Kraus
413-536-3511

AT&T American
Transtech
8000 Baymeadows Way,
Rm 53143
Jacksonville, FL 32216
800-241-3354 x2524

AT&T
Communications
International
1 Pierce Place
Itasca, Il 60143
201-221-6658

Ad Data Services
2075 Palos Verdes Dr. N
P.O. Box 399
Lomita, CA 90717
213-534-1860

Adovations
19 Brompton
Ste. A
Huntington, NY 11746
516-673-8741

Advanced
Telemarketing
8001 Bent Branch Dr.
Irving, TX 75063
Beverly McIntosh,
Natl. Accts.
214-830-1800

Advantage Direct
19860 Plummer St.
Chatsworth, CA 91311
Michele Madon
818-717-6149

Alan Hirschfeld DM
Consultant
8926 Ware Court
San Diego, CA 92121
Howard Webber
619-549-0505

Alford and Partners
126-13 101st Ave.
Queens, NY 11419
718-847-5200

Alliance Air Freight
110 W. Ocean Blvd.
#529
Long Beach, CA 90802
213-435-8454

American Telephone
Marketing Group
2070 Chain Bridge
Road, Suite 380
Vienna, VA 22180
703-790-3636

American Mail
Systems
211 Progress Dr.
Montgomeryville, PA
18936
215-628-9878

American Tele/
Response Group
401 Pilgrim Lane
Drexel Hill, PA 19026
Dennis Durkin
215-789-7000

Ameritel Corporation
124 W. Wisconsin Ave.
Neenah, WI 54956
Craig Leipold/Jim Bere
414-727-3900

Amrigon
25 W. Long Lake Rd.
Bloomfield Hills, MI
48013
Richard Smith
313-258-2300

Anderson Dunston
& Helene Inc
114 Mayfield Ave.
Edison, NJ 08837
William B. Helene,
President
201-225-5300

Answer Network
23015 Del Lago
Suite D2/D3
Laguna Hills, CA 92653
Reenie Robb
714-472-4444

Applied Telemarketing
Associates
2696 Chamblee-Tucker
Road
Atlanta, GA 30341
Michael J. Burke
404-451-4334

Assist Services
106 Robbins Ave.
Niles, OH 44446
800-524-3120

Automatic Marketing
Consult.
1346 Cove Dr.
Prospect Heights, Il
60070
312-541-8755

Beekly Corporation
Prestige Lane
Bristol, CT 06010
Peter Rodgers
203-583-4700

Bell Atlantic
1310 North Courthouse
Road, 8th Floor
Arlington, VA 22201
Ed Parker
609-987-7030 Ed

Bell Telephone of Pennsylvania
1 Presidential Blvd., Ste. 204
Bala Cynwyd, PA 19004
Barbar Swift
215-578-5040
202-392-1011

Bottomline Promotions
115-01 Lefferts Blvd.
Ste. 6
South Ozone Park, NY 11420-2488
Alan Reiter
718-843-5440

Burton Advertising Agency
203 N. Wabash Ave.
Chicago, Il 60601
312-332-0187

Businessmen's Mailing Service
193 Hillside Ave.
P.O. Box 278
Williston, Park, NY 11596
516-248-0573

CCI Telemarketing
555 W. 57th Street
New York, NY 10019
Adrian Miller
212-957-8520

Call Center Services
302 Knickerbocker Road
Cresskill, NJ 07626
Douglas Comfort
201-567-9314

Carlyle Marketing Corp
5850 N. Lincoln Avenue
Chicago, IL 60659
Joyce Igou, Creative Dir.
312-271-2700

Celebrity Sales, Inc.
7553 Green Valley Rd.
Placerville, CA 95667
916-622-9387

Chargit
60 Charles Linbergh Blvd.
Uniondale, NY 11530
800-645-4244

Communique Direct Marketing
250 N. Sunnyslope Rd.
Room 260
Brookfield, WI 53005
414-785-0400

Contact Telemarketing
120 Brighton Road
Clifton, NJ 07012
201-778-7722

Contel-A-Marketing
Division of Contel
509 Cherry Drive
Hershey, PA 17033
717-534-9417

Continental Cablevision
Pilot House,
Lewis Wharf
Boston, MA 02110
617-742-6140

Continental Marketing
13505 C Dulles Technology Drive
Herndon, VA 22071
703-471-7910

Creative Technical Services
40 Daniel St.
Farmingdale, NY 11735
516-752-9500

DAC Associates
A Jay Group Co.
60 N. Ronks Road
Ronks, PA 17572
717-687-8641
800-342-5322 Natl.
800-322-5463 PA

Daniels Productions
1155 New Britain Ave.
West Hartford, CT 06110
203-233-9611

Direct Marketing Services
11288 Hanover Rd.
Cincinnati, OH 45240
513-851-2745

Deerfield Associates
5060 North 19th Ave.
Suite 216
Phoenix, AZ 85015
602-246-2868

Dial America Marketing
135 Galway Place
Teaneck, NJ 07666
Nancy Katz
201-837-7800
201-843-6268

Dial Direct Inc.
230 S. Broad Street
Philadelphia, PA 19106
215-546-0216

Dialog Immediate
2300 East Devon
Suite 218
Des Plaines, IL 60018
800-624-7342

Ellis Singer Group
1035 Delaware Ave.
Buffalo, NY 14209
716-884-8885

Edward Blank Associates
71 W. 23rd Street
New York, NY 10010
Herbert Feldman
212-741-8133

Electronic Sales Professionals
31566 Schoolcraft Rd
Livonia, MI 48150
313-425-5551

FCS
23 Route 206
Stanhope, NJ 07874
201-347-9006

Fala Direct Marketing
70 Marcus Dr.
Melville, NY 11747
Greg Blower,
Adv. Director
516-694-1919

Fellers, Lacy & Gaddis
2211 S. IH 35, Ste. 400
Austin, TX 78741
512-445-3492

Financial Telemarketing
100 Fifth Ave.
Suite 1100
New York, NY 10011
212-206-0160

Floral Network
165 N. Canal Street
Chicago, IL 60606
312-930-2000

Flournoy & Gibbs
241 N. Superior Street
Toledo, OH 43604
491-244-5501

Foremost Telemarketing Group
15222 Keswick St.
Van Nuys, CA 91405
David Essex
800-225-5343
818-988-6900

Fortune 800
4050 Durock Rd.
Cameron Park, CA 95682
916-677-7171
800-451-0303 IO

Frank/James Direct Marketing
500 Chromally Plaza 120
S. Central Avenue
St. Louis, MO 63105
314-726-4600

GLS Credit Card Marketing
2000 Market Street
Philadelphia, PA 19103
215-568-1100

GLS Telemarketing
26899 Northwestern,
Suite 421
Southfield, MI 48034
Steve Shapira, VP
313-827-4700

GTE Spring
Burlingame, CA 94010
Ralph Sherman
415-692-5600

Garvan Advertising
501 S. Broadway
Hicksville, NY 11801
516-433-2573

Goodway Marketing
930 Benjamin Fox Pavilion
Jenkintown, PA 19046
215-887-5700

Harte-Hanks Telemarketing Services
65 Rt. 4 East
Riveredge, NJ 07661
Marcia Doron
201-342-6700
800-526-5368

Hunter Business Direct
8793 N. Port Washington Road
Milwaukee, WI 53217
414-351-5850

I. Market, Inc.
8240 Beverly Blvd.
Los Angeles, CA 90048
213-655-0133
415-968-1818

IXI
Box 26344 Park Station
Minneapolis, MN 55426
612-933-8758

Inquiry Handling Services
200 Parkside Dr.
San Fernando, CA 91340
Bernie Otis, Mktg. Cons.
818-365-8131

Inquiry Processing Center, Inc.
18016 Crenshaw Blvd.
Torrance, CA 90504
Jim Russel
800-252-4488 x799 USA
800-262-4488 x799 CA

Interactive Telemarketing Inc.
8585 Stemmons Fwy.,
Ste. 1107-N
Dallas, TX 75247
214-631-2277

Inter-media Marketing
201 Carter Drive
West Chester, PA 19382
Keith Brady
215-636-4646

**International
Telesystems
Corp.**
65 Jackson Drive,
Ste. 2000
Cranford, NJ 07016
201-272-1062

JF Glaser Inc.
999 Main Street
Suite 103
Glen Ellyn, IL 60137
Joseph Glaser
312-469-2075

John P. Walsh, Inc.
3024 Springboro West
Moraine, OH 45439
513-299-8777
800-531-3456

**John Ross Enterprises
Inc.**
23611 Chagrin Blvd.,
Ste. 101
Cleveland, OH 44122
800-223-5580
800-442-4545 OH

**Leading Edge
Telemarketing
Inc.**
8330 Old Courthouse
Road
Vienna, VA 22180
703-734-9505

**Learning
International**
P.O. Box 10211
Stamford, CT 06904
203-965-8477

**Mail Center Of
Edwardsville**
P.O. Box 364
Edwardsville, IL 62025
618-667-3656

**Management Services
Group**
100 Union St.
Brigdeville, PA 15017
412-221-2020

Marcon Inc.
831 Baxter St., Ste. 218
Charlotte, NC 28202
J. Wright
Clarkson-Director
704-333-5816

Mardex
150 Fifth Avenue
Suite 530
New York, NY 10011
212-675-1008
800-426-4000

**Market Resources
Corporation**
419 N. Harrison Street
P.O. Box 183
Princeton, NJ 08540
Kate Fogel
201-769-5224

Market Track Inc.
2110 Powers Ferry Rd.,
Ste. 301
Atlanta, GA 30339
Jamie Baskin
404-951-0681

**Marketing
Communications Inc.**
10605 West 84th Street
Lenexa, KS 66214
800-881-5536

**Marketing Solutions,
Inc.**
7335 E. Livingston Ave.
Reynoldsburg, OH
43068
614-764-7610

**Marsh & McLennan
Group**
3 Embarcadero Center
San Francisco, CA
94111
415-393-5484

Master Mechanic
280 S. Pine St.
P.O. Box A
Burlington, WI 53105
414-763-2428

**Matrix Marketing
Services**
6506 Schroeder Rd.
Madison, WI 53711
608-271-6888

Mediaworks
1400 Homer Rd.
Marketing Resource
Center
Winona, MN 55987
507-454-1400

**Midwest
Marketing/Lake
Geneva**
P.O. Box 165
Lake Geneva, WI 53147
414-248-8188

**Mercury Telemarketing
Services**
165 North Canal Street
Chicago, IL 60606
Ane L. Weston
800-341-7400
312-930-2023

Molin & Associates
18927 23rd NE
Seattle, WA 98155
Susan Molin
206-622-4707

**Nation-Wide Sports
Publication**
9255 Sunset Blvd.
Ste. 200
Los Angeles, CA 90069
213-273-9025

**National Fulfillment
Services**
100 Pine Ave.
Holmes, PA 19018
215-532-4700

National Data Corp
1 NDC Plaza,
Corporate Square
Atlanta, GA 30329
Connie Bates,
Mgr. Dir. Response
404-982-8477
404-329-8553

NICE Corp.
4357 S. Airport Park
Plaza
Ogden, UT 84405
801-621-6423

PSI Telemarketing
2945 W. Peterson
Avenue
Chicago, IL 60659
Barbara Borowsky
312-878-0800

**Pebblebrook
Associates**
5030 Northwind Drive
East Lansing, MI 48823
800-248-2746

**Phone Marketing
Services**
1823 N. St. Paul Rd.
St. Paul, MN 55109
Sallye Orlando
612-778-9169

**Professional
Telemarketing
Services, Inc.**
10 Corporate Hill Dr.,
Ste. 100
Little Rock, AR 72205
Carol Crain
501-221-3303

**Progressive
Marketing Services**
3649 W. 183rd Street
Hazel Crest, IL 60429
Kevin Lane
312-957-5200

**Publishers
Clearing House**
382 Channel Drive
Port Washington, NY
11050
516-883-5432

**Publisher's
Support
Services**
The Webb Company
1999 Shepard Road
St. Paul, MN 55116
Judy Jacobs
612-690-7422
800-428-4646

R.H. Marketing
555 E. 78th Street
New York, NY 10021
212-734-1497

Rainbow Trading
5240 Campo Rd.
Woodland Hills, CA
91364
818-348-0591

Rapid Data Processing
3000 Mt. Carmel
Avenue
Glenside, PA 19038
215-887-1129

Ring Response Ltd.
5309 W. Touhy
Skokie, IL 60077
Mike Centrella, Pres.
800-338-3338
212-244-4555 (NY)

**Ron Weber &
Associates**
727 Campbell Avenue
West Haven, CT 06516
203-776-3484

Schilling Sons
576 Main St.
Chatham, NJ 07928
201-635-6090

Select Marketing
7745 Chevy Chase Dr.,
Suite 350
Austin, TX 78752
512-450-0582

Seneca Marketing
P.O. Box 348
Merrick, NY 11566
516-378-2912

Service 800
90 Park Avenue
New York, NY 10016
212-286-9190

Singer Electronics Inc.
P.O. Box 1029
Sandy, OR 97055
Ernie Singer, President
503-668-5371

Smartline Corp
Main Place Tower,
3rd Floor
Buffalo, NY 14202
Mark Rieman, President
716-842-2141
716-842-2148 Sue

**Spirited Marketing
Concepts**
105 Fulfillment Street
Suite 300
Denver, CO 80206
303-320-3920

**Stephan Aaron
Enterprises**
32 Union Hill Rd.
P.O. Box 428
Morganville, NJ 07751
201-536-3869

Sturner & Klien
11900 Parklawn Drive
Rockville, MO 20852
301-881-2720

**Synergy Marketing
Group**
79 Sagmaw Drive
Rochester, NY 14623
Raymond Del Monte
716-232-1177

**System Vision
Corp.**
P.O. Box 281166
San Francisco, CA
94128
415-355-7308

Tanto Facet Ent.
P.O. Box 730
Temple Hills, MD 20748
301-420-7600

Techni-Cal
20775 Western Ave.
Torrance, CA 90501
Steve Noble
213-618-9994

Techno-Trak
1825 Chicago Avenue
South
Minneapolis, MN 55404
612-872-1616

Telemarketing
5306 W. Lawrence
Chicago, IL 60630
312-545-0470

Telerx Marketing
901 Bethlehem Pike
Spring House, PA 19477
800-438-3232

Toll Free Systems
P.O. Box 458
Allendale, NJ 07430
201-327-3858

Tele-One Corporation
132 Welsh Road
Horsham, PA 19044
Dick Ray
215-657-2075

TelAc
(Telephone Access, Inc.)
1725 K Street NW,
Ste. 210
Washington, DC 20006
John Jordan
202-393-8360

**Tele America,
Inc.**
1955 Raymond Drive,
Ste. 112
Northbrook, IL 60062
Larry Kaplan
312-480-1560

Tele Systems
10550 Westoffice Drive
Suite 100
Houston, TX 77042
Michael Burns
713-784-3439

**TeleForce (Formerly
Strategic International
Telemarketing)**
901 Campisi Way, #205
Campbell, CA 95008
David Marin
408-377-3800

Telecom Center
3240 Wilson Blvd.
Arlington, VA 22201
Read Debutts
703-247-2500

**Telecom Marketing
Resources Ltd.**
25 Greenwich Avenue
Warwick, RI 02886
Bill Rosenberg,
President
800-345-6733 ext. 11

**Teledirect
Telemarketing**
224 Parkade
Cedar Falls, IA 50613
319-277-6578

**Telemarketing
Concepts**
2013 Cronpond Road
Yorktownheights, NY
10598
Richard Penn
914-666-0016

**Telemarketing
Enterprises, Inc.**
2307 Oak Lane,
Suite 115
Grand Prairie, TX 75051
Diane Alexander
214-263-8120

**Telemarketing
Experience**
25072 Alicia Drive,
Ste. A
Dana Point, CA 92629
Robert Zack
714-240-4611

**Telemarketing Service
Bureau, Inc.**
20314 42nd Avenue, NE
Seattle, WA 98155
David S. Sutton
206-363-5230

Telemarketing West
Div of Harte-Hanks
Comm. Inc.
2830 Orbiter Street
Brea, CA 92621
Mary Weyland
714-993-9010
800-424-WEST

**Telephone Comm.
Canada Ltd.**
60 Bloor Street West
Suite 209
Toronto, Canada
M4W 3B8
416-961-1155

***Telephone Marketing
Services**
25354 Cypress Ave.
Hayward, CA 94544
Richard Herzog
800-227-1817
415-887-8555

**Teleservices
Center, Inc.**
2535 152nd Ave. NE,
Ste. A
Redmond, WA 98052
206-883-4006

Telespectrum, Inc
Box 94697
Schaumburg, IL 60194
301-987-7300
406 Headquarters Dr.
Millersville, MD 21108
800-824-1774

Tele Systems
10550 Westoffice Dr.,
Ste. 100
Houston, TX 77042
Michael Burns
713-784-3439

***Teletech**
15355 Morrison Street
Sherman Oaks, CA 91403
(818) 501-5595

**Teletrak Response
Center**
10297 Yellow Circle
Drive
Minnetonka, MN 55743
R. Slesinger
800-328-5727
612-935-3333

Telmark Inc.
5700 Broadmoor
Ste. 220
Mission, KS 66202
Joe Martin, Pres.
800-tel-mark

**The Direct Response
Corp**
1865 Miner St.,
2nd Floor
Des Plaines, IL 60016
Cooke Bausman,
Exec. VP
312-827-7170

The Great Tradition
750 Adrian Way
San Rafael, CA 94903
415-492-9382

**The Marketing
Machine**
436 Glendale Road
Glenview, IL 60025
312-724-9136

**The
Telemarketer**
200 Park Avenue,
Ste. 303 E
New York, NY 10166
Aldyn McKean
212-674-2540

**Trans-Continental
Telemarketing Inc.**
7968 Main St. NE
Fridley, MN 55432
Alan Beugen
612-784-0200

**U.S. Business
Services, Inc.**
14831 Bessemer Street
Van Nuys, CA 91411
800-237-7367

U.S. Topper Limited
1438 N. Gower
Courtyard 1
Los Angeles, CA 90028
Douglas Hoitenga
213-462-3321

USA "800"
6608 Raytown Road
Kansas City, MO 64133
Jeane Miller
800-821-7700 x 306
800-USA-WATTS x 2000

**Wats Marketing
Outbound**
9706 Mockingbird Drive
Omaha, NE 68127
800-348-1000
402-397-8660

World Line®
Division Worldwide 800
Rue De La Morache 14
1260 Nyon, Switzerland
Jacques Couvas
212-286-0944

Telephones

Newsouth Communications, Inc.
1925 Century Blvd.,
Suite 4
Atlanta, GA 30345
W.T. Littlehales
404-263-7050

Panasonic Company
Mail Stop 1F1 MTEC
One Panasonic Way
Seacaucus, NJ 07094
Ren Franse
201-392-4466

S&M Associates Communications
5721-J Bayside Road
Virginia Beach, VA
23455
804-460-5333

Toronto Research Centre
133 Torresdale Avenue
Suite 201
Willowdale, ON
Canada
M2R 3T2
Flora M. Rosen
416-665-5695

Webcor Electronics, Inc.
107 Charles Lindbergh Blvd.
Garden City, NY 11530
Ken Richenstein
516-794-6200

Telex

GTE Supply
P.O. Box 30402
Salt Lake City, UT
84130-0402
Ray Bufford
801-537-5222

Via Titus Inc.
475 E. Main Street
Patchogue, NY 11772
Donald MacLay
212-553-3542

Toll Restriction Equipment

Precision Sales Inc.
1434 Dumont
Richardson, TX 75080

David Floyd
800-543-3000

Power & Telephone Supply Co.
2668 Yale Avenue
Memphis, TN 38132
Laburn Dye
901-324-6116

Valor Telecom Ltd
378 Schuyler Ave
Kearny, NJ 07032
Joseph Pannullo,
President
201-997-2000

Training Aids (Audio and Visual)

AMA Film/Video
85 Main Street
Watertown, MA 02172
Robert Fraulo,
Mktg. Mgr.
617-926-4600

American Media Incorporated
1454 30th Street
Ste. 105
W. Des Moines, IA
50265
Patty Strong
515-224-0919 Iowa
800-262-2557 USA

Bell of Pennsylvania and Diamond State Telephone
555 City Line Ave.
Bald Cynwyd, PA 19004
Richard Schneider
800-492-2508
202-392-1011

CRC Information Systems
435 Hudson Street
New York, NY 10014
212-620-5678

Coffman Systems, Inc.
13140 Midway Place
Cerritos, CA 90701
Bill Bryce, Sales Mgr.
213-926-6653

Coronet/MTI Film & Video
108 Wilmont Road
Deerfield, IL 60015
Phil Joseph
800-621-2131

Dartnell Corporation
4660 N. Ravenswood
Chicago, IL 60640
Jim Vesely
800-621-5463
800-321-4001

*Fidel Communications
12611 Pacific Avenue
Los Angeles, CA 90066
Stan Fidel
213-390-7594

GTE Directories
P.O. Box 619810
DFW Airport, TX
75261-9810
214-453-6161

Ideabank, Inc.
P.O. Box 614
Salem, NH 03079
Joel Davis
603-898-7855

JOCOM International, Inc.
250 W. 57th Street,
Suite 701
New York, NY 10019
Patricia Crane
212-586-5544

McGraw-Hill Training Systems
P.O. Box 641
Del Mar, CA 92014-9990
619-453-5000 x213

MODAD Trainer's Aide
163-60 22nd Avenue
Whitestone, NY 11357
Carol Richman
718-352-2314

National Educational Media Inc
21601 Devonshire Street
Chatsworth, CA 91311
Susan Petrich
818-709-6009
800-245-6009

Profit Technology
39 Broadway Ave.
New York, NY 10007
Mary Manila
212-809-3500

Tele Techniques Consulting Company
7537 No. Ridge Blvd.,
Ste. A
Chicago, IL 60645
Linda P. Israel
312-338-2424

Telemarketing Management
1755 S. Claudina Way
Anaheim, CA 92085
Ginger Cupkie
714-535-2945

Telephone Selling Report
15427 Summerwood Drive
Omaha, NE 68137
Art Sobczak
402-895-9399

Terry Moore & Associates, Inc.
P.O. Box 177
Bloomington, IN 47402
Jennifer Nelson
812-336-3677

The Economics Press Inc.
12 Daniel Rd
Fairfield, NJ 07006
Debbie Franklin

The Fortune Group
4675 No. Shalowford Road
Suite 200
Lithonia, GA 30058
Dick Kubow
404-455-9451

The Harbor Company
P.O. Box 309
Santa Monica, CA
90406
Doug Davidson
212-393-6494

The Professional Educators Group
5407 Ridgefield Road
Bethesda, MD 20816
David Alan Yoho
301-320-4424

The Telexcel Co.
3004 Pacific Avenue
Marina del Rey, CA
90291
George Walther
213-821-4100

Training Consultants, Inc.
40 Skokie Blvd.,
Ste. 630
Northbrook, IL 60062
Andera Crane
312-498-4064

Training Services

Scott Ashby
2520 Grand Ave. #310
Kansas City, MO 64108
816-474-9038

**Bell of Pennsylvania
and Diamond State
Telephone**
555 City Line Ave.
Bald Cynwyd, PA
19004
Richard Schneider
800-492-2508

CCI Telemarketing
555 W. 57th Street
New York, NY 10019
Adrian Miller
212-957-8520

Care Call/Market Call
1728 Pounds Road
Stone Mountain, GA
30087
Carole Norman
404-469-1922

**ComTel Marketing,
Inc.**
288 Lancaster Avenue
Malvern, PA 19355
Jeff Wooden/
Clelia Salerno
215-647-8781

David Alan Yoho
10803 W Main St.
Fairfax, VA 22030
David Yoho
703-591-2490

Dial Services
4517 Minnetonka Blvd.
Suite 206
Minneapolis, MN 55416
612-929-4114

**Diamond State
Telephone**
555 City Line Avenue
Bald Cynwyd, PA
19004
Dick Schneider
215-578-5335

**Direct
Communications, Inc.**
1385 So. Colorado
Boulevard, Suite 506
Denver, CO 80222
Margie Pomerantz
303-691-9275

*Double Five, Inc.
P.O. Box 267
DeBary, FL 32713
Stan Billue
305-668-4058

**Drothier & Smith
Associates**
26021 Southfield Road
Lathrup Village, MI
48076
Mary Doris Smith
313-569-5430

**Expert Telephone
Techniques Inc.**
48 Earl Drive
N. Merrick, NY 11566
Catherine Blake
516-868-5588

GTE Directories
P.O. Box 619810
DFW Airport, TX
75261-9810
214-453-6161

**Inquiry Handling
Services**
200 Parkside Dr.
San Fernando, CA
91340
Bernie Otis,
Sr. Mktg. Cons.
818-365-8131

J&J Haimes
5940 Main Street
E. Petersburg, PA
17520
Joel B. Haimes
717-569-5549

**Learning
International**
P.O. Box 10211
Stamford, CT 06904
203-965-8477

**Market Motivators,
Inc.**
3725A No. 126th Street
Brookfield, WI 53005
Lawrence A. Pentler
414-783-6800

**McGraw-Hill
Training
Systems**
P.O. Box 641
Del Mar, CA
92014-9990
619-453-5000 x213

Molin & Associates
18927 23rd NE
Seattle, WA 98155
Susan Molin
206-622-4707

National Data Corp
1 NDC Plaza,
Corporate Square
Atlanta, GA 30329
Connie Bates,
Mgr. Dir. Response
404-982-8477
404-329-8553

Norcom Associates
685 Rock Oak Road
Walnut Creek, CA
94598
Jeannine K. Nordan
415-937-9144

**Peg Fisher &
Associates**
1201 S. Wisconsin
Racine, WI 53404
Peg Fisher
414-633-1675

**Prows
Communications**
13551 Emilie Drive
San Jose, CA 95127
Brian Prows
408-923-4841

**Redwood Training
Associates**
1115 Foothill Street
Redwood City, CA
94061
Michael A. Brown
415-364-2527

***Rockingham* Jutkins*
Marketing**
P.O. Box 1349
Venice, CA 90294-1349
Ray W. Jutkins
213-306-7901

**SNET Telemarketing
Consulting Services**
2 Science Park
New Haven, CT 06511
Luke Brennan
203-497-4866

**Southern Bell TM
Seminars**
7750 N.W. 50th St.
Bldg A-1
Miami, FL 33166
Ruth Pittman
305-593-7171
800-634-0303

**Sandy Smyth
Associates, Inc.**
35 Livingston Street
Fairfield, CT 06430
Sandra Smyth,
President
203-371-7329

SofTel
1974 Las Encinas
Los Gatos, CA 95030
Judy Lanier
408-866-2284

**Systematic
Telemarketing,Inc.**
6603 Queen Ave. South,
Suite H
Richfield, MN 55423
Dan Krueger
612-861-6157

**Tele-Networking
Associates**
165 Western Avenue N.
Suite 210
St. Paul, MN 55102
Joan Carver
612-291-8168

**Telemarketing
Experience, Inc.**
25072 Alicia Drive
Ste. A
Dana Point, CA 92629
Robert Zack
714-240-4611

**Telemarketing
Professionals
Inc.**
57 Tunnel Road
Berkley, CA 94705
Carolyn Mills
415-986-8981

**Telemarketing
Sciences**
15840 Ventura Blvd.
#450
Encino, CA 91436
Alex Goodman, Advisor
818-789-2888

**Telemarketing Service,
Inc.**
15840 Ventura Blvd.
Suite 450
Encino, CA 91436
818-789-2888

**Telemarketing
Systems**
221 Camaritas Ave.,
Ste E
San Francisco, CA
94080
Paul Braschi, Pres.
415-583-1640

**Telespectrum,
Inc.**
P.O. Box 94697
Schaumburg, IL 60194
800-824-1774

Tele Systems
10550 Westoffice Dr.,
Ste. 104
Houston, TX 77042
713-784-3439

**The Chambers-Weike
Group, Inc.**
500 Branard
Houston, TX 77006
713-630-0132

The Direct Response
Corp
1865 Miner St.,
2nd Floor
Des Plaines, IL 60016
Cooke Bausman,
Exec. VP
312-827-7170

The Telephone
Training
103 Forbes Road
Westwood, MA 02090
617-326-3430

*The Telexcel Co.
3004 Pacific Avenue
Marina Del Ray, CA
90291
George Walther
213-821-4100

Training Consultants
Inc.
707 Lake Cook Road
Deerfield, IL 60015
312-498-4064

UNISYS
130 Jamesburg Rd.
Dayton, NJ 08810
800-222-0966

U.S. Profiles
Corporation
6825 Manhatten Blvd.
Suite 500
Fort Worth, TX 76112
Sharon Haberer
817-496-6881

U.S. Telemarketing Inc
5300 Oakbrook
Parkway, Bldg 300
Norcross, GA 30093
Jean Villanti
404-381-0100

Visions
International,
Inc.
20 Seminole Avenue
Baltimore, MD 21228
Charyl L. Dayton
301-597-9238

Ziehl
Associates, Inc.
306 Jericho Tnpk
Floral Park, NY 11001
Joan E. Ziehl,
Sales Manager
516-437-1300

Turnkey
Systems for
Tele-
marketing

Affinitech Corporation
2252 Welsch Industrial
Court
St. Louis, MO 63146
Bryan Baehr
314-569-3450

Behavioral
Management
6 Pine Tree Drive
St. Paul, MN 55112
Mary Imgrund
612-483-5750

Bill Rosenberg &
Associates
3 Versallies Street
Cranston, RI 02920
Ryan Loveless
401-728-4929

Carlyle Marketing
Corp
5850 N. Lincoln Avenue
Chicago, IL 60659
Joyce Igou, Creative Dir.
312-271-2700

Data Station Systems
Inc.
2769 E Atlantic Blvd
Pompano Beach, FL
33062
Joe Cordney
305-942-0990

Dialogic
Communications Corp
1106 Harpeth Industrial
Court
P.O. Box 8
Franklin, TN 37064
Gary Fitzhughes,
VP Mktg.
615-790-2882

Early, Cloud, &
Company
Aquidneck Industrial
Park
Newport, RI 02840
Lisa Stapleton
401-849-0500

Finalsoft Inc
305 S. Main St
N Syracuse, NY 13212
Steven Bergere
315-458-8627

Information
Management Assoc
19 Lunar Dr.
Woodbridge, CT 06525
Andrei Poludnewycz
203-397-1100

Intellisys
Technologies
1933-#102 O'Toole
Avenue
San Jose, CA 95131
Hayes Kolb
408-435-0666

Interactive
Telemarketing
Inc.
8585 Stemmons Fwy.,
Ste. 1107-N
Dallas, TX 75247
Jeff Symon
214-631-2277

International
Computer Systems
8300 Greensboro Drive
McLean, VA 22102
Arun Batavia
703-442-9430

James Atherton, Inc.
149 Palo de Oro Drive
Islamorada, FL 33036
James Atherton
305-664-8100

Marketing
Information
Systems
411 North Rockwell
Chicago, IL 60618
312-491-3885

Melita Electronic Labs
P.O. Box 5120
Scottsdale, AZ 85261
Michael Domer
602-998-3600

Microdyne
Corporation
491 Oak Road
P.O. Box 7213
Ocala, FL 32672
904-687-4633

NICE Corp.
4356 S. Airport Park
Plaza
Ogden, UT 84405
801-621-6423

Peerless Technologies
Corp
11843 Starcrest
San Antonio, TX 78247
Janis Maxymof
512-494-3647

Peridata International
Division of Lantor
13650 Gramercy Place
Pasadena, CA 92315
Dave Callahan
213-217-9155

SRO Consultants, Inc.
1395 Marietta Parkway
Bldg. 500, Suite 110
Marietta, GA 30067
Barry Hoffman
404-423-1811

TBS
International
959 E. Collins
Richardson, TX 75081
Jack Zimmermen
214-690-9436

Teledirect
International Inc.
402 W. 35th Street
Davenport, IA 52806
Kenneth Ryan
319-391-5562

Telesys Associates,
MN
19214 N. 31st Lane
Phoenix, AZ 85015
Henry Schwarzberg
602-242-2727

Voice
Activated
Phones

Precision Sales Inc.
1434 Dumont
Richardson, TX 75080
David Floyd
800-543-3000

Power & Telephone
Supply Co.
2668 Yale Avenue
Memphis, TN 38182
Laburn Dye
901-324-6116

Valor Telecom Ltd.
378 Schyuler Ave.
Kearny, NJ 07032
Joseph Pannullo,
President
201-997-2000

Voice
Messaging
Systems

Applied Intelesys
4340 Campus Dr.
Ste. 3204
Newport Beach, CA
92660
714-852-1175

Audiocom, Inc.
8100 Oak Lane
Penthouse 401
Miami Lakes, FL 33016
Stuart Ginsberg
305-825-4653

**Brooktrout
Technology, Inc.**
110 Cedar Street
Wellesley Hills, MA
02181
Bethany Odence
617-235-3026

**Centigram
Corporation**
1883 Ringwood Avenue
San Jose, CA 95131
Kevin Burr
408-291-8200 x207

**Compass Computer
Systems**
319 N. Pottstown Pike
Exton, PA 19341
Bill Rivell
215-524-VOIC
215-363-8770

**Computer Research
Inc.**
3901 Nome Unit 2
Denver, CO 80239
Bill Hamilton
303-373-2331

Computertalker
Div of Computervoice
Inc.
1730 21st Street
Santa Monica, CA
90404
Ron Anderson
213-838-6546

Comtec
135 Ludlow Avenue
Northvale, NJ 07647
Steven Lampert
914-735-4000

Direct Voice Mail
184 Pompton Ave
Verona, NJ 07044
Fred LeComte
201-564-8878

Dukane Corporation
2900 Dukane Drive
St. Charles, IL 60174
Jim Shane
312-584-2300

**Granite Telcom
Corporation**
8 Continental Blvd.
Merrimac, NH 03054
Bill Hart,
VP Sales and Mktg.
603-424-3900
603-625-5403

**Micro
Peripheral
Corporation**
2565 152nd N.E.
Redmond, WA 98052
Mark Perrin
206-881-7544

Microvoice Systems
23362 Peralta
Suite 5
Laguna Hills, CA 92653
D.S. Amlotte
714-859-1091

**Northern
Telecom, Inc.**
P.O. Box 1222
Minneapolis, MN 55440
Joseph A. Scott,
Mktg. Mgr.
800-328-8800
612-932-8238 MN

Omni Communications
319 Lynnway
Lynn, MA 01903
Laurie, TM Manager
617-596-2000

Phoneworks
P.O. Box 9
Hackensack, NJ 07602
Brad Wendkos
201-343-0022

**Ring Group of North
America**
230 Community Drive
Great Neck, NY 11021
Paul Ruggieri, VP
516-487-0250

**TBS
International,
Inc.**
959 E. Collins
Richardson, TX 75081
Jack Zimmerman
214-630-3436

**Teleconnect
Company**
500 2nd Ave. SE
Cedar Rapids, IA 52403
319-366-6600

**Television
Telecommunications**
2723 Curtis Street
Downers Grove, IL
60515
Robert Groetzenbach
312-852-9695

**The Audiochron
Company**
3620 Clearview Parkway
Atlanta, GA 30340
Phylis McNell
404-455-4890

Voicemail International
19925 Stevens Creek
Blvd.
Cupertino, CA 95014
Nilda Lewis
408-725-7800

**Xerox
Corporation**
Xerox Square
Rochester, NY 14644
716-423-4024

INDEX

ABOUT THE AUTHOR

Stanley Leo Fidel is President of Fidel Communications, a Los Angeles-based consulting and training firm whose aim is to make the business world a better place in which to thrive through enhanced communications. Services provided by Fidel Communications include turn-key telemarketing programs; modular in-house workshops; presentations and talks at meetings, conferences, and conventions; and cassette training programs.

Your questions and comments are invited. The author may be contacted at:

Fidel Communications Company
One Wilshire Building
Suite 1210
Los Angeles, California 90017
213-622-5211